W9-DGL-782

What Makes Workers Learn

The Role of Incentives in Workplace Education and Training

SERIES ON
LITERACY: RESEARCH, POLICY AND PRACTICE

Series Editor:
Daniel A. Wagner

Associate Editors:
Richard L. Venezky and Vivian L. Gadsden

Editorial Advisory Board

Richard Anderson	Ingvar Lundberg	Scott G. Paris
Jeanne Chall	Susan L. Lytle	Stephen M. Reder
Iddo Gal	Mohamed Maamouri	Catherine Snow
Shirley Brice Heath	Larry J. Mikulecky	Thomas G. Sticht
Luis Laosa	John Ogbu	Brian V. Street

The series is co-sponsored by the National Center on Adult Literacy at the University of Pennsylvania, which is part of the Educational Research and Development Center Program (grant No. R117Q00003) as administered by the Office of Educational Research and Improvement, U.S. Department of Education, in cooperation with the Departments of Health and Human Services and Labor. The findings and opinions expressed here do not necessarily reflect the position or policies of the Office of Educational Research and Improvement or the U.S. Department of Education.

Volumes in the series include:

Literacy Among African-American Youth (*Vivian L. Gadsden and Daniel A. Wagner, eds.*)

What Makes Workers Learn (*Donald Hirsch and Daniel A. Wagner, eds.*)

Forthcoming

Adult Basic Skills: Innovations in Measurement and Policy Analysis (*Albert Tuijnman, Irwin Kirsch, and Daniel A. Wagner, eds.*)

Adult Literacy Research and Development Vol. 1: Learning and Instruction (*Daniel A. Wagner, ed.*)

Adult Literacy Research and Development Vol. 2: Programs and Policies (*Daniel A. Wagner, ed.*)

What Makes Workers Learn

The Role of Incentives in Workplace Education and Training

Edited by

Donald Hirsch
*Organisation for Economic
Co-Operation and Development*

Daniel A. Wagner
*National Center on Adult Literacy
University of Pennsylvania*

HAMPTON PRESS, INC.
CRESSKILL, NEW JERSEY

Copyright © 1995 by Hampton Press, Inc.

Printed in the United States of America

Library of Congress Cataloging-in-Publication Data

What makes workers learn / edited by Donald Hirsch, Daniel A. Wagner.
      p.   cm. -- (Literacy--research, policy, and practice)
    Includes bibliographical references (p. 193) indexes.
    ISBN 1-881303-23-3 (cloth) ISBN 1-881303-24-1 (pbk.)
    1. Occupational training--Psychological aspects. 2. Vocational education--Psychological aspects. 3. Motivation in education.
I. Hirsch, Donald. II. Wagner, Daniel A. III. Series.
HD5715.W5 1994
158.7--dc20   94-28030
                                                   CIP

Hampton Press, Inc.
23 Broadway
Cresskill, NJ 07626

Contents

Series Preface

Daniel A. Wagner
National Center on Adult Literacy
University of Pennsylvania

Although most peoples and cultures today utilize literacy as a way to conserve cultural knowledge, imbue contemporary information through education, and enrich their societal heritage, literacy—as a set of learned skills for producing and comprehending written language—is poorly controlled by large segments of many societies across the world.

Once thought to be a fully literate country—with a 1990 UN "literacy rate" at nearly 98%—the United States, according to recent studies, now is believed to have a literacy rate at which between one-third and one-half of adults are "functionally illiterate"! Similar findings are coming in from around the world. Some specialists say that these discrepancies have more to do with changing definitions of literacy, whereas others say that previous claims were simply conjecture or based on poor methodologies for assessment. Both views are probably correct in part. What we do know is that changes in the globalization of economic exchange, industrial production, and worker retraining has put the acquisition of basic skills—of which literacy is clearly the most critical—at the center of national and international concern about education and development.

Through what I believe to be an historical quirk of academic scholarship and arbitrary disciplinary divisions, research on literacy has tended to fall into a variety of unconnected research and specialty camps. Thus, under the rubric of "literacy," we find books on adult learning and adult education, cognitive dimensions of reading acquisition in children, oral versus literate societies, orthographies and psycholinguistic processes, the role of literacy in cultural preservation, the impact of literacy on income and social mobility, and so on. These scholarly specialties are all valid, but they are remarkably insulated one from the other. Indeed, even the references utilized for these different approaches often take little note of what scholars have produced in other areas.

The present series, *Literacy: Research, Policy and Practice*, is one attempt to break down the walls that partition literacy into such separate intellectual territories. We will try to find interconnections not only among the three major segments of literacy specialists as denoted in the series subtitle, but also across the life span (children and adults) and across ethnic groups and cultures. This series, we hope, will provide an opportunity to make connections across various knowledge bases and expand the possibilities not only to achieve a better understanding of literacy in the past, present, and future, but also to lead to a future which is a more literate place to live.

Daniel A. Wagner
Series Editor, *Literacy: Research, Policy and Practice*
Philadelphia, PA

Foreword

Jarl Bengtsson
Counselor, Centre for Educational Research and Innovation
OECD

Adult education and training will be a necessity rather than an optional luxury in advanced economies in the 21st century for three reasons. First, because of the accelerated pace of change in the global economy and the penetration of new technologies into nearly every aspect of daily life; second, because of demographic changes that increase the importance of adults in the population (when one or two children per family becomes the norm rather than four or five as at the beginning of this century, resource allocation to education and training needs to be reconsidered); and third, the consequences of neglecting the first two reasons will be greater than ever before. That is, if there are insufficient opportunities and incentives for adult education and training in knowledge-intensive economies, there will be a growing polarization between the "knows" and the "know-nots." The eventual result of such polarization could be a catastrophe for the democratic system.

Yet, although we increasingly agree on the need to engage adults in learning in order to create a "learning society," the problem is that we know little or nothing about the incentives—economic, social, and psychological—that are needed to encourage adults to return to education, or to take an interest in informal learning in ways that can change their lives.

Most Organisation for Economic Co-operation and Development (OECD) work on this subject, which has been going on since the late 1960s, has focused around changes in institutional structures, the content of education, and the interaction between education and work. There is now a need for a better understanding of the incentive structures that cause adults to learn in relation to their work. In making a first analysis of what is known about incentives, this book aims to encourage researchers in a range of disciplines, from economics to psychology, to address this issue. This will be particularly important as the degree of interest in adult education and training grows, particularly in the private sector. If we remain ignorant about the factors that cause workers to participate in education and training, there is a danger that measures to stimulate learning will have benefits for only a minority of already privileged workers.

We at OECD were pleased to collaborate with the National Center on Adult Literacy in Philadelphia on this important and timely topic.

Introduction

Donald Hirsch
Centre for Educational Research and Innovation, OECD

Daniel A. Wagner
National Center on Adult Literacy University of Pennsylvania

Children are sent to school and told they must learn. Adults do their learning on a mostly voluntary basis. School is traditionally intended to prepare children for adult life and to pass on the wisdom of previous generations. Adult education is traditionally intended to offer citizens the possibility of bettering themselves and of filling gaps in their initial schooling. School is life's compulsory initiation. Adult learning has often been seen as life's optional extra.

In recent years there has been a strengthening of the ideal that learning is a continuing experience for all adults, rather than concentrating education and training resources mainly for youth. Such an ideal has been long advocated on the grounds of individual opportunity. However, lately it has been enhanced by the fairly convincing case that there is also a strong societal interest in achieving it: The world has become more complex and more changeable and will function better if citizens and workers continue learning throughout their lives.

1

The perception that greater adult participation in education and training could be of benefit not only to individuals but also to society—and particularly to the economy—has caused many Organisation" for Economic Co-operation and Development (OECD) countries to consider devoting more resources, both public and private, to adult learning programs. As long as participation remains voluntary, a society of *lifelong learning* cannot simply be decreed by program providers in the way that universal youth education is decreed by legislators. An adult will learn when given sufficient motives to do so. Therefore, societies cannot promote adult learning for collective ends without keeping sight of individual motivations and incentives.

This book looks at what makes adults participate in education and training, particularly in relation to work. Effective participation depends on a suitable course being offered, on the offer being accepted, and on the learning being effective. The book, therefore, considers three kinds of incentives: to provide education and training, to accept learning opportunities, and to learn effectively.

In the chapters that follow it becomes clear that effective adult learning is being constrained by the failure these the incentives to exist simultaneously. For example, when workers are not offered the training that they would like, when educational programs are not accepted by target groups, or when workers learn little from training programs because their roles at work remain the same, incentives need to be brought into closer harmony. The remainder of this introduction describes three potential conflicts that need to be resolved to achieve this harmony.

SOCIETAL INTEREST VERSUS INDIVIDUAL OPPORTUNITY

The growing recognition during the past decade of links between a learning workforce and economic performance has strengthened arguments for increased education and training for adults, yet at the same time has changed the nature of the education and training offered.

Meeting in Paris in 1990, the education ministers of the 24 OECD countries described initial education as "a start to lifelong learning" (OECD, 1992b, p. 33) and identified one of their main aims as the development of new learning opportunities to allow adults to "participate actively in today's rapidly changing labor market and society" (p. 33). At the political level today, it is generally accepted that new technologies have reduced the need for unskilled labor and increased the need for a well-educated and well-trained workforce and that the desired results will not be achieved without considerable attention to the knowledge and skills of today's adults.

Twenty years ago, recurrent education and training were being advocated in rather different terms. Then the stress was on improving individual educational opportunities across the life span, as well as creating greater flexibility between experiences in learning and in work (see, for example, OECD, 1973). Now that it is widely recognized that an increasing proportion of new jobs requires greater basic and problem-solving skills, the quality of the workforce as a whole has replaced individual opportunity as the prime goal. At one level such a shift could be of potential benefit to individual workers: The result could be to make all jobs more interesting and rewarding. At another level, as the stress shifts from individual rights to the productivity of the firm or the whole economy, the interests of the individual worker could be neglected.

In practice, however, a strategy to raise the level of education and training among adults will fail if it neglects the benefits—and hence the incentives—to the individual. As discussed in the following two sections of this chapter, adult learners need clear incentives both to participate in education and training programs and to learn effectively within them.

There is an interesting contrast in the chapters that follow between those (by Puchner, Chapter 11, and by Stromquist, Chapter 12) focusing on lessons from the Third World and those directly addressing the perspective of developed countries. The former put significant emphasis on the role of literacy programs to give opportunities to members of disadvantaged groups; the latter tend to assume that adult learning is desirable from a more universal perspective, related in particular to economic performance. At the extremes adult learning might be seen, on the one hand, as a purely political process involving the empowerment of certain groups, or on the other, as a necessary tool for achieving economic efficiency. Although the *empowerment* perspective comes into sharpest relief in the Third World, where illiteracy clearly limits the power of large sections of the population, it can also be applied to marginalized groups in industrialized countries, sometimes referred to as the *Fourth World*.

However, the different perspectives may not conflict as much as it first appears. As mentioned above, individual interests need to be addressed in order to provide sufficient incentives for adults to learn, whatever the underlying social motive for wanting them to do so. In addition, the economic efficiency perspective is increasingly in line with the approach of targeting underserved groups. The existence of a large number of undereducated, underskilled workers creates serious problems in an advanced economy. Indeed, growing alarm about adult illiteracy in industrialized countries seems to be due less to declining education levels than to rising intellectual expectations of workers, as the need for unskilled manual labor declines. Although Western economies may be able to cope with the existence of relatively small marginalized groups, surveys finding that possibly more than one-third of the adults have difficulty applying literacy skills in complex situations raise justifiable concern (for example, see Kirsch, Jungeblut, Jenkins, & Kolstad, 1993, for a large-scale adult literacy survey recently carried out in the United States). Such high low-literacy levels have created a political desire to improve education and training opportunities for less advantaged adults, thereby enabling them to play a more useful and rewarding part in the workforce.

INCENTIVES TO PROVIDERS VERSUS INCENTIVES TO LEARNERS

Despite the broad coincidence of interest between economic efficiency and available education and training opportunities for individuals, the specific interests of employers and other potential education and training providers do not always match those of potential learners. Whereas the general education or training level of the population might affect a nation's productivity, the rewards to an individual are not always direct, in terms of pay, status, mobility, or responsibility. Training programs for the unemployed, for example, do not always lead to good jobs; employer-based training may not lead to a pay raise or a promotion. However, employers who support training of value to individuals may not always reap the benefit in countries and industries in which job mobility between companies is great.

A number of chapters in this book, in particular those of Ryan, Bishop, Mikulecky, Wells, and Luttringer, address the incentives conflict between providers and learners from different viewpoints. In terms of financial incentives, Ryan (Chapter 1) identifies an important distinction between the cases of training sponsored by employers and those sponsored by individuals or governments. On the whole, workers accept training when it is offered by their employers and appear collectively to want more of it than they get: thus, in the case of employer-sponsored training, incentives for providers need the most attention. *Self-sponsored* training, however, tends to incur higher costs to the individual and to offer less certain rewards; in this case, incentives to the learner become the most significant constraint.

A recurring theme in this book, addressed most directly by Bishop (Chapter 2), is the apparent failure of employers, left to their own devices, to provide an optimal level of training for their workers. Bishop examines reasons for *market failure* related to real externalities in terms of benefits to outside parties as well as to the distortions created, in the United States, by government regulations and tax systems. Looking at France, Luttringer (Chapter 3) argues, in contrast, that government is capable of boosting training provision through legislation to give direct financial incentives to employers to train their workers.

Mikulecky (Chapter 9) focuses on workplace literacy programs by identifying a number of incentives that may be needed to encourage individual participation and by giving examples of measures to provide them. He emphasizes the limited generalizability of any one incentive, as different individuals and groups face different constraints. Indeed, workplace literacy programs could be seen as an exception to Ryan's rule that generally employees welcome training: Many feel threatened by the offer of remediation for fear that the admission of reading difficulties could damage their job prospects. Nonetheless, Mikulecky concludes that employers who have committed themselves to workplace literacy programs have the ability to create strong incentives for employee participation.

One possible conclusion is that differences in incentives could increase polarization between more and less privileged groups beyond the differences caused by inequalities in access to education and training. Well-placed professional workers with secure jobs have strong incentives to accept employer offers of training when it costs them little or nothing in time and money and when they can see direct benefits in terms of prospects in their firm. Workers with literacy difficulties who feel insecure in their jobs and people outside of work who are uncertain of the future payoff of costly investments in their own skills may view the offers differently.

A crucial element in the concept, as offered by Ryan and by Rubenson and Schütze, is the role of qualifications. As Rubenson and Schütze (Chapter 7) point out, qualifications acquired in the context of work have many advantages over those resulting from external courses; yet, as Ryan (Chapter 1) points out, employers are understandably reluctant to certify skills acquired in house in ways that make it easier for workers to move to other firms. As on-the-job qualifications gain in significance at the expense of external ones, those outside or on the fringes of the labor market are likely to become more firmly excluded.

As noted above, such polarization is likely to hurt not only disadvantaged groups but the whole economy because advanced economies require high literacy and skill levels of the great majority of workers, not just of an elite. This is the case for public intervention to improve learning incentives where they are weakest and, in particular, to help excluded groups to undertake education and training in a context as close to the workplace as possible. Such public intervention does not necessarily imply across-the-board subsidies or legal obligations for employers who give training. Intervention may need to be done selectively and designed in partnership with employers to promote not only participation in courses, but effective and relevant learning.

LEARNING PARTICIPATION VERSUS EFFECTIVE LEARNING

Sending workers to training courses is no guarantee that they will learn skills relevant to their performance at work. This limitation is more important today than it was 20 or 30 years ago because of the increasing need for workers to acquire more than just narrow technical skills. Broader competencies, such as the effective use of literacy and communication skills and efficiency at problem solving and teamwork, are growing in relative importance. The acquisition of such competencies may depend less on the number of courses attended than on the context in which learning takes place and the circumstances in which it is applied. Thus, there are needs for incentives for providers and learners not just to carry out education and training activity, but also to ensure that it is effective.

The need for broader competencies emerges most forcefully in the chapters by Rubenson and Schütze (Chapter 7), Hirschhorn (Chapter 5) and Ford (Chapter 6), and also figures in those by Luttringer (Chapter 3), Sticht (Chapter 8), and Noyelle and Hirsch (Chapter 4). Rubenson and Schütze establish what—in their view—are the key requirements for effective learning in the context of the modern workplace, notably that work qualifications seem to be produced best at the workplace itself in the context of changes in the organization of work, and as far as possible, in informal everyday settings. The priorities juxtapose the kind of legislative approach to employer-sponsored training described by Luttringer, in which the key incentives for companies are to prove that a certain percentage of the payroll has been allocated to identifiable training activity. Luttringer discusses ways to make legal measures more flexible, making learning a cooperative venture between employer and employee at the workplace, rather than simply a managerial exercise in buying an externalized service. Such lessons arising out of the French experience of legal/fiscal measures are particularly relevant at a time when similar measures are being considered in the United States.

Hirschhorn (Chapter 5) uses a specific example to delve more deeply into the incentives needed for workers to create real learning within an organization. The key requirement identified is that workers need to feel authorized to use learning as a tool for bringing about change. In other words, training can no longer be seen as merely a managerial exercise in a world in which productivity depends more on effective performance by teams with clear roles than on an old-fashioned hierarchy of command. It is not possible to create an effective work organization without giving new incentives to workers in terms of authority to act and responsibility for their actions.

A strong conclusion emerging both from Hirschhorn's chapter and from the book as a whole is that learning increasingly must become a genuinely collaborative activity between employer and employee. The time of individuals regarding *human capital* purely as a personalized investment is over. At the same time, managers who regard labor simply as a *unit of production* to which training courses can add value have misunderstood the complex relationships that make a modern workplace function well. Luttringer calls for a shift to a concept of *co-responsibility* for training. Recognition by workers and employers that they have a mutual interest in creating effective learning in relation to work is the first step towards producing the incentives that will enhance worker and workplace learning.

*   *   *   *

This volume emanates from papers prepared originally for a roundtable held in Philadelphia in November 1991. Jointly sponsored by the Centre for Educational Research and Innovation (CERI) of the Organisation for Economic Co-operation and Development (OECD) and the National Center on Adult Literacy (NCAL) at the University of Pennsylvania, the roundtable brought together approximately 40 specialists and policymakers from a dozen countries to debate the issues described above.

In preparing the book, OECD and NCAL commissioned papers on six aspects of adult learning incentives: financial, legal, and organizational incentives; learning methods; incentives to provide and join literacy programs; and lessons from the Third World to the first. On the basis of the roundtable discussion, these papers were revised and given greater coherence. Under each of the six themes, a main paper and a response paper was presented. These have now been turned into 12 autonomous chapters, but each even-numbered chapter attempts to continue the discussion from the preceding (odd-numbered) chapter.

The interest of OECD in the topic of adult learning and worker training stems from the increasing concern found among many of the most industrialized nations. The status quo in first- and second-chance education as well as in workplace learning are inadequate to meet rapidly changing economies as we approach the year 2000.

NCAL has as a central part of its mission to increase the understanding of what adult skills are necessary for effective functioning in the workplace, how to improve those skills, and how well the United States is competing in the skills "marketplace" relative to its economic partners and competitors. Yet, the Center's mission, as indicated by its base in a university environment, is not focused inward, but rather is part of an effort to bring together many voices and points of view, and to share as broadly as possible the best information available.

Thus, there was a clear overlap in the interests of both OECD and NCAL in the incentives that lead workers to learn new skills. The 1991 Philadelphia roundtable was an expression of that mutual interest, as is the production of this book. Collaborations of this kind enable each organization to accomplish more with the available resources, and, more importantly, it provides opportunities for improved networking and sharing of ideas with specialists with diverse yet converging sets of needs.

SECTION I:
Financial Incentives

1

Adult Learning and Work: Finance, Incentives, and Certification*

Paul Ryan
University of Cambridge

Although the benefits of adult work-related learning are increasingly recognized by economists, little attention has been given to the important distinction between training sponsored (i.e., organized and financed) by employers and that sponsored by individuals.

From the individual's standpoint, employer-sponsored training is low cost, low risk, and apparently high benefit; self-sponsored training is commonly the opposite. Employer training is, however, rationed to and among employees by criteria that have more to do with trainability and retainability than with individual interest or willingness to pay. The availability of such training has increased, particularly among employers whose operations are affected by new technology and increased competition in product markets. But it remains scarce, partly because of its cost to employers, and partly because of the enduring nature of competition in labor, product, and capital markets.

*I am grateful to William Brown, Donald Hirsch, and participants at the Philadelphia OECD/NCAL Roundtable for comments on an earlier draft of this chapter; to Hilary Steedman and David Marsden for information on French and German payment systems; and to the Policy Studies Institute for access to unpublished data.

11

Individual sponsorship, by contrast, depends directly on individual interest and readiness to sacrifice, and, as such, it is impeded both by the constraint of its high cost to the individual and by market failures underlying credit rationing and lack of insurance. Public policy has done little to offset such disincentives outside the disparate contexts of unemployment and higher education.

Two intertwined issues of considerable interest in contemporary policy discussions—the certification of adult work-related learning and payment-for-skill—are open to question in terms of importance and feasibility. Certification is important, particularly for individuals and public policy, but it is also problematic for employer-sponsored training at least: the interest of employers in slanting its content and coverage toward their own requirements can easily render it narrow or meaningless. Payment-for-skill enjoys a mostly symbolic importance, as even without it employees have strong incentives to take up whatever training employers decide to sponsor for them; but it is most readily achievable when linked to the same independent certification of skill to which employers show distinct aversion.

The importance of increased adult work-related learning is now widely recognized in advanced economies. It reflects in particular the tendency of electronic technologies, increasingly variegated customer demand, and intensified international competition to favor skill-intensive production methods, reversing earlier tendencies toward deskilling. Although the extent of such tendencies remains controversial, there is little doubt about the overall direction of movement, and instances of corporate adjustment in work organization toward greater skill intensity have become widespread (Best, 1990; Brown, 1991; GB TA, 1989a; OECD, 1988, 1991a).

Public interest in increased workforce skills has concentrated primarily on initial training. The governments of advanced economies nowadays seek extensive, if not universal, vocational preparation among young people (Garonna & Ryan, 1991). Although adult learning has played second fiddle to youth training in this respect, it too faces calls for rapid improvement (OECD, 1991a). Public concern has been fostered *inter alia* by declines in the size of youth cohorts; in Germany, by near saturation in youth training; in the United Kingdom and the United States, conversely, by the weakness of youth-training improvement and the ensuing need to advance on both fronts; and in North America, by evidence of literacy and numeracy problems among adult workers, particularly ethnic minority members and immigrants (DeFreitas, 1991; Hirsch, 1991; Mikulecky, this volume; OECD, 1991a).

The importance of adult learning is underlined by the considerable benefits to individuals that are associated with training, such as improved employment probabilities, occupational status, pay, and job satisfaction, for private-sector training at least. Yet, despite substantial employer outlays, adult participation in training remains low in most economies (GB TA, 1989a; Green, 1991; OECD, 1991a, 1991b; Ryan, 1991a), particularly among less skilled and low paid workers (Greenhalgh & Stewart, 1987; Ryan, 1990).

The disparity between benefits and activities leads directly to questions about information and incentives. Is adult training held back by a lack of interest in or information about benefits? Or are individuals informed and aware, but unable to get training opportunities?

In response to these questions, this chapter argues that problems associated with individual interest and information are of secondary, and those associated with access to training are of primary importance. The incentives and opportunities facing individuals differ fundamentally according to whether the training available is sponsored by themselves or by an employer. The great majority of adult training opportunities are sponsored by employers, who do so on terms sufficiently favorable to individuals for the latter to need little or no further inducement to accept what is being offered. The incentive problem centers then on the employer, who, although subject to the training incentives associated with the "new competition," is also subject to the training disincentives associated primarily with labor mobility.

Individuals can and do sponsor training for themselves. Incentive issues then concern individuals, rather than employers, and are underlined by the scale of both costs and risks to the individual, relative to those in employer-sponsored training. Opportunity issues are, however, arguably more important in terms of the availability of both suitable courses and requisite finance and insurance.

The contrast between the economics of the two types of training sponsorship is not fully appreciated, particularly by economists. The distinction is, however, implicit in the everyday difficulty of choosing training terminology—should individuals be described as *taking* or *getting* training? The contrast between an active and a passive conception of the role of the individual corresponds broadly to the difference between self-sponsored and employer-sponsored training. (The distinction also comes out in Luttringer's chapter in this volume.)

The benefits of training to participants and the extent to which individuals are both aware of them and interested in acting on them are discussed in the next section. The issue of sponsorship is elaborated in the third section, followed by a discussion of training incentives under employer and individual sponsorship, respectively. Issues of assessment, certification, and monetary rewards are discussed next, followed by the conclusions in the final section.

The chapter deals primarily with the United Kingdom, although evidence is also taken from other countries, notably the United States, Germany, and France. Some parts of the analysis do not, however, apply directly to adult training in Japan (Dore & Sako, 1989; Marsden & Ryan, 1991a). The United Kingdom is singled out partly on the grounds of the author's familiarity, partly because other countries have already been studied in detail (Madigan, 1990; Clement, Drake, Fong, & Wurzburg, 1991), and partly because a recent British survey of individual training provides data on the nature and importance of training sponsorship (GB TA, 1989b).

The term *training* henceforth will be substituted for work-related learning for reasons of brevity, notwithstanding its typically narrower connotation, and should be interpreted as including both vocationally relevant education and learning by experience.

BENEFITS, INFORMATION, AND ATTITUDES

To what extent do individuals and employers both benefit from training and know that they benefit? This section draws primarily on British evidence to argue that the benefits of training depend strongly on the type of training involved and that, although knowledge of benefits may be defective for both individuals and employers, in neither case does it appear to be a major constraint on training activity. The discussion is oriented to individuals primarily.

Benefits

The main incentive for adults to undertake training is an expectation of gains in job rewards, supplemented sometimes by consumption and developmental benefits. This section concentrates on pecuniary gains, which are easier to measure than nonpecuniary ones and are expected to predominate within total gains for the more instrumental components of adult learning.

The benefits of training to individuals appear to depend on the type of training, with private sector training performing better than public training programs, and differences in purposes and quality an apparent reason for the gap between the two. Although the evidence is fragmentary and often indirect, receipt of training is closely related in British and American evidence to gains in employment probabilities, occupational status, pay, and job satisfaction. The best evidence available for Britain continues to relate to an earlier period. Having received any full-time training during the previous 10 years, for British employees in 1975, was associated with an increase in expected hourly earnings in that year of between 3% and 8% (from occupational mobility alone). Long duration added further to earnings, particularly if it led to a qualification, which was associated among males with a further earnings benefit of between 2% and 10%. Unmeasured increases in pay within occupational categories are presumed to have raised the benefits further (Greenhalgh & Stewart, 1987, Table 6; Nickell, 1982, Table 1).[1]

The existence of significant benefits to individual participants in employer-sponsored training in particular is affirmed by a range of recent U.S.-based studies. Earnings, employment rates, and occupational status proved to be regularly associated with previous participation in employer training (OECD, 1991b, pp.138-139).

The picture for public training programs is mixed. Participation in full-time, off-the-job training in Britain proves to be strongly associated with subsequent employment rates, job satisfaction, and earnings. Average gross hourly pay was 28%-34% higher for participants who worked subsequently in the occupation for which they trained, and the probability of finding such work increased by up to 25 percentage points (Payne, 1990, Tables 6.1, 7.4, 7.5).[2] Other public training is, however, associated with weak, even negative, benefits. Evaluations of U.S. manpower policies suggest modest improvements in employment rates and, to a lesser extent, pay for adult females, although not generally for males (Bassi & Ashenfelter, 1986; Ham & LaLonde, 1991; Maynard, 1991). The weakness of these benefits appears to reflect the weak training content and low per-capita funding of most of the programs, although the disadvantaged attributes of both the participants and their labor market options may be relevant as well (Doeringer & Piore, 1971).[3]

The benefits of training to employers also appear potentially great. At the level of the individual, the growth in productivity associated with employee training typically exceeds that in pay, thereby generating a return for the employer (Bishop, 1990). At the sectoral level, high

[1]Although econometric studies of individuals' training have mushroomed in Britain, they have focused on determinants rather than benefits (e.g., Green, 1991; Greenhalgh & Mavrotos, 1992). The extent to which the 15 to 25 years that have elapsed since the experiences were recorded in the 1975 National Training Survey have altered the benefits as well as the pattern of training in Britain remains uncertain (Marsden & Ryan, 1991b).

[2]The results of such research appear sensitive to the selection of the control group (Lalonde, 1986).

[3]Weak and even negative benefits for participants in public training programs for young workers in Britain are also likely to reflect to some extent low training quality (Dolton, Makepeace, & Treble, 1991; Main & Shelley, 1988; Marsden & Ryan, 1991b). These defects of youth-training policies may well have been extended to adult training with the institution of the Employment Training scheme in 1988.

levels of training and skill utilization have been associated with high productivity in a range of international comparisons (e.g., Prais, Jarvis, & Wagner, 1991; Steedman & Wagner, 1989). The evidence is far from being unambiguous, but it does suggest that many employers derive substantial benefits from training, at the margin as well as on average.

Risk

Even when the expected returns to training are favorable, agents cannot be sure of their actual returns. Some benefit exceptionally, others little or not at all. The risks facing individuals reflect the properties of human capital. It is highly illiquid and, even when transferable across employers, usually specific to a particular occupation, implying uncertainty about employment and earnings prospects. A particular person may fail to complete the course, fail to find a high paying job in the occupation involved, fail to find any job in the same occupation, or even fail to find any job in any occupation. Employers face the risk of losing their investment should the ex-trainee quit or have to be laid off.

Assuming risk aversion, such risks reduce the value of the expected net benefits of training, particularly as insurance-type options for reducing risk are largely unavailable with respect to human capital investment. The costs associated with risk bearing are expected to be greatest for individuals and for small businesses.

A sense of the training-related risks facing individuals is provided by British data. A majority of individuals who had in 1965 worked in the lowest of four occupational categories and who had received full-time training before 1975 had also during that decade moved into a higher occupational category, consistent with positive expected returns to training. The dispersion of outcomes was substantial. A significant minority (28%) showed no mobility, notwithstanding receipt of training; most moved up one or two categories; and a small minority moved all the way up to the top category (Table 1.1).[4]

Such data are best suggestive of the role played by risk, as they control neither for costs, nor for the dispersion of outcomes in the absence of training, nor for determinants of the benefits over which individuals can exercise choice (e.g., search intensity).

---

[4]As the dispersion of earnings after participation in full-time public training programs in Britain appears distinctly lower than that before it, some forms of training may reduce the total labor market risk facing individuals. Even so, the returns clearly remain uncertain, particularly in connection with finding a job in the relevant occupation, a contingency that increases expected benefits, but which a substantial minority of trainees fail to satisfy (Payne, 1990, Tables 6.1, 6.4).

Table 1.1. Occupational Mobility 1965-75 (Percentages Among British Employees in Lowest Occupational Categories in 1965, by Participation in Full-time Job-related Training, 1965-75)

(percentages in sex/training category)

	Training 1965-75	Number of categories moved, 1965-75[a]				
		none	one	two	three	all
females	any	27.1	31.0	33.5	8.4	100.0
	none	75.7	12.4	8.4	3.5	100.0
males	any	28.5	33.1	24.2	14.1	100.0
	none	68.5	16.2	7.9	7.4	100.0

Source: Greenhalgh and Stewart 1987, using author's calculations.
[a]Across four occupational categories, grouped by mean pay of male employees in category.

INFORMATION AND INTEREST

If the benefits of training for economic performance and individual job rewards indicate a need for training, that does not by itself create a desire for it. Both individuals and employers may be insufficiently aware of the benefits to generate an appropriate level of demand.

Evidence about individuals derives from two sources: statements and actions. The former involves attitudes, which economists often dismiss as soft evidence, untested by practice; the latter involves actual behavior, seen as hard evidence, tested in practice. However, as individual behavior is constrained by opportunities as well as influenced by information and interest, attitudinal data are potentially valuable, albeit somewhat suspect.

Most individuals indicate interest in acquiring training and have the expectation of benefiting from it. Only 9% of members of the British workforce are willing to describe themselves as not particularly interested in training. Although interest in training and career development is relatively low among females and falls off with income, educational level, and past training, in all categories a majority express interest, even when they have no expectation of taking training (GB TA, 1989b, Tables 11.15-11.20).[5]

---

[5]By contrast, 56% of an earlier sample of female employees had expressed a lack of desire for training (Martin & Roberts, 1984, Table 5.22). The higher incidence of interest in the later survey may represent changes over time. Attitudinal responses to a survey that focuses on training and implicitly treats it as a "good thing" may also be biased by halo effects.

The expectation of benefit is also widespread. Even though more than 40% of adult respondents do not expect to acquire training in the future, only 14% agree with the proposition that training would make little difference to their work prospects (GB TA 1989b, Table 7.6a; Ryan, 1990, Table 6.5). Nor does defective information appear to constitute a widespread obstacle to training. Although recent participants in training showed some dissatisfaction with the information that had been available to them concerning course availability, guidance, and finance, even people not considering training showed considerable awareness of sources of information about training (GB TA, 1989b, Table 7.7a-7.7e). At the same time, awareness of public funds for financing individual training has been found to be low among the low paid (FE UK, 1989).

The prevailing gap between potential benefits and actual activity in adult training appears, therefore, to reflect only secondarily a lack of interest and information among individuals. To the extent that there is a problem, it is particularly marked among unskilled and low-paid workers, many of whom have previously moved away from learning, and among married females, who often have more pressing claims on their attention.

Problems of information and interest may actually be greater for employers. British governments have long exhorted employers to increase their awareness of training's benefits for them. Even so, a formal training plan has been developed by only 20% of establishments and a cost-effectiveness analysis by only 3% of employers (GB TA, 1989a, pp. 42, 46). On the informational side, the costs and benefits of training to employers are intrinsically difficult to measure. The costs of on-the-job training are included with those of production and therefore difficult to separate. The benefits of training are intertwined with choices of products, processes, and work organization. The benefits of training to employers may well be great, but the evidence is far from strong enough to convince skeptics (Ryan, 1991b).

Adult learning is therefore adversely affected by inadequate benefits, particularly to disadvantaged participants in public programs; by poor information on its benefits, particularly among employers; and by a lack of interest, particularly among married females. At the same time, as none of these constraints appears to be of primary importance in the wider picture, the anomaly of large numbers of informed and interested individuals who could benefit from training alongside low rates of participation in it must be explained largely in other terms.

TRAINING SPONSORSHIP: MEANING AND PATTERNS

The financial attributes of training, and with them the incentives to offer or take training, differ fundamentally according to whether an employer sponsors it or not. *Sponsorship* in this case means having the primary responsibility for arranging and financing training.

The party who arranges training clearly need not be the one who finances it. For example, individuals who arrange to take vocational courses may receive financial help from public bodies or employers by way of tuition subsidies. Moreover, economic theory predicts that employers will not, under competitive conditions at least, finance any training that they arrange or provide when the skills involved are *general*, (that is, the skills can be transferred to other employers without cost (Becker, 1975)).

Nevertheless, in the United Kingdom in particular, arranging and financing training appear to overlap heavily when employers are involved. The British survey from which this chapter draws much of its evidence classified training events according to whether or not they were "arranged or paid for by an employer" and found that the two criteria largely coincided: "In virtually all cases employers paid the entire costs" of the training which they had arranged (GB TA, 1989b, 19).[6] Such behavior is rational when market competition is limited (Katz & Ziderman, 1990; Ryan, 1984).

The degree to which the two attributes of employer sponsorship—arranging and financing—can be separated is brought up immediately by proposals for increased sharing of responsibilities in training (Luttringer, this volume). Can individuals be expected to bear more of the costs, for example, by training on their own time or on reduced rates of pay? The former is the norm in adult training for *Meister* and higher work-related qualifications in Germany (Streeck, Hilbert, Van Kevelaer, Maier, & Weber, 1987). The latter is, however, rare outside initial (youth) training, and even then it is problematic. Other employees and trade unions are averse to special trainee pay rates unless training is externally regulated and trainee status is clearly distinguished from employee status (Ryan, 1984, 1993). The scope for such developments in adult training appears slim.

In the absence of such features, *employer sponsorship* is used here to denote a broad fusion of the two roles of arranging and financing training. Its key attribute is that training takes place on the employer's time, whether at the workplace or elsewhere, and whether or not the employer actually provides the training. Other types of training may then be grouped together under *other sponsorship*, as long as it is understood that

---

[6]Doubts have been raised concerning the accuracy of the picture of training produced by the *Training in Britain* survey as a result of the absence from the data set of all details for a large minority of the training experiences mentioned by respondents (Greenhalgh & Mavrotos, 1992). It is assumed here that the attributes of training in the published results of the survey are not systematically distorted by such difficulties.

arranging and financing are less closely aligned than in the former category, in that individuals, public bodies, and even trade unions show varied
degrees of involvement in the arranging and financing of training.

Incidence and Content

British employers do not sponsor training on any comprehensive basis.
Only one-quarter of the British labor force reports that it has during the
last three years received any employer-sponsored training; at least one-
third says it has never had any at all (Table 1.2; see also GB TA, 1989b, p.
19). Employer-sponsored training has risen sharply in recent years (GB
DE, 1991, Table 14), but as late as the mid-1980s, it was still available to
only a minority of British workers.[7]

At the same time, employer sponsorship dominates adult training. About three-quarters of adult training events are sponsored by
employers. Only 1 in 11 British workers undertakes training without
employer sponsorship during a 3-year period (Table 1.2).

Patterns of participation in training in the 1987 survey follow
patterns common in the wider literature, falling with age and rising with
occupation, previous qualification and income (Table 1.2; Green, 1991;
Greenhalgh & Stewart, 1987; OECD, 1991b; Payne, 1990). What is less
well known is the association between the incidence and the sponsorship
of training. The decline in training activity with age is much less sharp
for employer-sponsored training than for other training. The lower incidence of training among females reflects lower participation in employer-
sponsored training; there was no difference for other training.[8]

The duration and location of training also differ markedly by
sponsorship (Table 1.3). Employer-sponsored training is more intense
but of shorter duration than other training. Nearly three-quarters (73%)
of it occurs on a full-time basis, as opposed to only one-half of other
training. Yet, only 38% of employer-sponsored courses last more than
three weeks, as opposed to 91% of other ones. Employer training is

---

[7]Although the *Training in Britain* survey defined training to respondents as "all
types of training or education that you think might be relevant to a job or getting
a job," recall error and inconsistent interpretation of the definition undoubtedly
bias the estimates downward to an unknown but probably substantial extent.
The reported incidence of work-related learning doubled when individuals were
offered a wider definition, including talking to co-workers and attendance at lec-
tures (GB TA, 1989b, pp. 17, 54).

[8]Multivariate analysis, separating the pure associations of age, and so on, with
training incidence, confirms the importance of age, sex, and occupation (Green
1991; Greenhalgh & Stewart, 1987). Analysis of the *Training in Britain* data suggests
similar results, although data censoring (exclusion of the unemployed) and small
sample size makes it difficult to pin down the differences between training incidence functions for the two sponsorship categories (Greenhalgh & Mavrotos, 1992).

Table 1.2. Incidence of Training by Sponsorship, British workforce aged 19-59, 1987 (percentages in category with training)

Criterion	Subgroup	Sponsor		
		Employer	Other	Any[a]
All		25	9	33
Age	19	28	47	73
	20-21	34	30	58
	22-24	31	21	47
	25-34	30	8	36
	35-44	25	6	31
	45-54	18	4	23
	55-59	11	1	12
Sex	female	22	10	31
	male	27	9	34
Income[b]	<4	14	5	18
(£'000	4-10	28	7	32
yearly)	10+	42	6	46
	all	29	6	33

Source: Based on GB TA (1989b), Tables 2e, 5.3b, 11.4 and unpublished results.
Note: Base is all training taken during last 3 years by 19-59-year-olds ("all", "age" and "sex") or training with a cumulative duration of 3 or more days taken by 22-59-year-olds ("income").
[a]Not equal sum of previous columns as some training was jointly sponsored.
[b]At time of interview.

clearly the more likely to be conducted at the workplace and on the job, notwithstanding the exclusion of informal, brief training, as shown in the data in Table 1.3.

There is less evidence about training content. Employer sponsorship normally teaches the trainee how to do an existing job, whereas other training is more commonly oriented toward a new job or occupation. Only 1 in 3 trainees sponsored by their employers gain a qualification; data are not available for other sponsorship, but the rate is surely much higher (Table 1.3). These features are consistent with a picture of employer-sponsored training as less formal and more geared to immediate job requirements than are other types of training.

Table 1.3. Attributes of Training by Sponsorship, British Workforce, 1987 (percentage of trainees in relevant category)

Attribute	Employer	Other	All
		Sponsor	
DURATION AND LOCATION			
Full time[a]	73	50	59
Duration 3+ weeks[a]: full-time training	22	94	61
full and part time	38	91	51
Location[a]: at job	(22)	(0)	16
off job, on premises	(11)	(0)	8
off employers' premises	(65)	(100)	75
Content: to do existing or past job	87	36	73
to do new or different job	10	60	24
CHOICES AND FINANCE			
Employee status throughout training[b]	(100)	33	65
Employer expectation to take training	46	(0)	36
Cut in normal pay while in training	3	n.a.	n.a.
Payment of training fees: employer	70	<2	50
public body	5	38	14
self/family	2	43	14
none charged	21	15	19
Sources of income[b]: earnings	(100)	44	(78)
grant or allowance	(0)	34	(13)
family	(0)	14	(5)
loan	(0)	(4)	(2)
OUTCOMES			
Expect improved earning ability	61	61	61
promotion prospects	71	56	67
job satisfaction	75	59	70
Asked not to quit after training[b]	44	(0)	(23)
Qualification obtained	35	n.a.	n.a.

Source: Based on GB TA (1989b), Tables 5.3b, 5.6a, 5.11b, 5.12b, 5.13a, 5.9b, p. 52, and unpublished results.
Notes: *Training* defined in survey as "all types of education and training that you think might be relevant to a job or getting a job" (p. 17); *base* is "all training events" unless indicated as otherwise:
[a] events lasting 3 or more days
[b] events lasting 3 or more weeks.
Numbers in parentheses estimated from reported status or interpolation rather than direct responses.

Financial Attributes

The costs of training sponsored by employers fall by definition mainly on the employer. The costs of other types of training may be absorbed by individuals, governments, unions, and even employers. Incentives to train differ greatly between the two categories of sponsorship.

Employer-sponsored training involves low, or even no, pecuniary sacrifices. Such trainees are presumed to enjoy employee status during training. Only 3% report having received less than their normal pay during training; only 2% have paid any course fees themselves. Other modes of sponsorship involve much higher costs to trainees. As only one-third of trainees are continuously employed during training which is not sponsored by an employer, many forego significant earnings while training. Course fees are almost never paid by an employer: public and personal funds share the load. A significant minority relies on family resources and loans to fund living expenses (Table 1.3).

Low costs to individuals for employer-sponsored training should be associated, according to competitive theory, with low benefits as well, complementing high costs and returns in other forms of sponsorship and equalizing rates of return to individuals. Although there is little evidence on how benefits vary by sponsorship, equalization of rates of return appears unlikely. The proportion of trainees who expect to increase their earnings is similar for the two sponsorship modes; the proportion expecting improved promotion prospects and job satisfaction is actually higher under employer sponsorship (Table 1.3). U.S. evidence suggests that wage growth following training may even be higher under employer sponsorship (Tan, 1989, cited in OECD, 1991b, p. 139).

On the other hand, only 1 in 3 trainees enjoying employer sponsorship gained a qualification, and a smaller share of such trainees expected a *great* increase in earning ability (25% and 34% respectively; GB TA, 1989b, Table 11.11).

More information on benefits by sponsorship is clearly needed. To the extent, however, that the benefits to trainees of employer sponsorship relative to other modes appear not to be lower in proportion to the cost to the trainee, the rate of return to the trainee is commensurably higher. In that case, the equalization of rates of return across sponsorship modes that is predicted by competitive theory fails to materialize, a not implausible outcome in segmented labor markets with rigid wage structures. In effect, competition for access to employer-sponsored training does not sufficiently depress starting pay and raise opportunity costs to employees who receive it; the result is non-price rationing of the job vacancies that bring access to training. Various theories attempt to explain such patterns, but little attention has been paid to their implications for training access and incentives.[9]

The attributes of training suggest also that risks are significantly lower in employer-sponsored training than in other training. Employment rates during and after training are higher, occupational change is less common, and the share of the costs falling to the individual are much lower under employer sponsorship.

TRAINING INCENTIVES: EMPLOYER SPONSORSHIP

The favorable financial attributes of employer sponsorship, from the standpoint of trainees, make incentives to trainees secondary to those to employers. In non-employer sponsorship the reverse is the case: employers matter only indirectly, as potential employers of workers whose training is sponsored by others and incentives to individuals are central. This section considers incentives in employer-sponsored training (a later section considers other forms of sponsorship).

Trainee Decisions

Patterns of employer-sponsored learning can certainly be affected by decisions made by employees, who may avoid or decline such training. Reluctance among older and less qualified workers may contribute, alongside employer reluctance, to low training incidence in those groups. At the same time, almost one-half (46%) of the trainees sponsored by their employers stated that they had little or no choice about participation or content in the face of employer expectations (Table 1.3). Although the British survey did not search explicitly for evidence of employee refusal, no evidence of it surfaced and it is expected to be rare, given favorable financial attributes for trainees.

The evidence also suggests excess demand for employer training. The principal reasons given by the 65% of British employees who could envisage training but who faced obstacles to it all take for granted low access to employer-sponsored training: inability to quit work or get time off work, lack of financial support and time, lack of employer support, and lack of relevance to work prospects (GB TA, 1989b, Table 7.6b). Employees may

---

[9]Evidence suggesting high individual rates of return in employer-sponsored initial training can be found in Jones (1986) and Marsden and Ryan (1991b); the low costs born by employed trainees are discussed by Bishop (1990), Lynch (1992), and Ryan (1984). It should be noted here that skill specificity is expected not to cause individual rates of return to vary by sponsorship, but rather to alter the distribution of training costs between employers and trainees.

wish for different types of training than employers offer (e.g., greater access to qualifications) but rejection of what is available appears unusual.[10]

Employer Decisions

The incentives facing employers are complex and contradictory. On the one side stand those associated with the requirements of the *new competition* (Best, 1990). Driven by intensified and altered competition in product markets, many employers increase training as part of wider strategic adjustment. On the other side stand those associated with what might be termed the *old competition*. Driven by the desire to reduce unnecessary and even damaging expenditures, many employers limit and mold training in order to restrict both training outlays and employee turnover.

The influence of the new incentives facing employers has risen rapidly during the last two decades. The impressive inroads made into many product markets by leading Japanese and German firms from the mid-1960s onward drew attention to their business strategies, which involved radical departures from those associated with the names of Taylor and Ford. Economic turbulence after 1974 forced the pace of learning, as failures and near-failures cropped up repeatedly among established businesses whose adjustments had lagged behind. Electronic technologies increased the potential of decentralized, knowledge-intensive organizations, as long as their human resources were sophisticated enough to meet the challenge (GB TA, 1989a, 1989c; OECD, 1988; Winch, 1983).

A key ingredient in these changes has invariably proved to be human resource development. Successful competitors seek to realize the concept of the *learning enterprise* on an unprecedented scale. Flexible, multiskilled work organization replaces the previous subdivision of labor. Skill requirements are identified on a comprehensive basis; skill gaps are diagnosed and training programs are devised to fill them. Complementarily, employees are encouraged to think of themselves in developmental terms, with a career plan and a learning program to support this (Finegold, 1991; GB TA, 1989a). The main incentive to make such changes is product competition from rivals who have already implemented them.

Far reaching though the new incentive may be, it will not carry all before it. Not all employers feel its force. In some markets there is no great force to be felt in the first place: Mass production and subdivided, detail labor remain viable and may be expected to remain so indefinitely (Nolan, 1990). Such businesses probably employ many among the one-

---

[10]Employee willingness to take up employer-sponsored training however, may be lower for literacy programs than for more vocationally oriented training, possibly because drawbacks associated with self-esteem and group identity are stronger in the literacy context.

fifth of British employees who expect their employers not to be support-
ive of any interest that they might express in training (GB, 1989b, Table
7.6b). Nor have all of the employers subjected to the new incentive been
willing or able to respond.

More generally, there is the enduring importance of the old competition. Commentators who welcome its new counterpart often idealize
the enterprise of the future and overlook the enduring training disincentives associated both with competition in the labor market and with other
aspects of competition in product and capital markets. The costs to the
employer of realizing in full the ideal of the learning enterprise would be
vast, given that it is the employer who must bear most or all of the costs of
the training involved. For example, a metal-working apprenticeship costs
the sponsoring employer in excess of £20,000 per head (Jones, 1986), and it
produces a skill that the employee is free to sell without compensation to
other employers. Employers naturally consider the cost—whatever they
say to the contrary (e.g., GB TA, 1989a)—and quite rationally desire to
limit the size and the exposure of their investment in training.

The most direct method of curbing the old competition is to
develop internal labor markets. Internal markets, in contrast to occupational ones, rely on job-based training whose content is limited in
breadth, depth, generality, and duration, and which is made available to
employees in an episodic sequence of doses throughout a long-term
employment relationship. Such personnel practices limit the cost of training by giving it only as needed and on the job when possible, by limiting
its educational and occupational content, by giving it to senior employees
whose propensity to quit is low, and by discouraging trained employees
from taking their skills elsewhere. Such practices reduce both the size
and the exposure of the outlays involved in employer-sponsored training
(Marsden, 1986; Marsden & Ryan, 1990, 1991a, 1991b; Ryan, 1984).[11]

Competitive constraints on employer training involve product
and capital markets as well. When a business increases its sponsorship
of training, it reduces short-term profitability in order to achieve higher
long-term profitability. The reduction in profitability is essentially an
accounting phenomenon. Although economic theory treats training as
an investment, which may be financed out of current profits but which
does not reduce them, as accounting practice enters training outlays on
current account, increased training reduces reported profits. Accounting
conventions would matter little if financial investors would perceive

---

[11]Employers who operate sophisticated internal markets may even find that
offering more training, including potentially transferable elements, may reduce
turnover, for example by signaling a long-term commitment to the trainee's
career within the organization (Sadowski, 1982). Training in transferable skills
has indeed been associated in some results with either only low increments to
turnover or lower turnover (Elias, 1991).

accurately the concomitant increases in the stock of human capital at the firm's disposal and therefore in its long-term profitability. Yet, such gains remain relatively invisible in the absence of intangible assets from corporate balance sheets (Finegold & Soskice, 1988; Flamholtz, 1985).

The fall in short-term profitability associated with a greater training effort can debar such a move under particular conditions in product and capital markets. Employers who sell in product markets characterized by intense price competition and low profitability may face the prospect of going out of business if they sponsor more training, even if it would be to the long-term benefit of the enterprise. Examples abound in sectors such as clothing, textiles, leather, and metal goods, in which employers report intense pressure to subdivide work and reduce training requirements (James, 1987).

A decline in short-term profit would, however, matter little if employers were able to borrow on the strength of improved future profits. That is when capital market constraints come in, associated in particular with markets for corporate control in the United Kingdom and the United States. The threat of takeover requires businesses to maximize accounting measures of short-term corporate performance. Higher spending on training—along with spending on research, advertising and other intangible investments that do not show up on the balance sheet— may be debarred by the concomitant increase in the firm's exposure to hostile takeover. The relative immunity of German and Japanese enterprises to such problems contributes to their high training sponsorship relative to their U.S. and U.K. counterparts (Finegold & Soskice, 1988).

It is the enduring influence of this range of disincentives that accounts for the low overall incidence and uneven distribution of employer-sponsored training in the United Kingdom and the United States. Even employers who square up to the new competition and give high priority to training at the same time adopt most of these practices. Recent field research in the United States suggests an enduring reliance on on-the-job training, lacking wider educational or occupational content, even among such businesses (Brown, 1991).

The key question for employer sponsorship is, therefore, how to expand it and even out its availability. The balance between the incentives and the disincentives that face employers must be altered in favor of the former.

TRAINING INCENTIVES: NON-EMPLOYER SPONSORSHIP

Training may be sponsored by governments, individuals, and trade unions as well as by employers. The parties that matter most are governments and individuals. Governments in most advanced economies sponsor training for the unemployed and the disadvantaged, but, those groups excepted, individuals who want training and cannot obtain it from employers typically have to arrange and finance much or all of it themselves. This section concentrates primarily on self-sponsorship.

Employers show little interest in assisting self-sponsored training beyond helping employees with fees for work-related courses taken after working hours. Even that form of assistance appears unimportant in Britain, where the fees for less than 2% of courses of other-sponsored training are defrayed in whole or in part by an employer (Table 1.3). The responsibility falls otherwise to the individual, with or without help from public funds. The incentive to sponsor one's own training resides in the expectation of improved job rewards (discussed previously). It is often offset by three obstacles to self-sponsorship: unavailability of suitable courses, inability to finance training, and low expected benefits.

Taking access first, although self-sponsorship has the advantage of avoiding the narrowness and specificity of much employer-sponsored training, suitable courses may not be available. Difficulties are associated in particular with the following factors: location, particularly for rural and small town residents; the unavailability of occupational qualifications which adults might use to gain employment, particularly in many craft and technical occupations for which training depends heavily on employer sponsorship within internal markets; and gender, particularly through discriminatory admission and poor female eligibility for unemployment-oriented public programs (Payne, 1991).

Such difficulties are reflected in the fact that 10% of the British workers who see obstacles to training specify a lack of suitable courses as an obstacle (GB TA, 1989, Table 11.21). The British government has promoted distance learning through the Open Tech, Open Learning, and Open College initiatives, in order to improve individual access to training, although the number of individuals sponsoring their own training appears to have remained low (GB TC, 1988b, pp. 45-47).

Even when suitable courses are available, personal ability to pay for course fees and living expenses during training may be limited. The failure of capital markets to deal with the financial requirements of self-financed training is well recognized (Becker, 1975). Individuals who lack other assets are consequently so rationed in borrowing potential as to be excluded from the longer and more expensive forms of training. Adults with family responsibilities are particularly poorly placed to forego regular earnings in order to sponsor their own training.

These difficulties are reflected both in the diversity of funding sources and in the importance of public funds reported by the limited number of individuals who manage to sponsor their own training (Table 1.3). A lack of funds or time are predominant among the obstacles perceived by the 60% of British individuals who would like to undertake training in the future (GB TA, 1989b, Table 11.21). The least difficulty is undoubtedly faced by both the most and the least advantaged members of the labor force: the former because of their wealth position, the latter because long-term unemployment brings with it, for males at least, eligibility for public training programs (Payne, 1991).

Finally, even when neither access nor finance are serious problems, particular individuals may be deterred by anticipating substandard benefits from training. Low expected benefits are likely in several situations: low educational achievement and motivation, poor health, an expectation of leaving the labor force in the near future, and, for women and minorities, discriminatory exclusion from intended occupations.

More generally, risks are usually higher and the costs of bearing them commensurably greater in self-sponsored rather than in employer-sponsored training. The lower incidence of continuous employment under self-sponsorship implies higher risks of both unemployment and inappropriate employment. Given the absence of insurance, the costs of bearing the risks associated with many long and expensive training courses will deter even well-endowed individuals if they are sufficiently risk-averse. Risks are particularly high in self-sponsored training related to occupations in which internal labor markets predominate and employers may not value the qualifications involved.

Concern that one's own benefits may be low can be found in the obstacles to training reported by the 1987 survey. The issue of risk was not explored, but as many as 13% of British workers saw a personal lack of qualifications as an obstacle to training and 10% a lack of interest and motivation (GB TA, 1989b, Table 11.21).[12]

Individual sponsorship of training therefore faces a variety of obstacles, notably front-end costs and risky benefits, which are largely absent under employer sponsorship and which make self-sponsorship much the scarcer of the two, particularly among adults.

Lack of incentives to individuals can therefore deter participation in training, but the importance of that problem is lowered first, by broadly favorable employment and earnings benefits and second, by the fact that incentives should be low, from an efficiency standpoint at least, for groups such as the old and the unmotivated. What holds others back is principally a lack of opportunity: in the labor market, the opportunity to acquire jobs that involve employer-sponsored training, and in capital, insurance, and labor markets, the opportunity to fund their own training and bear the risks involved.

---

[12]However, individual variation in expected benefits is limited. In particular, the actual short-term benefits that participants derive from publicly provided full-time training depend only weakly on such individual attributes as sex, age, and previous qualifications (Payne, 1990).

CERTIFICATION

Although most adult work-related learning has traditionally remained uncertified, interest in its assessment and recognition has recently grown considerably. Certification of adult work-related learning is normal, indeed often crucial, for success under individual sponsorship, in that it is typically a prerequisite for entry to occupational markets, as in nursing, typing, and driving jobs. It also helps workers enter internal labor markets, to the extent that employers use qualifications as guides to ability, motivation, and requisite skills, although not all qualifications pass muster in this respect, and vocational ones often stand at a discount.

Certification is, however, problematic under employer sponsorship, particularly when upgrade training in internal markets is involved. Employers prefer to train for their own needs and are consequently averse, if not to assessing, then at least to certifying the resulting skills. Employer dislike reflects partly the costs of assessment and certification; partly the short, episodic, and specific nature of most of the training that they sponsor, which makes it unsuited to codification (Mehaut & Clement, 1989); and, above all, the external regulation that inevitably accompanies certification. When an external accreditation agency inspects and evaluates the training provided within the firm, an area hitherto reserved for managerial prerogative is encroached on and pressure is exerted to train toward wider educational and occupational goals, not simply for the firm's own needs. The transferability to other employers of employee skills is both increased and made more visible, threatening on each count to raise the cost of labor turnover (Katz & Ziderman, 1990). Finally, employers may expect certification to promote the values and interests of the occupation rather than the employer—to the detriment of the productivity of workers who remain—as well as to encourage pay rises unrelated to gains in productivity.

A striking example of employer avoidance of certification is provided in a U.S. shipyard in the mid-1970s. The company was spending heavily on the training of manual arc welders, whose basic proficiency had to be certified by a U.S. Coast Guard test before they were even allowed to do production work, by which time the company had spent $1800 (1975 prices) per trainee on average. The possibility of formal certification was not announced to those who passed the test: Those trainees who asked for a certificate were brushed off as far as possible, and only a persistent handful obtained the small beige card that stated tersely that they had qualified. Through such measures management sought explicitly to reduce employee quits and their associated training costs. Ironically, the test involved only manual proficiency, without educational content, but even a certificate limited to that was of recognized value in the wider occupational labor market (Ryan, 1980, 1984).

Not all considerations point employers toward opposing certification, if only because the value that employees and unions have come increasingly to place on certification makes it useful both as a fringe benefit and as a bargaining chip. There is also the potential value to the employer of the skills audit that certification both facilitates and encourages for the internal assessment of training requirements and possibly even for presentation to the stock market as evidence of the human capital at the company's disposal (OECD, 1991a).

Such benefits have not, however, induced much employer support for external certification. Even leading knowledge-based companies such as IBM and Motorola, who have demonstrated extensive commitment to career-long learning opportunities for their employees, prefer to avoid certification of the resulting skills (Madigan, 1990). German employers, who have acquiesced in an elaborate tripartite regulation of initial training, have fought long and hard—thus far largely with success—to retain unfettered jurisdiction over adult training at the workplace (Madigan 1990; Streeck et al., 1987).

Only in two contexts have employers accepted certification. The first involves external educational qualifications for which employees can study, usually on their own time, and which are of value for career development within the firm as well as outside it. The favorable attitude of German employers toward the certification of such learning reflects partly the fact that the primary responsibility for sponsoring such training lies with the employee, and partly the benefits that employers perceive for themselves within the exceptional combination of occupational and internal labor markets which has developed there (Marsden & Ryan, 1991b; Streeck et al., 1987).

The second context involves learning at the workplace, which constitutes the core of the problem. British employers support the efforts of the National Council for Vocational Qualifications (NCVQ) to certify existing employee skills, largely because through sectoral lead bodies staffed overwhelmingly by their representatives they retain collective control of assessment criteria and methods. Similarly, in France, where institutions to assess and accredit adult work-based learning have been developed over the past two decades, the predominant influence enjoyed by employers over adult training has allowed them to slant certification more toward job requirements than toward the educational and occupational criteria favored by unions and government (Colardyn, 1990).

Controversy over the methods adopted by the NCVQ illustrates the problematic nature of certification in workplace learning. The NCVQ has attempted to base certification on the continuous assessment of employee learning by workplace supervisors, with performance in relation to job requirements as the central criterion. It claims that its focus on *competence* and *outcomes* is preferable to standard, examination-based assessments by an external agency, in that it avoids wasteful, purely academic knowledge and draws on the broad knowledge of trainees' skills which is possessed by their supervisors (Jessup, 1991).

The NCVQ approach is itself open to serious criticism for the high cost of its multidimensional assessments of trainee competence, when properly conducted, and, alternatively, for the high probability that they will not be properly conducted. Biased and unreliable assessment is to be expected when supervisors face incentives to certify defective learning and when, in the absence of external assessment, they enjoy the scope to do just that (Lee, Marsden, Rickman, & Duncombe, 1990). In either case, the NCVQ's approach pays inadequate attention to wider educational and occupational knowledge, as opposed to narrow job competence, particularly in offering qualifications for possession of the limited skills required for menial jobs (Jarvis & Prais, 1989; Prais, 1991; Wolf, 1990).

The prospects for the certification of adult learning are thus favorable for self-sponsored training in which it is often essential, but generally unfavorable for employer-sponsored training in which it runs up against widespread employer reluctance unless its content and procedures are subordinated to narrow employer interests.

PAYMENT SYSTEMS

The desirability of linking employee compensation to learning by paying higher wages and salaries for additional skill, competence, or qualifications has also become prominent in discussions of adult training. The motive is to encourage work-related learning: If an employee will be paid more for learning more, the argument goes, he or she will want to learn more.

Basing compensation on work-related knowledge and skill is in one respect far from novel. Management normally seeks to place the more qualified and skilled workers in jobs that both require more skill and offer higher pay. Earnings rise with skills and qualifications both within organizations and in the wider labor market, even if the adequacy of skill differentials is often questioned.

What is novel about contemporary proposals is the idea of a *direct* and *automatic* link between skills and pay within organizations, with job content as a secondary rather than a primary consideration. Workers are to be paid by their skills, independently of whether their job requires those skills. Management then faces strong incentives to use those skills effectively in practice, but that is an indirect consequence of, rather than a precondition for, paying workers at a skilled rate.

The contrast to mainstream practice in Europe and North America is sharp, as, under the job evaluation systems that have come to dominate most payment systems in large and medium-sized establishments, pay is determined by the skill (along with the responsibility, effort, etc.) requirements of the job rather than by the skill characteristics of its occupant. Unneeded and superfluous skills are not rewarded under job evaluation (Brown, 1990; Milward & Stevens, 1986).

Some payment systems already embody an element of direct payment for skill. Large Japanese employers pay their employees by skills and knowledge as well as by rank and length of service (McCormick, 1991). Sectoral collective agreements in both France and Germany widely stipulate that individuals with particular qualifications—notably intermediate craft ones (e.g., *Facharbeiter* "in trade" in Germany, *Certificat d' Aptitude Professionel* in France)—be paid, subject in some instances to a limited period of grace, at skilled rates irrespective of job assignment.

Payment for skill is also on the rise in English-speaking economies. Eight percent of large U.S. employers have already implemented some form of payment by skill somewhere within their organization (Gupta, 1988, cited in OECD, 1991a). Some British employers have negotiated higher rates of pay for multiskilled craft employees independently of the actual work that they perform. One goal of *awards restructuring* in Australia is to permit the development of direct links within enterprises between employee learning and pay, an option previously debarred by rigid occupational boundaries (OECD, 1990). Practical interest in payment for skill is clearly on the move.

At the same time, both employers and trade unions often resist payment by skill. Employers fear increases in hourly labor costs as a result of paying for unused and underused skills. If the upskilling of jobs lags behind that of employees, unit labor costs will rise as well, to the extent that labor productivity grows more slowly than wages. British employers who, as part of a business strategy of deskilling work and cutting hourly labor costs, fought historic battles with craft unions to break the latters' insistence on payment by skill, are not easily persuaded to reverse direction and pay for skill when it is not of immediate value.

Sophisticated employers require payment systems that are widely accepted by their employees and therefore not a source of discontent and demotivation. Payment by job content has widely ousted payment by results because of the anomalies and everyday frictions that were induced by the inequities of piecework and its derivatives (Brown, 1973). Payment by skill may also be capable of commanding widespread employee allegiance, but difficulties have been thrown up by attempts to implement it in the United States. Older, senior, and less qualified employees resist having to pass tests to demonstrate skill and acquire higher pay (Brown, 1991). Employees fear that managers and supervisors may use informally assessed competence as a form of favoritism and division. In addition, some trade unions, notably in Sweden, oppose payment for skills as disruptive of solidaristic and egalitarian wage structures, even when fairly administered (Clement et al., 1991).

The key difficulty involves the link between payment and certification. Employees and unions are most receptive to payment for skill when its objectivity is fostered by basing it on formalized assessment with external guarantees of quality. Employers find external assessment and certification unappetizing, preferring informal indicators and discretionary payment for skill. Faced with a need to develop certification alongside payment for skill, most employers prefer neither, or at most the weak linkage between learning and pay that results from periodic supervisory reviews of employee performance and which places learning and development among the criteria for the award of discretionary merit bonuses.

Nor is it clear that payment for skill is important for the expansion of learning at the workplace. It does encourage employees to accept employer-sponsored training, but as discussed previously there is little resistance on their part to overcome in the first place. Self-sponsored training is more likely to be encouraged by payment for certified skill, as the costs and risks are then directly defrayed by higher earnings after training. But there too the benefits to individuals are often limited. Most self-sponsored training occurs apart from continuous employment and much is geared to a change of occupation and employer. There is then less assurance of acquiring a job in which pay will be raised by gaining a qualification than were the trainee already employed under such a payment system.

Perhaps the main prospective benefit of payment by skill is the extension of the limited overlap which exists at present between employment and self-sponsorship, insofar as employees are encouraged to sponsor their own learning outside company time by a clear prospect of higher pay and promotion within the company. Such patterns, familiar in adult career development in Germany, would be encouraged more generally by paying employees directly for certified skills and knowledge.

Finally, insofar as payment for skill visibly increases labor costs while providing only indirect or concealed gains in productivity, it may marginally discourage employers from sponsoring training at the workplace. The primary function of payment by skill then is as a signal of employer intent, stating that human resource development is a high priority and backing up the statement by paying directly for it. More generally, payment for skill is a secondary issue for the development of adult learning at the workplace.

CONCLUSIONS

Finance and certification pose difficult issues for the development of adult work-related learning. The particular shape that they assume in practice depends heavily on whether adult work-related learning is sponsored, that is, initiated and financed, by employers or by individuals and government.

The functioning of *markets* for adult training is impaired by the gap between the financial attributes of the two types of sponsorship. Employer sponsorship means low cost and low risk for the employee; self sponsorship, high cost and high risk. Benefits to participants may even be higher under employer sponsorship, although evidence on the issue is limited. Access to employer-sponsored training is rationed on essentially nonprice criteria, both at entry to the organization and in selection for upgrade training and promotion, with trainability and retainability the key criteria in employer decision making (Thurow, 1975). Access to self-sponsored training is rationed on the orthodox criteria of willingness and ability to pay. In addition to its high cost, both absolutely and relative to employer-sponsored training, self-sponsored training is held back by the problems both of financing training and of using one's training to find suitable employment when internal labor markets predominate.

Whether or not incentives to training are adequate, therefore, concerns primarily the employer, as the predominant sponsor of adult learning. Employers are subject to conflicting incentives: On the one hand there are the considerations of labor turnover and short-term profitability that favor limiting the extent and quality of adult learning; on the other, there are the motivational and strategic benefits of extending employee learning. Although the net effect of that conflict varies by time and place, even learning-oriented employers seek to shape employee learning to the requirements of jobs and careers in internal labor markets. The employee and public interest in wider learning, geared to occupational and educational goals, consequently exerts little influence.

There is therefore a need for public policy and collective bargaining to tip the balance in favor of broader and deeper learning at work. The era of employer sovereignty over adult learning at work will not end rapidly or easily, but it should be prodded toward joint regulation, embodying employee and external interests and centering on the assessment and recognition of acquired knowledge and skill. A broad framework of national vocational qualifications is currently being installed in several countries. Certification can improve both the market for and the collective regulation of adult learning at work if it develops in suitable directions.

There must also be a *quid pro quo*. For both economic and political reasons, workplace learning cannot be exposed to public scrutiny and regulation without offering employers incentives to extend and improve it. Employers who develop their employees' skills to meet jointly determined standards must be rewarded. The fiscal, statutory, and tripartite interventions practiced in France and increasingly in Australia point toward the range of pressure points needed to push employers in the desired directions (Clement et al., 1991; GB TA, 1989a; Madigan, 1990).

Incentives to individuals require consideration as well. Sponsoring one's own training remains a subsidiary part of adult learning in all economies, consistent with its cost and riskiness. There is scope for the extension of a public subsidy beyond its traditional associations with unemployment and formal schooling in order to provide more loans and grants to individuals sponsoring their own learning. The need is particularly clear in Britain, with its solitary, underfunded Career Development Loans scheme (GB DE, 1988; Ryan, 1990).

The two strategies are complementary. Helping individuals to sponsor their own training increases the pressure on reluctant employers—who either do not train or who train only for narrow job needs—by shrinking their labor supply, in both quantity and quality. Workers who can see not only the benefits of training but also a way of obtaining it will less readily tolerate a workplace that offers them little or no training at all.

2

Do Most Employers and Workers Underinvest in Training and Learning On the Job?

John H. Bishop
Cornell University

Many economists question the need for social intervention in training, arguing that the benefits accruing to employers and employees create sufficient incentive for private financing. Research findings indicate that in practice this means depending on employers because it is they who pay for the bulk of employee training, even when the skills being taught are useful at other firms. Yet in practice, private incentives for on-the-job learning and training do not currently generate broader results that are in the public interest. This chapter looks at the theoretical and empirical evidence of market failure in training provisions. It argues that the training market in the United States is failing to provide a socially optimal quantity and quality of employer training. Specifically, it examines four potential sources of market failure: real externalities, tax-induced distortions, liquidity constraints, and government regulatory interventions that discourage training. Each of them are found to operate to some degree in some training markets.

REAL EXTERNALITIES

Public control and subsidy of schooling and public involvement in other forms of education and training is justified because the individual who gets the education and training receives only part of its benefits. There are social benefits as well. When deciding on the type and amount of education and training to undertake and how hard to study while at school, most individuals are taking only private benefits—the higher after-tax income and the prestige and consumption benefits of having an education—into account. These private benefits account for only part of the total benefits to society of education and training, however. People who have received more or better education and training or who achieved more during the experience benefit others in society by paying higher taxes, by making discoveries or artistic contributions that benefit others in the society, by being more likely to give time and money to charity, by being less likely to experience long periods of hospitalization that are paid for by insurance or government, and in many other ways (Haveman & Wolfe, 1984). Economists call social benefits such as these *spillovers* or *externalities*. Private decisions will lead to an insufficient quantity and quality of education and training and insufficient achievement by students, unless public agencies intervene and partially subsidize the cost or add to the rewards. The appropriate amount of public subsidy is closely related to the size of the spillover or the externality benefits of education and training. Two kinds of real externalities produced by training are discussed next.

Discoveries and Disasters Attributable to Training

High-quality training benefits customers and the public as well as the trainer and the trainee. When, for example, the dancers of the New York City Ballet receive excellent training, the company benefits through greater ticket revenue, but the audience benefits as well because they derive a larger consumer surplus from the performance. The COMSAT employee who figured out how to double the lifetime of communication satellites by judicious use of the rocket fuel remaining on board benefited customers and competitors at least as much as he benefited COM-SAT. The Aloha airlines pilot who landed the plane after an explosive decompression and the loss of a major section of the plane certainly raised the lifetime earnings of the passengers. On-the-job training (OJT) and experience were critical to the COMSAT discovery and the safe landing of the Aloha plane.

When a worker makes mistakes because of poor training, the

customers and the general public often lose as much as the worker and the company. Examples of disasters caused or contributed to by poor training are legion: Chernoble, Three Mile Island, Exxon Valdez, the shoot-down of the Korean Airlines 747 flight (pilot error caused the plane to be off course), and Greyhound bus crashes in New York State. Tort law internalizes some but not all of these costs. A study of egregious physician errors in New York State found that only one-eighth of them resulted in a malpractice claim. Damage awards are typically paid by insurance funds that are imperfectly experience rated. Where the public interest in insuring top quality training is manifest to all, training is often regulated or subsidized by government. The Federal Aviation Administration, the Department of Transportation, and the Nuclear Regulatory Commission, for example, engage in such regulation.

However, for every big discovery or disaster that gets media attention and generates a political response, there are millions of little discoveries, unrewarded services, or unanticipated product failures that directly effect consumers that do not generate political responses. Because customers lack low-cost access to accurate information on the quality of what they are buying, the prices paid do not fully reflect quality differentials between different providers. As a consequence, training that enhances quality and reliability often generates benefits to customers that are not recognized or rewarded by the market.

Poor Signaling of General Skills to Other Employers

The training provided by one employer benefits other employers and consumers, not just the trainee and his or her employer (Bishop, 1991). The worker is more productive in future jobs, but these employers do not perceive accurately the quality of the general OJT received by the worker and, as a result, do not fully compensate the trained worker for their higher productivity. Bishop's (1994) study of the relative productivity and profitability of new hires obtained results that are consistent with this hypothesis. New hires who had received formal off-the-job training sponsored by a previous employer made significantly more suggestions designed to improve productivity, were more productive, and profitable and were less likely to be fired. If one accepts these findings as valid, the implication is a market failure that reduces the payoff to worker investments in OJT. The ultimate cause of this problem is the lack of effective signals of the quantity and quality of training.

Institutions for signaling occupational competence—a comparison. In the U.S. labor market, hiring decision makers have a very difficult time assessing the quality of the general human capital obtained from OJT.

Such assessment difficulties increase turnover, lower wages, and lower productivity. Because part of the reason for getting general training is to improve the worker's marketability with other employers, not recognizing the benefits of training reduces the incentive to invest in general OJT.[1] Doing an especially good job of training employees will benefit the trained workers when they leave the firm, only if the firm develops a reputation for being a good trainer.[2] Past experience with the former employees of a firm is probably the primary determinant of a firm's reputation as a trainer. Large firms that turn over a reasonable share of their trainees are likely to develop a reputation (good or bad) for the training that they provide. It is well known, for instance, that IBM and General

[1]Lack of information about the quality of general OJT received can increase investment in general OJT only under the very unlikely circumstances of very high retention rates and large differentials between the rates at which employers and employees trade off present before-tax income for future before-tax income. Under these circumstances the employer's desire to invest in general training may be stronger than the worker's desire. Because the wage will have to be increased by an equivalent amount, employers cannot benefit from (and therefore do not pay for) general training that is visible to other employers. Consequently, as such training becomes more visible to other calculus that determines the amount of training shifts to give greater weight to the very high discount rates faced by the worker, possibly reducing investment in general training. The condition that would have to be satisfied is that the retention rate would have to be equal to or greater than the ratio of the firm and worker discount factors. Even if the worker were to face yearly interest rates that were double the firm's rate (e.g., 30% rather than 15%), the yearly retention rate would have to be above 85%. Retention rates for the first year at a job are seldom above 50% and average yearly retention rates for all employees new and old seldom exceed 85%. Yearly retention rates of employees who have been at the firm for many years may exceed 85%, but these more mature workers will typically have better access to capital markets than younger workers and face a tax regime that is neutral to OJT. This discussion has been based on the theoretical analysis of the training decision presented in Bishop and Kang (1984, 1988).

[2]Well-trained employees who leave the firm that provided the training may benefit if their new employer eventually learns of their greater-than anticipated productivity and makes later adjustments to their wage or bases a promotion on it. In the model presented in Bishop and Kang (1984, 1988), high renegotiation costs prevent such adjustments from occurring at the first employer. If a third period was added to the model and retention in the second job modeled, the same assumption of high renegotiation costs would prevent the worker from benefiting from better-than-expected training in the second job. If one were to relax the assumption that post-training wage rates are prespecified and analyze a multiperiod model, the size of the distortion to training investment decisions would be reduced, but it would not disappear. Productivity is measured with error so one could never expect the new employer to perceive the full value of the worker's greater-than-anticipated training. Furthermore, other employers remain ignorant of greater-than-anticipated productivity. For all intents and purposes this greater productivity is specific to the firm, so the worker will only receive a small share of this greater productivity in higher wage rates.

Electric provide excellent training to their newly recruited junior executives. The positive reputation helps the separating employees find better jobs, and, in turn, helps the firm recruit the best possible candidates when it is hiring. Even though a good reputation as a trainer forces them to pay higher wages in the posttraining period, most firms have a strong interest in establishing such a reputation. The armed forces are aware of the positive training reputation and consequently spend millions of dollars advertising the quality and civilian usefulness of their training.

Most young workers without a baccalaureate degree, however, do not obtain jobs at the large firms with established training reputations. The smaller lesser known firms in which they find their first job typically have unknown reputations when it comes to the quality and general usefulness of their training.

The lack of full reward for improvements in general skills if one leaves the current employer affects the incentives for the trainer and trainee to devote time and energy to learning general skills. The higher the worker's likelihood of leaving the firm, the lower is that worker's incentive to devote him- or herself to learning general (or specific) skills that are not immediately visible to other employers. As a result, the underinvestment in general OJT is greatest for temporary and seasonal employees and for young people as a group.

The poor quality of the information about a job candidate's general skills and the resulting underinvestment in general training (both on the job and in schools) is a major institutional flaw in U.S. labor markets. Formal systems for certifying the competencies gained through OJT exist in the United States, but they have not achieved the widespread usage they deserve. The apprenticeship systems of Switzerland, Austria, and Germany are probably the best examples in the world of widespread and effective systems of OJT and competency certification. One of the most important features of these apprenticeship systems is the requirement that the apprentice pass written and practical examinations covering the occupation's curriculum. If an employer cannot provide training in all the skills included in the curriculum, it must arrange for its apprentices to receive instruction at another firm or at a special employer-run school. The examinations are set and scored by a local committee of masters (skilled workers) and employers, so the quality of the training provided by the master and the firm is put to a public test. Passing the apprenticeship exam is of benefit not only to the trainee, but it is important to the masters as well. Their reputations among their peers and their abilities to recruit high-quality apprentices depend on it. As a result, 90% of German apprentices remain at one employer for the full 3-year apprenticeship period, and 90% of these apprentices pass the test (on the first or second try). The apprenticeship systems of the

English-speaking nations are based on *time served* rather than on *competencies achieved* and are considerably less successful in standardizing and upgrading the training that occurs.

The examination at the end of the training process is the key to maintaining quality control. In the late 19th century, the Swiss educational/training system went through a period of crisis and self-examination not unlike what is now happening in the United States and the United Kingdom. The nation had to export to survive, but the quality of workmanship was low and deteriorating. The Swiss assigned blame to their apprenticeship system and proceeded to reform it by ending apprenticeship based on time served, establishing a standardized curriculum, and instituting written and practical examinations set by local committees of employers and workers. The high standards of workmanship for which Swiss workers are renowned are not an inherent trait of national character, but rather are the consequence of the institutions that teach, test, certify, and publicize the workmanship.

The standardized curricula and the proficiency exam at the end of the apprenticeship mean that the quality and nature of the training is well signaled to employers in Germany, Switzerland, and Austria. The result is that the worker can count on benefiting from doing a good job in his or her apprenticeship, even if the training employer does not retain them. Because the future payoff is certain, German apprentices are willing to start out at a wage that is only about one-quarter of the wage they will be able to command at the end of the apprenticeship. If the apprentices were adults, they could not afford to accept so low a wage. They are, however, teenagers living at home who are heavily subsidized by their parents. Consequently, the liquidity constraint that is such a barrier to heavy investments in general training in the United States is much less of a problem in Germany.

TAX-INDUCED DISTORTIONS OF THE TRAINING MARKET

The Nondeductibility of Some Training Expenses

The benefits of training are taxed, but not all of the costs are deductible.[3] Some of the time that trainees devote to employer-sponsored training comes from reducing leisure time. Employees taking job-related college

---

[3]If training an employee causes a reduction in output or necessitates an increase in hours paid, profits, and thus taxes, are reduced. If workers pay for training by accepting lower wage jobs, individual income tax payments are reduced. In both of these cases, training costs are effectively deductible in the year they are incurred. If all individuals pay taxes every year at the same marginal tax rate,

courses typically attend classes and do their homework on their own time. Japanese workers frequently take correspondence courses related to their job and, when they are rotated to a new job, the meticulous description of how the job is done, written by its previous occupant, is studied at home. Japanese supervisors are expected to fill slack time with training. When Ronald Dore presented his passport at an out-of-the-way port of entry that seldom sees British passports, the supervisor called his younger colleagues over and taught them about its intricacies while Dore looked on (Dore & Sako, 1989). Such a training session delayed passengers somewhat and necessitated a sacrifice of on-the-job leisure, but output—the number of passengers processed—did not change. Incentives to undertake training are distorted if government does not share in the costs of training to the same degree it shares in its rewards.

The Progressive Income Tax

The second tax-induced distortion arises from the fact that investments in OJT are typically made at a time when the individual has no tax liability or a lower-than-normal marginal tax rate, and the benefits are received when earnings and marginal tax rates are higher. As a result, the after-tax benefits of an OJT investment are reduced more than the after-tax costs, and such investments are discouraged. Firms, on the other hand, train continuously, so the marginal tax rates faced when the costs of training are incurred and deducted are no different from those faced during the payoff period.

HIGH BORROWING COSTS AND LIQUIDITY CONSTRAINTS

The third reason why society subsidizes schooling is the failure of the free market (in the absence of publicly funded loan guarantee programs) to offer loans to young persons seeking to invest in their education. The government recognized long ago that people going to school needed access to low-interest, government-guaranteed loans. Workers investing in general OJT have a similar need but are not eligible for such loans unless they happen to be part of a training program run by an accredited educational institution. Because of the fear of turnover, employers are reluctant to pay for general training that is visible and useful in other

---

the tax system would not distort decisions to invest in OJT. In fact, however, some training costs are not deductible and tax rates are generally higher when benefits are being received than when costs are being incurred, so the tax system discourages training investments.

firms. If the employer is not willing to pay for general training, it will be offered only to those workers who pay for it by accepting a lower wage during the training period than could be obtained elsewhere. The more intensive the training, the greater the required reduction in wages will have to be. Many workers are unwilling to accept a large reduction in their current standard of living, and because they are unable to borrow at reasonable interest rates, they forego the investments in general OJT.[4] If they fund such investments, they do so only if extremely high rates of return can be obtained.

Most young workers are liquidity constrained, that is, they are unable to shift as much consumption from the future into the present as they would like because they have neither assets that can be depleted nor access to credit at reasonable terms. Half of the households headed by someone under 25 years old have less than $746 in financial assets, and 19% have no financial assets at all. Half of the households headed by someone between 25 and 34 years old have less than $1514 in financial assets, and 13% have none (Survey of Consumer Finances, 1984). Subsidized or guaranteed student loans are not available to finance OJT, and banks will not lend money for training purposes without collateral. Borrowing against the equity in one's home is a possibility for some, but only 34% of the households with heads under 35 years old own a home, and many of the houses have been owned for only a short while, so that the equity that can be borrowed against is small. Even with collateral, the loans available to individuals usually carry higher interest rates than those charged businesses. Studies of the willingness of consumers to substitute consumption over time have all concluded that the intertemporal elasticity of substitution is no higher than 1, and most studies conclude it is .5 or below (Friend & Blume, 1975; Hall, 1988; Hubbard & Judd, 1986). A substitution elasticity of .5 implies that reducing a liquidity that constrained a worker's wages by one-half (in order to pay for general training) roughly quadruples the worker's marginal utility of consumption. Such a worker would be willing to give up $4.00 of future income in return for $1.00 of current income. The liquidity constraint phenomenon has little effect on the wage profile of jobs requiring no general training

---

[4]Becker clearly recognized the existence of liquidity constraints in his 1962 article. "Since employer specific skills are part of the intangible assets or good will of firms and can be offered as collateral along with tangible assets, capital would be more readily available for specific than for general investments" (p. 42). He did not, however, explicitly how such constraints might influence the tenure profile of wages and thus induce employers to share the costs of general training. Parsons (1972) points out that "The worker's . . . discount rate will affect the firm's choice of wage policies. . . . It can be shown that firms will decrease the worker's share of specific investment as the workers discount the future more heavily" (p. 1129).

and which, therefore, have a flat productivity profile. Where significant general training is occurring, however, it comes into play and may result in an employment contract in which the employer shares the costs of general training (Feuer, Glick, & Desai, 1987; Glick & Feuer, 1984).

Firms are thus more willing than workers to trade future earnings for present earnings. The compensation packages that result from the asymmetric access to capital markets and the progressive tax structure reflect the worker's strong preference for compensation now rather than later. In effect, firms offer new hires a loan that will be canceled if a separation occurs. Firms do not require repayment of the loan when separations occur for the same reasons that banks do not offer large unsecured loans without a government guarantee of payment. The administrative costs of obtaining repayment are extremely high, and bankruptcy is a real option for someone with zero assets. Firms, however, undertake to finance some of the costs of general OJT only when their investment yields a return sufficient to pay for the cost of capital and the risk of turnover. Such justifications reduce employer investments in general OJT below the level that would have prevailed if workers were able to borrow at the same interest rates as employers.

REPAIRING GOVERNMENT-CREATED DISTORTIONS

A fourth justification of public efforts to encourage greater OJT is to undo the damage done by other government interventions in the labor market that discourage it. With respect to investments in OJT, the two most significant of such interventions are the minimum wage and barriers to employer use of basic skills tests and high school grades as devices for selecting new workers.

Minimum Wage

The minimum wage prevents unskilled American workers from offering to pay for general training by accepting a subminimum wage during the training period. Providing training to a new employee is costly. The new employee is not very productive at first, and other workers must take time away from their regular activities to give instruction to the new hire. Many of the skills that the new employee learns have application in other firms as well. To avoid losing the worker to another firm, the employer providing the training must raise the wage as the trainee's productivity increases. Jobs that offer training and the prospect of future wage increases are more attractive than those that do not. The competition for these jobs will enable employers offering general training to obtain workers at lower wage rates.

Minimum wage legislation, however, prevents wage rates from falling below the legislated monetary figure. Lacking the ability to get new employees to pay a major share of the costs of general training (by accepting a low wage during the training period), employers will adopt production technologies that minimize the skill requirements of the job. The evolution of the diner and the small, family-operated restaurant into franchised fast-food operations using specially designed machines and prepackaged food is an example of how this is accomplished. By reducing the skills required to do the job, the employer shortens the time it takes for new employees to reach maximum productivity. The same people may have the job, but they are taught less, and what is taught is useful only in that firm, not elsewhere. Opportunities for promotion are minimal, and wage increases are small or nonexistent.

A second impact of the minimum wage is that the forced increase in the starting wage is partially compensated by a fall in wage rates during the posttraining period. The fall in wages increases the quit rate, which in turn reduces the payoffs that employers receive from formal training and, therefore, their willingness to make such investments or to hire individuals who require substantial training investments. The predictions of theory have been confirmed by at least two studies (Hashimoto, 1982; Leighton & Mincer, 1981).

Barriers to Careful Selection of Entry Level Workers

In the United States, governmental institutions and regulations are an important reason why American employers do a poor job of selecting entry-level workers and experience very high rates of turnover. Employers are not able to obtain good information on the skills and competencies of young job applicants. Employers believe that school performance is a good predictor of job performance[5], but they have great difficulty getting such information. If a student or graduate has given written permission for a transcript to be sent to an employer, the Federal Education Rights and Privacy Act obligates the school to respond. Many high schools are not, however, responding to such requests. In Columbus, OH, for example, Nationwide Insurance sent over 1,200 requests for transcripts signed by job applicants to high schools in 1982 and received only 93 responses.

An additional barrier to the use of high school transcripts in

---

[5]Policy capturing experiments have found that employers give substantially higher ratings to job applicants with high grade point averages (Hollenbeck & Smith, 1984).

selecting new employees is that when high schools do respond, it takes a great deal of time. In most high schools, the system for responding to transcript requests has been designed to meet the needs of college-bound students rather than the students who seek jobs immediately after graduation. A 1987 survey of a stratified random sample of small- and medium-sized employers who were members of the National Federation of Independent Business (NFIB) found that transcripts had been obtained prior to the selection decision for only 14.2% of the high school graduates hired.[6] Only 15% had asked high school graduates to report their grade-point average. The absence of questions about grades from most job applications reflects the low reliability of self-reported data, the difficulties of verifying it, and the fear of Equal Employment Opportunity Commission (EEOC) challenges to such questions.

Hiring on the basis of recommendations by high school teachers is also uncommon. In the NFIB survey, when a high school graduate was hired, the new hire had been referred or recommended by vocational teachers in only 5.2% of the cases and referred by someone else in the high school in only 2.7% of the cases.

Tests are available for measuring competency in reading, writing, mathematics, science, and by EEOC guidelines, which made it prohibitively costly to demonstrate the validity of tests assessing competence in English and mathematics.[7] Before such a test could be used, the firm had to conduct a very expensive validity study of the proposed test and alternative tests at their own work sites. Separate studies had to be done for men and women, blacks, Hispanics, and whites. Most firms did not have enough workers in each category to do a reliable study (Friedman & Williams, 1982). Litigation costs and the potential liability are substantial. Using an event study methodology, Hersch (1991) found that corporations that were the target of a class-action discrimination suit which was important enough to appear in the *Wall Street Journal* experienced a 15% decline in their market value during the 61-day peri-

---

[6]The survey was of a stratified random sample of the NFIB membership. Larger firms had a significantly higher probability of being selected for the study. The response rate to the mail survey was 20%, and the number of usable responses was 2,014.

[7]The Supreme Court's decision in the Wards Cove Packing Case has made it easier for employers to defend the use of selection methods that produce adverse impact and has therefore opened the door for increased use of employment tests. It appears that employers will be able to justify the use of employment tests without having to undertake costly validity studies in their own firm by citing validity research done for similar jobs in other firms. Congress is considering legislation that would reverse Wards Cove and make it even harder to defend the use of selection procedures that have adverse impact than under the Griggs precedent. If this legislation passes, the ability of firms to make wise hiring decisions will deteriorate even more.

od surrounding the announcement of the suit. Companies became extremely cautious about testing, and the result was to greatly diminish the use of tests for employee selection. A 1987 survey of the membership of the National Federation of Independent Business found that basic skills tests had been given in only 2.9% of the hiring decisions studied.

Other countries handle the signaling of high school accomplishments to prospective employers much more effectively and have much lower turnover rates as a result.

CONCLUSION

Turnover affects the stock of trained workers in three ways. First, high turnover necessarily implies that a given rate of investment in firm specific skills yields a smaller stock of workers with such skills. Many of those trained have moved on to other firms at which the firm specific components of training wield no benefits.

Second, turnover has a powerful effect on employer decisions to provide training to employees. Employers, not workers, finance most of the training that is undertaken in U.S. firms (see above). Employers will not invest in training unless they believe it will generate a monthly return that exceeds the sum of the monthly turnover rate (generally above 2% per month in the United States and sometimes greater than 8% per month) and the cost of capital (which is about 1.5% per month or 18% per year). Monthly turnover rates are typically much larger than the cost of capital and are also much more variable. If turnover is 5% per month and the cost of capital is 1.5% per month, the cash flow yield of the training investment rate of return must exceed 78% per year if the investment is to make economic sense. Even when turnover is very low—2% per month—required cash flow yield is still quite high—42% per year. Training thus becomes a sensible investment for an American employer only when it yields very rapid and very large returns. The amount of training employers are willing to finance is negatively related to the projected turnover rate of the trainees.

The third reason why turnover is so critical is its impact on the process of teaching and learning. Turnover disrupts learning regardless of whether the skills being learned are generic or firm specific. Schools teach general skills and follow a common curriculum, yet have great difficulty when students transfer from one school to another during the school year. Teaching must be adjusted to the special needs of the learner, and it takes time for the teacher to learn of those special needs. Learning occurs best when instructor and learner have a close personal relationship, and it takes time to build such relationships.

The high rates of turnover in America, then, help explain why investments in OJT are lower in this country than in Japan and Germany.

SECTION II:
Legal Incentives

3

Worker Access to Vocational Training: A Legal Approach

Jean-Marie Luttringer
Caisse des Dépôts, France

This chapter considers the application of legal requirements to develop vocational training for workers. It focuses particularly on experiences in France, where a strong legal framework of employer obligations has been in place for two decades.

It is argued that the system has served an important purpose by creating far more vocational training than would otherwise have existed. However, a system based solely on employer obligation will not provide the right incentives for effective training of the workforce of the future. Furthermore, new initiatives are beginning to emerge in France that give employees more responsibility for their own training in partnership with their employers.

The concept of incentives for training needs to be changed in a new "post-Tayloristic" work environment. When work becomes less hierarchical, the idea of requiring managers to order workers into training needs to be revised. The concept of "co-responsibility," discussed here, relates closely to the theme developed by Hirschhorn in this volume: that learning within organizations is likely to be ineffective unless it is linked to individuals' capacity and authority to make decisions. Therefore, training may need to become more integrated into organizational change than has been practiced in France, where much training has been imposed externally by employers. Legal incentives for training should not be discarded, but rather adapted to meet new requirements.

THE INTERNATIONAL CONTEXT

Awareness of the strategic importance of continuing training for workers is strong in industrialized countries. The general educational level of individuals and their qualifications are determining factors not only for economic competitiveness but also for the optimal functioning of democratic societies.

International Agreements

Such an imperative has been incorporated into international treaties and national legal systems during the past two or three decades. For example, UNESCO organized four international meetings on continuing training that took place in Elsinor (in 1949), in Montreal (in 1960), in Tokyo (in 1972), and in Paris (in 1985). These meetings led to recommendations to foster the development of continuing training. The International Labor Organization (ILO) adopted conventions and recommendations on paid educational leave and on career guidance.

    The European community has followed recommendations of the Treaty of Rome (1957) for integrating young people into working life through vocational training in which formal study and work are alternated (*alternance*). The European Council (EC) of Ministers has offered financial and technical support for such training to member countries. An EC directive that aims to promote access to training is being implemented within the framework of the European Social Charter passed in 1990. Although it has no prescriptive power in this field, the Organisation for Economic Co-operation and Development (OECD) has been very influential. Its work on recurrent training and the individual's right to training, on the integration of young people into the workplace, and on the close link between training and human resources management has considerably influenced supranational as well as national legislation.

National Legislation in Europe

Most European national legislation tends to encourage workers' access to continuing training. The legislation establishes rules relative to the setting up and financing of such training. Some significant features of the European position in this field include:

- *European national legislation on continuing training remains heterogeneous*. It is closely subordinated to three factors: first, to the position and orientation of the educational system (Is it centralized or decentralized? Is it a public service monopoly? Is it allowing a role for private initiative?); second, to the orientation of the industrial relations system (Is there a tradition of conflict between employers and trade unions or a tradition of collective bargaining and joint management?); and third, to the country's level of development (i.e., Northern Europe contrasts with Southern Europe). Furthermore, the application of legislation depends on each legal system's characteristics. For example, public policies have focused their attention on access to vocational training for jobless people who have been laid off or young people without qualifications.

- In all, three subsystems can be distinguished within the training system: the integration of young people, unemployed workers' training, and vocational training for workers in jobs. Conditions of access to training, the status of beneficiaries, and financing all vary according to the subsystem.

Although this chapter focuses on the subsystem of workers in jobs, there are overlapping areas among the three subsystems that are worth mentioning. Thus, youth integration increasingly involves *alternance*—alternation between training and work—under contracts that have both elements built in. Companies are also asked to take in young people for practical vocational training without any work contracts. The same legal techniques are used to bring back to work long-term (more than 12 months) unemployed people.

- *Several European countries use legislation for individual training leave* (Germany, France, Belgium, Italy). However, the quantitative impact of such a legal tool remains limited. Less than 1% of the potential beneficiaries have access to it. Even though the tool could certainly be improved, it cannot be the main answer to the problem, which is the necessary development of access to vocational training for workers.
- *Many firms have become aware of the double necessity of the elevation and evolution of labor force qualifications.* Thus, the training of their employees becomes a strategic stake. Newly developed initiatives rely mainly on collective bargaining and on firms' agreements.
- Legal structures and financial inducements set up by European countries to facilitate vocational training have left a number of issues unresolved. For example, training most commonly consists of short courses without recognized certification. Almost everywhere there is a tendency to concentrate training on a privileged few, resulting in an increasing dispar-

ity between those who are trained by firms and those who are not. Moreover, worker attitude surveys indicate that some "structural brakes" to training participation remain: fear of management refusal, fear of losing one's job, fear of disruption in family life, and fear of failing.

THE FRENCH MODEL: BUILDING INCENTIVES THROUGH A LEGAL AND FINANCIAL ENVIRONMENT

A 20-year Process

Although the French system has existed for 20 years, it is continually undergoing change. Both the government and private industry have viewed worker training as a priority and have struggled to promote legislation that facilitates incentives. They deal with a number of ongoing issues, such as:

- Should employers be obliged to train their employees or, on the contrary, should they remain free to make this choice as a corollary of freedom to hire and to manage?
- Should employees' vocational training be a compulsory subject of bargaining with the employees' representatives? Should joint management be set up in this field, or should the employees have the last word?
- Should training become an object of collective bargaining with unions? If so, at which level: the firm, the professional branch, or both? Should this collective bargaining be compulsory or should it remain optional?
- Should the development of a training provision by the firms and their professional organizations be encouraged, or, on the contrary, should a diversification of training supply be encouraged?
- What should be the share of responsibility for financing training among firms, employees, the government, and other public professional bodies?

As early as 1970, answers to these questions had been produced—by management and labor through collective bargaining, and by the legislature through the law—but they have been regularly reconsidered over the past two decades by collective agreements or new laws. In July 1991, the first interprofessional agreement of July 16, 1970 was renewed after a 1-year negotiation process. A new law is in preparation to legalize the interprofessional agreement. The system stemming from the decade of progress is on the way to long-term stability.

The initiative led by the French government was a precondition to the development of workers' continuing training in France, especially because room for initiative in the social and economic sphere is limited. Such a precondition seems to be especially true in a field such as education and training—the foundation of French republican ideals—and, therefore, are seen as the responsibility of the state.

Specific French cultural factors that underlie the new legal, institutional, and financial environment are: the rediscovery of free enterprise values during the past 10 years, the ebb of the ideology of a class struggle between trade unions and bosses, and the rehabilitation of private businesses from *predatory* to *creative* behavior.

The French System: Who Pays for Training

French legislation is one of the few in the world in which an obligation to finance the employee's continuing training is borne by the firm. (Other examples are Belgium and Greece.) The obligation was conceived by the legislation instituted in 1971, precisely as an inducement to develop continuing training by firms.

Added to the central mechanism of training finance are joint financing systems that have been implemented by the government to support the training of certain priority categories of worker. Several of the financial mechanisms are described next.

The employer contribution. Every French firm employing at least 10 persons is obliged to give a certain percentage of its wages to the financing of staff training. The percentage is currently 1.2% of the payroll. Labor proposes that the legal minimum should be fixed at 1.4% in 1992 and 1.5% in 1993. It also proposed that firms employing less than 10 people make a smaller contribution of about 0.15%.

Such a financial mechanism has been much debated. Is it bureaucratic and unnecessarily restricting or, on the contrary, has it played an incentive role? After a 20-year experience, it appears that the second opinion prevails because management and labor have both suggested its extension to small firms. One attractive characteristic of the system is its flexibility. Firms have three possibilities to free themselves from the obligation: They can organize in-service training, delegate training to external bodies, or mutualize part of the training insurance funds established for the firms of a particular branch or region by employers' organizations and trade unions.

Whereas part of the legal obligation can be used freely, 0.15% out of the 1.2% must be used to pay for individual training leave through specialized funds of joint management mutualization, and 0.3% (0.2% from 1993) must be allocated to the financing of *alternance* devoted to young people who are less than 26 years of age. This incentive becomes a tax only for firms that do not engage in training.

The average expenditure of French firms for the training of their employees is now about 2.90% of the payroll, 32.9 billion francs in 1989. (It was 1.35% in 1972.) Some budgets even reach 8%-10% of the payroll. An insignificant number of firms have to pay the unused sums to the public revenue department. But it is important to stress that firms' behavior is very different according to their size and to the sector to which they belong. Eighty percent of the firms employing between 10 and 19 workers remain close to the minimum level.

The financial mechanism has strengthened and professionalized company training and has developed a training market worth 40 billion francs. A dialogue and collective bargaining on training relies on stable financial means.

Joint financing mechanisms—private and public. The French government has its own training policy and its own budget. Its priorities are to support unemployed and unskilled young people and also job seekers. Therefore, its direct intervention for the financing of employees' training is marginal. On the other hand, its indirect intervention in firms to benefit their staff is quite significant. The intervention strategy has several goals and takes various forms:

- To encourage the firms to increase their training expenditures and tax credits for vocational training enabling firms to receive a tax reduction. The credits cover 25% of training expenses above the 1.2% minimum. To qualify, firms must show that their workers have benefited by obtaining higher qualifications or reducing their risk of maladjustment.
- To increase planned employment and vocational training, there are several public legislative instruments. They are structured within the framework of conventions established among the public authorities, the firms concerned, and the representatives of professional associations. The government particularly encourages the development of training, professional equality between men and women, the reduction of working hours, the prevention of redundancy, and a general modernization of the firm's management. Training activities can be financially supported by the government. For instance,

a major study on the future needs of truck drivers was financed in this way.

- To support the access of less qualified workers to training, a system of training credits was created in 1989, restoring an impetus for the idea of equal opportunity to employment and training. The state recognizes that it owes unqualified workers access to training. To fulfill this responsibility, the state pays 50% of all costs of mutual organizations in charge of the financing individual training leave. This is meant to increase the company contributions, to the benefit of less skilled workers' access to training placements.

Employee contributions to their own training. The debate on the issue of employee contributions recently opened in France. It is a very sensitive theme in French culture, heavily influenced by the prevailing idea that initial training should be free of charge and that it is the firm's exclusive responsibility as to whether to continue training. In fact, many workers already contribute to the financing of their own training.

However, a poll carried out at the request of the Confédération Française Démocratique du Travail (CFDT) (the second largest trade union confederation) shows that workers are far from being opposed to the idea of a contribution to the financing of their own training. The theme has found a concrete translation in "co-investment." Article 70-7 of the new French interprofessional agreement echoes this. It stipulates that a training program leading to a recognized qualification can take place, with the consent of the worker, outside work hours and without payment, but for no more than 25% of the training period.

The same agreement mentions the use of training penalty clauses. The employer agrees to finance the employee's training, provided that the latter commits him- or herself to remaining on the staff for a certain length of time, which should be long enough to pay off the agreed training investment. If the employee leaves before the due date, the employee is compelled to reimburse the firm for part of the training expenditure that was paid. This kind of contract is subject to legal control, and a judge can decide to reduce the amount paid by the worker in cases of disagreement.

Three other systems of encouraging employees to help finance their own training have been discussed, but have not been legally accepted. These include: (a) payment of subscriptions to training insurance funds by employees themselves, (b) favorable tax treatment of training savings programs on the financial markets, and (c) income tax exemption for the expenses of employees' continuing training. Clearly there is a wide range of possibilities that still could be developed. They have not yet been implemented for cultural and ideological reasons, and also because the market for this kind of financial bond is still unexplored.

According to studies by the OECD and EEC, a number of factors, such as demographic shifts and the pace of change, predict an increasing demand for employee training within the coming decades. Further, imaginative approaches to help workers finance part of their own training will likely be developed.

Strengths and Weaknesses of the French System

Today, most of the actors—firms, workers, unions, and the government—feel strongly that vocational training is important for the future of France. As much as 85 billion Francs (about $15 billion), about 1.4% of the gross national product, are spent each year in France to finance vocational training, including public spending. But the system is facing three main difficulties:

- Public money is mainly used to train unemployed people.
- Firms often finance short training periods with a short-term view. No new qualifications are gained by the worker in such training.
- Vocational training financed by the firms benefits mainly those who are already qualified. This is true also in other European countries; in Germany, for instance, 50% of the trainees have received some university-level education.

The French vocational training system is characterized by the fact that, probably more than anywhere else, it is organized through public and collective bargaining control. This is quite different from the situation in other countries in which the firm or the worker are *consumers* of vocational training. In France, it is generally agreed that the involvement of workers and managers in vocational training needs to be encouraged by social and state regulation. This is reinforced by the nature of contractual relations between employer and employee, which is considered in the following section.

ACCESS TO TRAINING AND THE FRENCH WORK CONTRACT

The French employee's status is characterized by dependence. Indeed, the employee is under the employer's orders to carry out a specific job corresponding to an agreed qualification for a specific length of time and for an agreed wage. Unless there is some specific stipulation, however, the regulations of work contracts do not include a duty of training. Thus, in two cases, the French Cour de Cassation (Court of Appeal) ruled that the employer had no definite training obligation because there was no apprenticeship contract. The decision was based on the principle of the autonomy of the employer, who is the only judge of the employees' skills. It was declared a constitutional principle by the Constitutional Council in 1982. The principle hardly encourages workers to receive training, nor does it leave much room for initiative. Rather, the concept implies that the professional qualifications of employees must essentially be acquired outside the workplace.

The underpinnings for this contract was long-standing theory about the scientific organization of labor. But the times are changing, and training—for a long time external to labor relations—is on the way to becoming its new framework. The components defining the work contract—qualification, work and its organization, time—are no longer fixed features. Thus, training now tends to become an integral part of the work relationship. The idea that training is not something a worker is "owed," but that it must be employee-invested as well as employer-invested, is gaining ground. Thus, a new right to training, characteristic of the post-Taylorist era, is emerging in France. It is characterized by improved integration between work and training, one feeding on the other, instead of externalized vocational training.

The following section addresses the place of training in classic labor relationships; the concluding section identifies some new perspectives.

The Traditional Place of Training Within the Workforce

Characteristics. The classic model—in effect the French *droit positif*—can be summed up by the following seven characteristics:

1. In accordance with the managing power conferred, the employer is bound to look after the safety of the staff and to provide them with the equipment and tools needed for work, but is not held to a general obligation to train employees. If the work contract or the legislation do not expressly stipulate it, the employer has no training obligation. Nevertheless, there needs to be agreement by all concerned over a definition of the training concept in cases in which the purpose of training is to provide increased qualifications.

2. On the other hand, the courts consider the employer to be

bound by a training obligation in the case of induction into a job, whether it be the first job or a new job. The rule is implemented particularly when the employer decides to transfer an employee or when the work organization is modified. So, when an airline company changes the type of planes it uses, it has to allow pilots to acquire the qualifications required to operate the new aircraft. Such an obligation, acknowledged by judges as an integral part of the general power of the employer, can be included in collective bargaining.

3. Whereas the training obligation of the employer remains limited, the duty of the employee to be trained when work organization demands it is much more clearly established. The employee who refuses to be trained or who does not make enough effort may be laid off for professional inadequacy. Judges do not sanction the refusal to be trained in itself, but rather the consequence of this refusal, that is, the professional inadequacy it implies. And the employer is the only one entitled to decide on this, subject to the ruling of a judge.

4. In some occupations, employers propose additional clauses to their workers' contracts called "training penalty clauses." The effect is to compel the signatory to reimburse employers' training expenditure if they quit before the agreed investment is amortized. The application of the clause is a function of the labor market situation. When the qualification acquired is in scarce supply and the training expensive (computing, aircraft industry, etc.), then the firm tries to avoid a turnover of its staff and to protect itself from competition.

5. A certain number of firms encourage their employees' access to training as they do their access to leisure activities, sport, and culture, as part of a social policy. In concrete terms, there is some payment of training expense for workers trained outside working hours or payment of a bonus when they pass an examination, or even granting days off that are allocated to a vocational training schedule outside the legal training period. The various compensations are given by the employer according to free choice. It does not affect the work contract.

6. Work contracts of specific types combine a job with training. In this case, the initiative does not belong to the firm but to the public authorities wishing to help unskilled younger people get a first job or people excluded from the labor market for a long time to return to work. The initial subject of the work contract is to provide jobs in return for adjusted remuneration for the workers. A job with training is provided in exchange

for a lower wage and financial support from the government. In this type of contract, the training incentive is the main goal. First, there is a financial incentive from the government (through firms' reduced salary costs, social security contribution exemption, and subsidies through the training). Second, there is an invitation for the employee to be trained, namely the granting of a work contract, that is, the recognition of a legal and social status, that of *alternance* training, which means the acquisition and enhanced value of knowledge for people who cannot go back to school. Such contracts recognize a right for the worker to make mistakes.

7. French law has adopted and developed the idea of training leave. The separation between work and training is the legal technique used here. The work contract is suspended during the period of training. The access to training was encouraged by the relevant international organizations in the early 1970s.

Exercising the right to training leave is characterized by the employees' free choice of training program. Employees may choose to attend courses other than those suggested by the employer. The incentive for training relies on the principle of free choice of paid training. However, experience has shown some limits to the system. On the one hand, employees face the risk of being separated from the firm during the training, and, on the other hand, the resources available are too small to allow a significant number of workers to be trained (about 30,000 a year participate in France).

All things considered, such a contractual tool, while needing improvement, remains an important means of access to the training of employees. Legal and financial systems with enough incentives to favor the access of a significant number of employees to training must be found within the work contract.

Critical Assessment

The model described here is strongly influenced by a conception of the employer's extensive power with respect not only to the running of the organization but also to the management of the labor force and especially to the management of collective and individual qualifications. The ability of an employer to use power to evaluate the professional fitness of a worker's adaptation to employment shall not be contested, judges contend.

According to the "scientific organization" of work assumed in the model, the individual qualifications of the worker are simply left to the opinion of the employer. So careful attention is given to proficiency and to the evaluation and fitness of individual qualifications. The only thing that matters is the capacity to adapt to the job.

Employees who wish to improve their skills on their own initiative must do so outside the firm, through evening courses, training leave, and so on. The acquisition or the transformation of qualifications are not usually linked to a contractual relationship. That happens only when worker qualifications are rare on the labor market and when their acquisition is long and expensive. In other words, the logic of *responsibility* is now substituted for the logic of *obedience* which underlies the juridical system in France.

New Perspectives

In connection with the "post-Taylorist" approach to human resources management, it is possible to find new legal perspectives related to the concepts of investment and co-investment.

From Training Investment to Co-investment

The idea of training as an investment appeared in the 1980s in France and was accepted by the trade unions in 1987. More and more, firms now see the training of their employees as an investment in addition to the investment in physical capital. For management, vocational training has become of strategic importance, and its goals, implementation, and feedback need to be well organized. On the employee's side, too, one's future career in the firm or elsewhere relies on training: The employee is now expected to manage self-skill development.

All this has juridical consequences. Collective agreements are being signed that include stipulations on training based on the future qualification needs of the firm. Obviously, the employees are asked to be prepared to be trained.

To summarize, a list of future qualifications in the firm is required. An individual's right to a skills assessment is needed, and contracts have to specify that the employee agrees to train him- or herself with higher qualifications in return.

Juridical Approach

In the July 1991 interprofessional collective agreement that may soon become law, each employee receives a right to an individual skills assessment, which includes an analysis of the employee's potential future, including vocational training. Every five years, an employee has the right to 3 days' training leave, with the company paying some or all of the cost. The same agreement provides for co-investment training: A maximum of 25% of training time can be taken outside working hours, with no wage during that period. It is restricted to training courses that last more than 300 hours.

It has also been agreed that a contract will be discussed in collective bargaining, at the occupational branch level, stipulating that employees who get a long but costly training from their company must remain in that company for a certain number of years (or repay the cost of training). Also, it has been agreed that at least every five years, management and unions will negotiate the vocational training at the industry level, especially its priorities, according to industry needs and individual qualifications. At the company level, management has to set up a program of training, including a precise description of the qualifications needed in the future.

Finally, before this nationwide agreement, some firms, many of them large, had already developed this kind of program. And, in many cases, the courts decided that management has a duty to train its workers. But this is true only for trainee contracts for young people, financially assisted by the government. Such a duty could nevertheless be recognized more broadly in the future by the courts, especially when a company creates skill redundancies that could have been avoided through vocational training that has not been carried out.

CONCLUSION

What is the role of public policy and legal tools in encouraging training? In France, two nonjuridical conditions must be met:

1. To continue to develop modern methods of human resource management: participative management, organization based on skill qualifications, anticipating future skill needs, and regular and individual assessment of skill levels.
2. To continue to develop the role of collective bargaining as distinct from the government role, which is historically too strong. In the words of Crozier, "a modern state is a modest state" (Crozier, 1987).

Once these two conditions are fulfilled, it is possible to stress some ideas on a more legalistic level. The legal tools for organizing training outside work, which frequently imply no link with work, are not efficient enough to respond to the rapid change of skill qualification needs that we face. These same tools can be improved by developing training time-sharing between employee and company and by developing new financial resources, especially to encourage employees to invest in their training (tax breaks, training saving funds, or insurance).

At the heart of the matter is the role of management with respect to qualifications. The constantly evolving skill qualification requirements are in the employee's interest as much as that of the employer. The work contract must reflect that. The training work contract for young people in *alternance*, which has been established by public policy over the past 10 years, should now be extended to adults.

4

Legal Incentives and the New Workforce

Thierry Noyelle
United Nations Conference on Trade and Development, New York
Donald Hirsch
Centre for Educational Research and Innovation, OECD

Legislating incentives or sanctions to encourage companies to train their workers is a tempting but problematic way of improving a country's human resources: It is tempting because the perceived private return from enterprise-based training can be limited by labor mobility, whereas the perceived social return can be considerable; and it is problematic because training is not a uniform process that will always bring benefits if delivered in sufficient quantities, and because it is difficult to construct legal incentives that reward only effective training. In recent years, the temptation to invoke legislation has been boosted by a realization of the importance of worker skills to national economies. At the same time, potential problems have grown as the relationship between skills and productivity has become more complex and more closely intertwined with the organization of work within individual companies. Jean-Marie Luttringer's report in this volume touches on several important issues concerning education and training related to work (hereafter referred to as vocational training). These include: (a)

Who are or should be the target populations for vocational training? (b) Who pays for vocational training? and (c) Does a system based on legal incentives create the kind of training that workers need? Luttringer's particular concern is to understand how the French policy and legal framework has addressed these issues since the early 1970s. The picture in France is one of a system that has fulfilled an important function, but which is being subjected to underlying tensions that are growing in importance. The problem might be summed up by noting that a system that gives clear, legalistic answers to the question of who pays for training does not necessarily provide satisfactory answers to the questions of who should be trained and what training they should receive.

TARGET POPULATIONS

Luttringer is careful to emphasize from the outset that the issue of vocational training is one that concerns not simply the employed labor force, but, equally importantly, underskilled youths facing difficulty getting work and the unemployed. He also points out that within the employed workforce there is a tendency for training to be concentrated on those who have received high levels of education and training in the past. It is worth pursuing the matter of target populations because the case against concentration on privileged groups has recently been strengthened by several developments including: the changing nature of work, which produces rising skill needs across the entire employment spectrum; increasing job mobility; aging labor forces; and limited literacy levels among a wide section of the population.

As work becomes more complex and less hierarchical, the skills required of ordinary workers are changing dramatically. No longer is it adequate to train, as in the Taylorist model, a few senior managers to be thinkers and problem solvers, who give commands through a management hierarchy to the mass of workers with, at most, narrow technical skills. The wider competencies needed in post-Taylorist production of both goods and services has been well-documented by the Organisation for Economic Co-operation and Development (OECD) and others (see, for example, Bertrand & Noyelle, 1988). Thus, there is a need to spread training among a wider selection of employed and potential workers than in the past.

Furthermore, developments in labor markets make traditional training strategies less appropriate than in the past. For a start, the diminishing numbers of new entrants into the labor force makes overdependence on youth training unwise. In many OECD countries, new entrants account for slightly over 2% of the workforce, and it may take 20-25 years for half the workforce to be replaced. In addition, it is not possible to train a new entrant for life, if only because the rate of job change is now so high. In Canada, for example, 8 million workers, or 55% of the workforce, changed jobs (including within their companies) during 1986 and 1987, according to a longitudinal survey by Statistics Canada (quoted in Ross, 1990). In short, there is a pressing need to provide continuing education and training for the adult labor force.

The need for continuing education and training is particularly strong with respect to employed and potential workers whose literacy skills are limited. Recent studies have revealed that this group is larger than previously thought if literacy is defined as possession of the reading competence needed in everyday life. A recent international study of adult literacy and economic performance in OECD countries concluded that literacy was a limiting factor for a substantial section of the workforce everywhere, mainly as a result of the widening competencies needed by workers (Benton & Noyelle, 1992). Again, telling evidence comes from Canada, where a 1989 survey found that 38% of adults had less than full functional literacy (Statistics Canada, 1989).

Legislation for vocational training does not always target the low-literate group. The tendency is to make a division between continuing training for those in work—in large part for professional and already-trained groups—and special state-funded training for the unemployed and young entrants to the labor market. Meanwhile the large number of employed workers whose performance is limited by a lack of certain basic competencies are largely left out.

WHO PAYS?

Most countries have become well aware of the importance of labor force retraining. Luttringer points to two competing models for providing it: in one, *consumer-driven*, demand expresses itself freely on the market; in the other, *interventionist*, the state intervenes to force the creation of vocational training.

In consumer-driven training, firms choose to invest in their labor force because it is in their economic interest: Training boosts productivity which, in turn, boosts competitiveness and profits. Similarly, individuals invest in their own training because training increases their lifetime earning expectancy. The state supports certain retraining costs because it lowers the long-term welfare costs associated with supporting unskilled youths and unemployed people.

Under the interventionist model, the state steps in to dictate to each firm its degree of involvement in the training process. Presumably, the United States epitomizes the first model, France and other European countries the second.

Luttringer suggests that the second model has great advantages over the first. In France, the state makes a major effort to assist in the retraining of unskilled youth and the unemployed, and enterprises are required by law to invest at least 1.2% of the value of wages and salaries in the training of their own workers. The result is an expenditure of approximately 85 billion French francs, or 1.4% of Gross Domestic Product (GDP), on vocational training.

The superiority of the interventionist model, however, remains to be proven. The 1.4% of GDP spent on training in France is no more than the amount spent in the United States, which is estimated at approximately $80 billion for a $5.2 trillion economy, or 1.5%. Furthermore, current fashion is to point to the Japanese model of industrial training as ultimately the most successful, and Japan is much closer to the consumer-driven than the interventionist model. Luttringer argues that France's strategy was dictated by its particular culture and traditions, and it might be that an initial impetus from the state is indeed needed in countries that traditionally look to government for a lead. More needs to be known about the comparative effectiveness in terms of costs and benefits of the two models.

CAN LEGAL INCENTIVES BE SATISFACTORY?

Luttringer argues that French policymakers and social partners need to move away from a training model anchored in a Taylorist emphasis on insuring that workers are provided with the necessary set of relatively narrow skills to perform relatively narrowly-defined jobs. A post-Taylorist system, on the contrary, must prepare workers for ever more broadly defined jobs.

By its nature, the interventionist model is best equipped to influence training that is typically formal and off the job. In contrast, informal on-the-job training is difficult to measure, thus difficult to influence through legislative or regulatory incentives. As a consequence, we think that the interventionist model risks falling short of its intended target.

Certainly, the legislated changes that Luttringer suggests are potentially useful, but much of what has been learned in recent years about the retraining of both poorly skilled and better prepared employed workers is that contextual learning and a strong learning environment are the two important ingredients to successful labor force retraining. Both are difficult to legislate because they stress, to various degrees, merging training and retraining with daily work. This discussion is more than simply the old debate about the merits of *on-the-job* versus *off-the-job* training. It is no longer about using supervisors to teach new recruits a relatively narrow and unchanging set of skills. It is about creating work environments in which the routine part of the daily job is largely subsumed into well-identified procedures and/or technologies and in which dealing with the nonroutine becomes the norm. The successful firm is that which can create an environment in which workers can identify abnormal situations and design and implement solutions to them as part of their normal activities.

Such fundamentally organizational, on-the-job transformations are very difficult to write into law. A system that rewards companies for providing off-the-job training is bound to distort the pattern of training expenditure. Compared to a system that allows companies to spend money as they think best, it may slow the move toward the new approaches to learning emphasized here and identified elsewhere by Sticht in this volume.

On the other hand, it should not be taken for granted that there is a fixed pot of money that employers are bound to spend on training. Luttringer has argued that legislative measures have boosted the total expenditure in France. Perhaps there is a tradeoff between legal incentives that help build companies commitment to training and a consumer-led development of the most appropriate training strategies by firms. One would hope that in time the terms of this tradeoff might improve, in favor of the consumer-led path. As companies develop a better understanding of the importance of workforce training in postindustrial economies, they might learn to develop appropriate training strategies without having to be told to do so by governments.

SECTION III:
Work Organization Incentives

5

Organizational Change and Adult Learning

Larry Hirschhorn

Center for Applied Research
Philadelphia, PA

As organizations face increasingly complicated settings and decisions, researchers, consultants, and managers have examined how and when organizations can learn. Organizational learning has acquired a new importance in discussions about human resources development. The usefulness at work of the education and training of an individual can no longer be divorced from the context of the work setting. In a post-Tayloristic work environment, it is the work team's ability to operate effectively as a group, not simply the skill level of individual workers, that determines performance.

Organizational factors also have an impact on learning incentives. Factors such as pay and job prospects often encourage workers to enroll in training programs offered by their employers or external trainers. Yet, the greatest incentive actually to learn something at work (beyond simple attendance of a course) is the prospect of using that learning to make work more worthwhile, either by enabling one to do one's job more effectively or by improving one's position within the organization.

Discussion of organizational learning has often been far too general. People frequently equate organizational learning with the maturity, wisdom, and intelligence of the organization's members. These discussions and ideas are sensible and even provocative, but they fail to highlight how organizational life shapes learning and fail to pay attention to the tools people may need to learn more effectively within their organizational settings.

This chapter explores a more concrete approach to organizational learning. Working from the sociotechnical tradition, it emphasizes how learning tools—the technical domain—and groups—the social domain—interact to create learning opportunities. Each domain has its own texture and properties.

———

This chapter is presented in three sections. The first describes a case study of a group of people within an organization who could not use a tool to learn and analyzes the aspects of the social and technical domains that contributed to the problem. The second describes and analyzes a case study of a group who used a tool successfully at one stage of their work, but failed to use it at a later stage. The third section summarizes what can be learned from the two case studies.

CASE ONE: WORKING WITH A COMPUTER MODEL

I and my consulting team were asked to help a large metropolitan transit organization (MTO) assess how its maintenance operation should be reconfigured so that mechanics and inspectors could repair and maintain trains with many more electronic parts. Ten prototype cars, incorporating the most advanced electronics, would arrive in the barns within the year. The leaders of the MTO wanted to prepare inspectors and mechanics for these prototypes and for the subsequent fleet of cars they would be ordering in the mid-1990s.

To begin our work, we asked the leaders of the maintenance organization to form a steering group and then to create a design team that would work closely with the consultants in developing a picture of the maintenance organization of the future. Composed of inspectors, mechanics, general supervisors, information specialists, reliability engineers, and training professionals, the design team represented a cross section of the maintenance organization. The work with the design team was intense. Team members wrestled with the dilemmas of whether technology would complicate or simplify repair work, whether maintenance workers should repair electronic boards, and whether software would help them anticipate rather than simply react to failures.

As one component of our work with the MTO we began developing a schematic model of the maintenance process itself. We wanted to understand, for example, how cars entered the shop, what affected their turnaround time, and how preventive maintenance affected the rate at which cars needed repairs. Following our principals of consulting, we decided to work collaboratively with members of the design team and the maintenance organization to build a computer model of the organization and obtain basic data that would allow the usefulness of the model to be tested.

We used *Stella*, a systems dynamic computer program that allows people to model the interactions of a complex system, to develop a rough sketch of the maintenance process. Stella is a very flexible program. It uses icons to show causal loops; positive, negative, and multiplicative relationships; and it can be easily modified as the user develops a conception of the system under study. It produces graphs that show the changing value of variables over time.

For a two-day workshop to test our first draft, we met with Sam, a superintendent who had come up from the trenches; his subordinate Paul, who was a general supervisor; Bill, a mechanic from another barn; and Phil a technical analyst, who could provide rough estimates of certain variables. After we introduced the model and its purpose, the discussion grew suddenly hostile. Sam, the superintendent, was suspicious and said that the ebb and flow of work in the shop could never be modeled—things were just too variable there, there were too many exceptions, and therefore one could never predict what would happen in the barn. Sam also worried that the model would get into the wrong hands, that decision makers would make predictions based on the model, and that the shop would suffer in turn. High-level decision makers simply could not be trusted. He worried as well that we, the consultants, did not understand the complexities of the environment and would support destructive decisions. When asked, for example, about average turnaround time for a train to get in and out of the shop, Sam noted that a motor operator once had a heart attack bringing a train into the yard, the train rammed the barn door, and it took several days to remove the train from the tracks. How could one talk of average anything?

We tried to explain that the model was hardly as nefarious as he imagined it to be—that it provided a mental picture of relationships and that it could not be used to run a shop. It was a tool for thinking, for sense making, not a tool for operational decisions. Sam would not be persuaded and seemed convinced that we would develop a decision tool that would ruin the shop. The model was viewed in concrete terms and could not be seen as an aid to conversation, a mind-expanding medium for clarifying how to think about the maintenance process overall and for exposing potentially hidden relationships.

Sam's attack on the model made it difficult for others to work as well. Paul, the general supervisor who worked under the superintendent was quiet, while the analyst Phil struck a cynical pose about what could possibly be learned. Bill, the mechanic, was most revealing. When asked during the first morning's break for his opinion of the model, he responded, "The model is totally worthless." Asked why, he said, "Well, you can only use averages." We tried to explain that indeed the model did not just use averages, that it could use random numbers to generate variability and unpredictability, but soon realized that it did not matter what we said. From Phil's rigid perspective, the model was either perfect or worthless, good or bad. There was no room to explore, to learn.

Analyzing the Case Study: The Social Domain

What was going on here? The superintendent and the group took *Stella* too literally, too concretely. Viewing it as an engineering tool, they believed that it would distort the functioning of the shop. It was a bad engineering tool, dangerously out of sync with the complexity and variability of work on the shop floor. The superintendent could not see the tool as the consultants saw it—as a model, a metaphor, a mind-expanding device that could amplify thinking about the general properties of the maintenance shops, not any one shop in particular.

But why was the superintendent so rigid? I suggest that the model provoked Sam's anxiety and uncertainty about his own authority, his superiors were irrational, they could destroy his shop, and disregarded his know-how. The superintendent lived in a complicated bureaucratic world, one in which superiors were unpredictable, budgets were maddeningly tight, and policies were frequently changed. Indeed, the design team had struggled to find its voice in the project, and at several joint meetings with the steering group, several design team members had been frightened by some senior managers' unpredictability. The superintendent had reason to worry. But the model was not to blame. Instead, *the superintendent did not feel authorized in his role. He felt powerless, with no freedom to learn or to play with ideas.*

Indeed, Sam's rigidity and overly literal conception of the tool were connected. This suggests a fundamental hypothesis: When people feel unauthorized, they take a learning tool too literally, and consequently, they cannot play and cannot learn. Consider the practice of brainstorming. Facing a problem, a work group will brainstorm suggestions to solve it. To do so successfully they must not censor their own ideas or evaluate other people's contributions. If they are worried about the quality of their suggestions, if they believe that their bosses or peers will evaluate them, they cannot contribute fully to the brainstorming process. If they do not believe that they are full members of the group, authorized to think and contribute equally, they are inhibited. Consequently, they take the brainstorming suggestions of others too literally. They focus on their apparent impracticality and on their direct fit with the current situation, rather than see them as springboards or as germs of a powerful idea. They cannot treat the brainstorm suggestion abstractly as a metaphor for another thought or feeling. Because they feel unauthorized, they think too literally.

Consider the following analogy. Adults can reshape their emotional stance, they can, for example, rework grief so that it is ordinary sadness, by watching a touching film. The film functions as a model or tool, creating a metaphor for their lives. Because the film is not their lives, they are free to experience feelings and thoughts that might otherwise frighten them. Alternatively, if they are too frightened to begin with, the film will feel too close for comfort, they will take it too literally, and they will consequently not be able to learn from it. It will neither touch nor change them.

As these examples suggest, when effectively used, a tool for learning creates models that function as metaphors. A model of an environment, whether it be computer-generated, a mock-up, or mathematical, provides an alternative domain, a context with a different set of rules that helps people discover connections and patterns that cannot be seen nor understood in the real world. Thus, for example, the Stella model helped us expose the links between preventive maintenance and turnaround time, shorn of all typical exceptions in the real world. A model is more transparent than the domain it mimics, and this gives it its power. At the same time, the model is not the real world. By abstracting from the real world the model gives the freedom to "play" with the world without doing it damage. Thus, the model is and is not of the real world, and by occupying this transitional space it helps people play and learn. However, if people feel unauthorized, if they do not feel potent in their roles, the model's power to reveal connections is frightening. Taking it literally, they imagine that it will show them up, rob them of their knowledge, reshuffle their setting, and thus further reduce their authority. That is why the superintendent emphasized the ubiquitous exceptions in the shop to the point of telling the story of the motor operator with the heart attack. He had to stake out an untouchable domain of knowledge and action.

Sam's anxiety, however, was not simply rooted in his personality. On the contrary, he worked in a highly bureaucratic setting in which policy was unpredictable, maintenance managers could feel undercut. Representing and enacting the limits of the MTO as a potent system, Sam also inhibited others. Paul, his subordinate, could not afford to disagree with him, while Bill, the mechanic, was probably frightened by Sam's response. In addition, the superintendent deauthorized the consulting team, making it harder for us to take up our roles as consultants and teachers. We all experienced Sam's powerlessness, and consequently, the group as a whole lacked potency.

I remember most poignantly, Paul's reflections after two days of work. He said he was disappointed that he had not been able to play with the model as he had expected and desired. I sensed how restricted and inhibited he felt and said a few encouraging words—yet, shared his disappointment and sense of defeat.

Analyzing the Case: The Technical Domain

The tool itself, the *Stella* program, may have contributed to the difficulties. To be effective a learning tool must amplify the ability to imagine. For example, brainstorming amplifies the ability to free-associate, to connect two ideas that have no overt links to each other. However, three properties of a tool are critical: its *transparency*, the degree to which the tool matches people's common and ordinary ways of thinking (what is meant by "user-friendly"); its *power*, the degree to which it exposes critical relationships; and its *flexibility*, the degree to which it helps a person change, revise, and edit ideas. Brainstorming is transparent. Because everyone daydreams and fantasizes, it is easy to free-associate if not inhibited. But brainstormng is not very powerful; it sets up potential connections among issues or objects in the world, but does not really highlight or clarify them. In addition, it is too flexible. Thoughts and connections can be easily disregarded as a list of ideas is built. It does not help to develop understanding.

Stella is a powerful and flexible tool, but at the MTO it may have been insufficiently transparent. Although people throughout the shop were familiar with computers and used data to analyze their operations, they lived in a mechanical world in which they related to objects and prized their own custom-designed hand tools. *Stella* challenged the norms of the work culture. It was a tool that represented relationships abstractly through graphs, arrows, and loops in an environment that valued objects and physical things. In the shop, people acquired knowledge by touching, moving, and sizing objects. They did not learn by moving concepts around on paper. Thus, even if they had felt fully authorized, they would have had to work hard to use the tool, though they might have been more eager and excited by the challenge and less angry at the difficulty.

This brief case thus points to the rudiments of a sociotechnical conception of organizational learning. On the social side, people's experience of their authority will affect how they approach and use a learning tool. The feeling of authority is in turn rooted in the organization's process. People feel authorized when they have elbow room to do their work and freedom to invent solutions to practical problems. If, by contrast, they feel unauthorized and powerless, if they have little elbow room and freedom to accomplish their work in their own way, they will take the tool too literally and be unable to play and learn with it. On the other side, people will be unable to use a tool that is insufficiently transparent and powerful and inappropriately flexible. As Figure 5.1 shows, the social and technical dimensions must be appropriately combined to create an effective organizational learning situation.

CASE TWO: BUILDING A SCALE MODEL

Consider the following vignette at the MTO. The design team worked with us to create *the ideal shop of the future*. Using sketches they had developed over several sessions, they met for two days to build a scale model on a 4 x 8 footboard. They used foam core (a light plastic material that is easily cut but retains its shape), toy train tracks, and other props, and worked with the help of a designer, John, who joined our consulting team. On the first day, June, the head of the capital facilities group at the MTO, and a member of the steering group joined the design team.

The design team worked rapidly. They decided how many tracks the shop should have, which should be used for inspection and which for repair; the width of deployment of lockers, computer stations, electronic wall displays, and work tables in the wide main aisle; the distribution of grease, air, and water through a trough rather than from overhead cables; the deployment of a crane that could move freely on an overhead track; and the use of an overhead walkway to stop visitors from traveling through the shop.

As people stood around the board talking, arguing, and pointing, the conversation was intense, rapid-fire, and concentrated. The designer John and an assistant hustled to keep up with the suggestions,

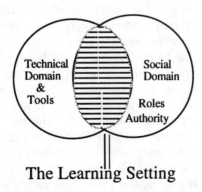

The Learning Setting

Figure 5.1. Interaction Between Technical and Social Domain

cutting foam core, moving tracks, measuring distances. June, the head of capital planning, the most senior member of the group, played a critical role in the discussion. She challenged them, asked them to clarify their assumptions, and made her own suggestions. Far from being inhibiting, June's presence stimulated everyone to think sharply. Indeed, in the course of one complex discussion in which she pushed and cajoled team members, the group solved a problem that had stymied architects for years: how to construct a platform that extended the length of several cars so that car cleaners could get easily in and out of a car with their cleaning equipment. One person argued that if you built a platform the width of half a track on both sides of the car, one could not get under the car easily to put out the rare but dangerous fire that might start under the track. If a platform was put on only one side of the car, the cleaners and others would be exposed to a live third rail. Working intensely, the group rapidly came up with several solutions involving electrical switches for taking power off the third rail. Rejecting these designs because they seemed unsafe, the group then hit on a simple compromise: Construct a permanent platform on each side of the car one-quarter the width of the track, thus covering the third rail, and then build trapdoors on the sides of the platform so a mechanic or cleaner could get under the train if necessary. The solution seemed simple, but it had evaded engineers and architects for a long time. Recalling her earlier skepticism, June now noted how much fun she was having working with the team.

Analyzing the Case Study: Linking the Two Domains

What was going on here? I suggested that the social and technical domains were appropriately combined. On the one hand, the learning tool—the grid and building materials—was sufficiently transparent, powerful, and flexible. The tool was transparent because team members immediately and naturally understood how to view and work with a scale model. It was flexible because the foam core could be easily cut and sized, and the tracks and props could be quickly moved about. Finally, it was powerful because people could look at spatial relationships in context, linking, for example, track width to the number of tracks, crane movement to the placement of grease and lubrication hoses in troughs, and the overhead walkway to the station floor.

In addition, the tool enabled the team to think metaphorically. With the exception of the designer, team members rarely touched or handled the grid and the materials. Before the work had begun, I had assumed that as craft people, team members would readily and eagerly build with the foam core and play with the trains. Instead, they used the model to think, to turn inwards toward the mind's eye and create ideas. Because the model could represent the physical space to them in so clear and secure a fashion, they could use it as a springboard for reconfiguring the space and the objects within it. They needed to keep their hands off in order to imagine. Thus, as they created a design, they moved back and forth between the model and their ideas, using the model to stimulate thinking and then watching the designer embody their thoughts in the evolving model. Had they worked with the scale model directly, their thinking would have been more inhibited. They would have experienced the model as a system of concrete materials rather than as a metaphor.

The group also felt authorized. Two factors are critical in this case. First, having worked together for eight months, team members had begun to experience their capabilities as a working group and had wrestled some authority from the steering group of senior managers who reviewed their work. Second, June, the head of capital planning authorized them by challenging them, giving them hard problems, and then working with them. Representing senior management at the MTO, she communicated by the way she took her role, that senior managers expected the team to solve tough problems. If June had taken her role differently, she could have deauthorized the team. For example, she might have remained quiet and watchful, communicating that she was evaluating the group or represented harsh reality by suggesting that proposed solutions could not work.

Analyzing the Case: The Failure to Learn

Surprisingly, the appropriate integration of the social and technical domains during the model building quickly fell apart. When the model was finished, John the designer suggested it was time to tear it down, turn the board over, and work with the grid on the other side to create a redesigned *shop of the present*. The group was horrified. How could they tear it down? On the contrary, they wanted to present it to the steering group as a valuable product. The designer countered that it was common practice to build a mock-up, take pictures of it (as had been done), strip it, and then start over. What counts, he said, is not the model but the ideas. The group would not budge. What would they have to show for all their effort and months of work? How could their ideas be enough? No, they wanted to keep the model; indeed, they wanted to embellish and beautify it. They wanted to construct part of the roof using colorful red model brick, complete the walkway, and build a cutaway of the offices. In short, they wanted to make their scale model attractive and realistic. John relented.

John's suggestions had clearly mobilized the group's anxiety about their authority and competence. The steering group would not honor their ideas, but would demand a product. Consequently, they began to look at their model in concrete, literal terms. It was no longer a metaphor, a springboard that could evolve as they created new ideas. It was a product. Now they needed to get their hands on it and make it look complete and finished.

Like Sam the superintendent, group members had reason to worry about their authority. All had experienced the dilemmas of working within the MTO bureaucracy. Accountability was diffuse, and policies were unreliably implemented and followed. The leader of the steering group had changed midstream, and design team members were uncertain about who supported them. It was necessary to be cautious. Feeling uncertain of their power and authority, the design team short-circuited its learning. They took a model rich in ideas but rudimentary in appearance and decided to embellish it, thus insuring it could no longer be a wellspring of ideas. Thus, even though the scale model was a transparent, powerful, and flexible tool, the team could no longer use it as a vehicle for learning. Instead, treating it literally, they killed it by making it pretty.

Table 5.1 highlights the ways in which the social and technical domain interacted in our three different vignettes.

SUMMARY: THE DILEMMAS OF AUTHORITY

Organizational learning takes place when people feel authorized in their roles and use learning tools that are transparent, powerful, and flexible. Bringing these two domains together in the future poses new and important challenges. Analysts and researchers imagine that the new computer technologies will simplify the challenges of organizational learning. By painting a picture of the new employee hooked into a computer network through which he or she participates in conversations, contributes ideas, and learns from others, they imagine that the quintessential flexible tool, the computer, will solve all the dilemmas.

This technocratic image of organizational learning confuses an individual's thoughts with an organization's competence. Organizations ultimately learn through action, through taking steps to rearrange work, establish a new policy, or test a new strategy. New ideas must ultimately be joined to someone's capacity and authorization to decide. To promote organizational learning, in other words, the idea must be embedded in a set of role relationships through which people experience the potential links among what they are thinking, what someone will decide, and how resulting role relationships might change.

Table 5.1. How Social and Technical Domains Interact

Vignette	Technical Domain	Social Domain	Key Issues
Stella	Tool is powerful, flexible, but not transparent	Sam feels powerless, others are inhibited by Sam's anxiety	Model is taken literally, is assumed to be an engineering tool, and therefore powerful in the practical sense. People cannot play with the model.
Building the scale model	Tool is transparent powerful, and flexible	Group feels authorized particularly by June's presence	Model is taken as a metaphor, people do not put their hands on the model. People have fun.
Preparing to present the scale model	Tool loses its flexibility	Groups feel unauthorized and helpless	People take the model literally and embellish it. They invest it with power, just as they deauthorize themselves.

Thus, the design team at the MTO could learn because it was accountable to the steering group for producing plans and ideas. The steering group, in turn, had the authority to act on the basis of the design team's ideas. The relationship between the two groups transformed a potentially abstract and lifeless activity into one charged with feeling and thinking. When thinking is not embedded in role relationships, people's creative capacity is dulled. This is why very creative technicians and workers in factories and offices can feel and appear deskilled. This is also why people who go to training events where authority relationships are suppressed rarely apply the ideas they learned. In both cases they feel cut off from the sources of authority and consequently feel powerless themselves. When thinking is joined to authority, the results can be dynamic. The presence of the head of capital planning at the design team meeting created stakes and added juice to the work. She charged up the meeting. Certainly computer networks can help people generate ideas, but if these ideas are not linked to the system of role relationships, to the challenges of working in and through authority relationships, they may well be ignored and devalued.

The field of sociotechnical systems has been remiss in this regard. Its original thinkers and practitioners, such as Trist and Emery, hoped to authorize workers by creating self-managing teams. In such settings, it was imagined, the supervisor, engineer, and plant manager would function as a support system for the team. Increasingly, this is seen to be a fantasy. People are keenly aware of the authority relationships in their setting, however much they are suppressed or stage-managed, and they respond accordingly. Moreover, as the number of managerial levels throughout organizations is reduced and workers collaborate increasingly with engineers, programmers, and other staff specialists, people will need to think, work, and collaborate in settings in which authority differences are ever present. New sociotechnical designs are needed to link teams to their bosses through their shared contributions, while helping each retain a sense of authorization and potency.

A final vignette is striking. After two days of work on the computer model, Sam and the superintendent and his group were leaving our offices. I introduced them to my boss, Vinnie Carroll. Bill looked quizzical and said, "I'm surprised. You don't act like you have a boss." He could not imagine that someone who had the authority and the freedom to accomplish tasks could have a boss. His comment reflected the difficult, and sometimes dysfunctional, relationships between bosses and subordinates at the MTO. The mechanic seemed to imagine that one was free and the other enslaved. In reality, if the bosses at the MTO failed to authorize their subordinates, they too would become victims, slaves of the new technologies and their changing environment.

To promote organizational learning, the dilemmas of authority must be wrestled with. It is no longer possible to choose between *good, self-managing, task-oriented* organizations and *bad, hierarchical, politically embroiled* ones. A more sophisticated vocabulary and a more supple organizational design are necessary. If this problem is not solved, it will not be possible to take advantage of the wide range of effective learning tools, based both on computers and group process, that are rapidly emerging.

6

*Workplace Learning in Changing Environments: A Researcher/Practitioner's Viewpoint**

Bill Ford
Industrial Relations Research Centre
University of New South Wales

The multidimensional and often multidirectional changes affecting many people's working lives are often not the central concerns of traditional education and training research. The idea of getting involved in participate development of workplace learning is often outside the "comfort zone" of many educators, as well as of large numbers of people facing technological, organizational, and industrial change. However, to develop the lessons of organizational change, researchers must learn to face the changing technological and market environments of people in their workplaces. This report describes how that new

*This report draws on my work with the OECD's Centre for Educational Research and Innovation; my official review of the Swedish Development Program in New Technology, Work, and Management; my Japanese enterprise research over the past two decades, and my involvement in conceptual and cultural change in chemical processing and Australian construction enterprises.

85

approach might be formulated to the OECD Centre for Educational Research and Innovation (CERI) cross-cultural research program and to work carried out with two enterprises in Sydney.

LEARNING AND SHARED VALUES

The multidimensional and often multidirectional changes affecting many people's working lives are often not the central concerns of traditional education and training research. The idea of getting involved in the participative development of workplace learning is often outside the "comfort zone" of many educators, as well as of large numbers of people facing technological, organizational, and industrial change. However, to develop the lessons of Hirschhorn's chapter in this volume, researchers must learn to face the changing technological and market environments of people in their workplaces. This chapter describes how that new approach might be formulated to the OECD Centre for Educational Research and Innovation's (CERI) cross-cultural research program and to work carried out with two enterprises in Sydney, Australia.

CONCEPTUAL CHANGES AND INTERDEPENDENCIES

To help refocus and reframe their changing work environments, people may be encouraged to use diagrams that highlight key conceptual shifts and interdependencies. Such visual tools are designed to help people shift from traditional static mindsets to more dynamic and interactive models of their changing environments. The tool is similar to Hirschhorn's use of the software program *Stella*. Rather than attempt to compare the two tools, this section discusses how Hirschhorn's analysis brings out a number of key conceptual shifts that are critical for workplace learning.

Computer-Aided Learning ⟶ Sociotechnical Learning

Hirschhorn's first case study shows there is a need for educators to shift conceptually from computer-aided learning to sociotechnical learning. The lack of success in the use of *Stella* did not indicate the need for more development in the technology, but the need to develop a better fit between the technical and social domains of learning. This is of increasing significance as workplace learning is developed within diverse organizational technocultures.

The successful use of any educational technologies, like production and maintenance technologies, requires an understanding of the environment in which they are used. In Hirschhorn's case study, the use of innovative educational technology was blocked by the established technoculture of the plant.

Training and Development ⟶ Integrated Enterprise Learning

In an earlier case study, one of Hirschhorn's conclusions was that:

> We cannot think of training as a narrow activity confined to classroom experience and designed to give workers particular technical skills. This image of training is not wrong, rather it is too limited. Training is a vehicle for organizational development and therefore facilitates organizational functioning in many ways. It helps people take up new roles rather than just new skills, it helps link roles and levels together in new ways, it creates a shared language of problem solving which helps people from different functions work together, it helps shape a climate in which people believe that in fact management *cares* about its people. Technical skill acquisition is one important subset of training's broad purposes, but it is only a subset. (Hirschhorn, 1989, p. 7)

Such a mindset is a massive conceptual shift from the traditional notions of training. Indeed, Hirschhorn's new vision cannot be transmitted in terms merely of "training." He has clearly enunciated a much broader, deeper, and changing phenomenon. Language can lock people into traditional mindsets. To break them out of such mindsets, it is necessary to use concepts that more clearly evoke the new reality.

Hirschhorn's perspectives relate to the interlacing of work and learning. The perspectives have nothing to do with formal attendance at classes; with trainer-controlled, designed, and driven processes; or with separation of theory from practice. Hirschhorn highlights an important conceptual shift from traditions of training and development to ideas for integrated enterprise learning.

Other conceptual shifts which follow from the above analysis are:

- instruction and training ⟶ involvement and learning
- individual training ⟶ team and network learning
- occupational training ⟶ career learning
- functional training ⟶ organizational learning
- demarcated training ⟶ shared learning
- technical training ⟶ sociotechnical learning
- skill profiles ⟶ skill dynamics

Each of these shifts needs to be developed and operationalized to support integrated enterprise learning.

The OECD/CERI Studies of Conceptual Changes and Integrated Innovations in Skill Formation at the Enterprise Level

During the decade of the 1980s, the Centre for Educational Research and Innovation (CERI) organized a series of enterprise-level studies on technological change and human resources development in the manufacturing sector and in the services sector in a variety of industries and countries. The studies showed that an enterprise's dynamic comparative advantage is increasingly related to its ability to absorb, adapt, and implement conceptual changes, to integrate innovations, and to learn as an organization. How does one enterprise learn faster than another? Such questions are critical to understanding the issues faced in workplace learning.

The CERI field research showed that leading enterprises have conceptually shifted in their development of human resources. What are some of the key shifts?

Education and training ⟶ *skill formation.* Perhaps the most critical conceptual shift for understanding human resource developments in many leading enterprises, particularly in Germany and Japan, is the shift from the traditions of education and training to the concept of skill formation. The dichotomy between education and training has strong class connotations. Teachers are educated, craftsmen are trained. The dichotomy is not very helpful for understanding the needs of people in a changing employment environment.

The concept of skill formation has its origin in Germany, but it has been adopted and perhaps more broadly developed in leading Japanese enterprises. It covers on- and off-the-job learning and initial and continuing skill upgrading. It is not constrained by institutional arrangements and thinking about curricula and methods of teaching nor is it constrained by *front-end* models of education and training. It is above all a learner-centered concept, essentially concerned with how skills are formed over a lifetime.

At the enterprise level, concern for skill formation has led to a more systematic interlacing of theory and practice, particularly through the development of learning-based work organization and career systems. This, in turn, has led to a concern for more systematic combinations of on-the-job and off-the-job learning. These shifts are critical if enterprises are to establish processes for the just-in-time development of skills to meet changes in markets, technologies, and organizations.

In many Western societies the professionalization of training has resulted in a separation of practice and theory, work and learning, and off-the-job training and on-the-job learning. Such separations continue because many people are locked into traditional notions of training.

Restrictive work practices ⟶ *open workplace learning.* In many traditional enterprises, industries, and occupations, learning is constrained by restrictive work practices created and maintained by management, unions, and occupational groups. These barriers to learning are sustained by reference to custom, precedent, and tradition.

To free people and enterprises, it is necessary to shift from narrow notions of job preservation and their resulting restrictive practices to the idea of skill formation through open workplace learning. Such a shift means redefining demarcations to show how they:

- restrict learning opportunities
- restrict employment and market opportunities
- restrict mastery of new systems technologies
- restrict human and organizational development

The conceptual and practical shift to open workplace learning is essential to support the development of work teams. It is critical also for supporting the shift from:

- skills hoarding ⟶ skills sharing
- information control ⟶ information sharing
- division of labor ⟶ balance of skills

Training leave ⟶ *learning time.* Training leave assumes that people need to leave work to learn. It also assumes that there are appropriate external skill providers. Both of these assumptions may be false. Shift workers in Australia provide an example. Shift workers have always been second-class citizens in terms of their access to structured skill formation in Australia. No public technical or further education system has catered for the needs of shift workers, nor were traditional shift systems designed in terms of the learning needs of the shift worker. This is, however, of increasing concern to shift workers who operate complex technologies and are required to meet continual improvement in quality and service.

The Journey to the Learning Enterprise

The 1987 National Congress of the Australian Council of Trade Unions (ACTU) was held under a banner that proclaimed "skill formation is the key issue." The banner was a modified version of one of my conceptual tools showing the interlinking of new technologies, quality markets, industrial democracy, work organization, and skill formation. The vehicle by which these changes were to be developed was award restructuring. (An industrial award in Australia is similar to a labor contract in the United States.)

However, although there has been considerable national debate and policy formulation around the issue of skill formation since that Congress, the rhetoric has not been matched by innovative practice. Australian public and private enterprises and skill formation providers are still restricted by conventional training concepts. They have yet to break down many of the strong barriers of custom, practice, and tradition.

A major barrier to reform is the policy focus on industry-wide and national agendas. Conceptual changes and innovations in skill formation require commitment and cultural change. These are more easily developed and delivered at enterprise and workplace levels. The chemical industry in Australia provides an example. As in other Australian process industries, there has traditionally been no structured learning program, even though operators may be responsible for hundreds of millions of dollars worth of processing equipment. Until 1991, attempts to get such programs across industry had constantly failed. However, change is taking place because of the workplace reform and conceptual changes and innovation at ICI Botany Operations. In recent years, the ICI plant has been transformed from a center of long-term conflict to a national example of workplace reform.

Central to the change has been the range of innovations in skill formation that are emerging on site. The innovations have led to the development of a recognized industry qualification of an *Advanced Certificate in Chemical Industry Technology*. The site's innovations are spreading across the chemical industry. Industry reform often requires the commitment and resources of a leading enterprise.

National focus ⟶ *international focus.* Critical to achieving skill formation and workplace reform in Australian enterprises is the widespread understanding and acceptance of international standards. The OECD/CERI enterprise studies clearly illustrate the dominant importance of the internationalization of economies. Enterprises in different cultures and industries are increasingly required to meet international standards of quality, adaptability, reliability, improvement, innovation, customization, service, and leadership.

To meet these diverse demands, enterprises need to create processes for achieving a diversity of conceptual changes and integrated innovations in participative work organization, technology, skill formation, and employment relations. Such changes require a *learning enterprise.*

A learning enterprise. A learning enterprise is one in which individuals, teams, and the enterprise itself are continually learning. In a world characterized by multidimensional and often multidirectional, changes, the long-term survival of enterprises is increasingly dependent on their ability to learn to integrate and meet old and new customer demands, effectively use and improve new technologies, develop and improve new work organizations, and change and improve their balance of skills and knowledge. The incentive to create the learning enterprise is the survival of the enterprise itself and the jobs it provides.

The Lend Lease Corporation (a construction, property, and finance conglomerate) is facilitating the development of workplace reform and the learning enterprise. In the groups construction and insurance companies, concept teams have been established (a) to identify and develop the conceptual shifts that the Lend Lease culture, need to make to continue their leadership in dynamic markets, and (b) to facilitate the development of participative processes to foster shared individual, team, and organizational learning.

The composition of the teams depends on the size of the company, available resources, and the priorities of key managers and their perception of the urgency for change. The teams may have full-time, part-time, and short-term members. The teams provide important participative learning opportunities for the people involved in their activities, including the opportunity to develop and integrate theory and practice, concepts and processes, and, above all, work and learning. Conceptual thinking in the organization is no longer the exclusive province of consultants, academics, and senior management.

The concept teams have provided participative processes to encourage people to challenge openly the conventional wisdoms and practices based on success in the past and to pursue new concepts and visions based on desirable futures for individuals and their organizations.

The teams have developed a concept team network to share their experiences, learning, and knowledge sources. Team networking has accelerated their own learning. Full-time members of concept teams move back into line leadership roles and are replaced by people from line positions. The revolving roles ensure that team members do not develop into traditional planners or trainers. The concept team members are assessed on their ability to develop and integrate theory and practice in relation to the changing organizational business environment.

Comparative advantage ⟶ *dynamic comparative advantage.* Nations such as Australia, Canada, and the United States are blessed with bountiful natural resources such as vast farmlands, minerals, and energy. Their citizens have grown up believing that their physical inheritance is central to their comparative advantage, failing to understand that such a mindset is a static concept of comparative advantage. The world economies are now led by nations and enterprises that do not rely on a physical and static concept of comparative advantage. Rather, countries such as Japan, Germany, and Sweden rely on a concept of dynamic comparative advantage. The dynamic comes from both their broad-based skill formation and more participative work organization.

Such dynamic comparative advantage is not sustainable by isolated centers of research and learning. Leadership in dynamic markets comes with real time integration of theory and practice; technical and social domains; individual, team and organizational learning; and work and learning.

The learning enterprise creates a dynamic comparative advantage by *just-in-time* adaptation to complex and changing environments and achieves continual improvements, reliability, and the absorption of new concepts and systems innovation.

Such timely responses cannot be achieved in traditional command-based enterprises or by reliance on traditional, independent education and training institutions. They come from enterprises in which individuals and teams are able to reframe their perceptions of reality and create processes for continual learning.

CONCLUSIONS

The wide range of emerging conceptual changes and integrated innovations in work organization and skill formation within enterprises has developed in response to changing technologies, organizations, markets, and international competition. There is a need, therefore, for individual enterprises and industries to reconceptualize their traditional incentive systems to provide support for new work organization and skill formation. As Hirschhorn points out, incentives for individuals to learn must involve authorization to play new roles within the firm. As this chapter has attempted to show, the incentive for the organization itself is its very survival in a competitive international economy.

SECTION IV:
Incentives and Learning Methods

7

Learning at and through the Workplace: A Review of Participation and Adult Learning Theory

Kjell Rubenson
Hans G. Schütze
Centre for Policy Studies in Education
University of British Columbia

———

Although much of the material and instruction at the workplace is written in a language that is so technical or legalistic that it defies easy comprehension, the lack of easy readability is not the principal cause for widespread workplace illiteracy. Rather, it is the work setting themselves that lack opportunities or incentives for the workers to continue to learn or use the whole gamut of skills that they acquired during their school years and initial vocational training. The organization of the workplace, characterized by the strict division of labor, the concomitant disaggregation of work skills, and the complete lack of autonomy on the part of the workers/leads not only to alienation (stressed by Karl Marx) and hence a lack of motivation but also to a steady regression of knowledge and skills (also noted by Adam Smith). Further, the whole area of education and training of the workforce needs to be addressed. The latter aspect is the focus of this chapter. The traditional way of approaching the issue encourages instruction to be treated within a narrow learning-teaching focus. This leaves out broader contextual factors that influence who gets what kind of education and training under what conditions. More than 50 years of research in education has shown that not only is the same method not suitable for all groups, but more importantly, education and training of the workforce covers an enormous scope, from simple job task training to the most advanced education at the postgraduate level. Broad principles are necessary that inform strategies to address a major problem, namely, how to engage a larger section of the workforce, particularly the undereducated, in effective forms of education and training.

The man whose life is spent in performing a few simple operations of which the effects too are, perhaps, always the same, has no occasion to exert his understanding or to exercise his invention in finding out expedients for removing difficulties which never occur. He naturally loses, therefore, the habit of such exertion and generally becomes as stupid and ignorant as it is possible for a human creature to become.

—Adam Smith, *The Wealth of Nations*

On October 17, 1991, the *Globe and Mail*, Canada's leading daily newspaper, reported on page 1 in its headline that a recent study had found that less than half of the sawmill employees in the province of British Columbia could read well enough to understand the written material they encountered in their job. The study by the B.C. Council of Forest Industries and the Woodworkers' Union, IWA-Canada (1991), found that 56% of 227 employees tested at eight sawmills had difficulty reading at mid-4-grade-level. Only 26% were found fully functional at a 12th-grade level. Almost 40% of those found to have reading problems had completed the 12th grade. The study stressed that the poor showing was not due to a lack of intelligence or abilities on the part of the employees. In fact, the study group found that "many people who have difficulty understanding certain written materials are very intelligent and often develop extraordinary skills to compensate for their shortcomings in reading."

One cause of the poor showing that was identified was the lack of readability of written materials—such as operating manuals or material on dangerous substances—in the workplace that are a part of everyday life in a sawmill. Much of the material and information the study group found was not easy to understand. The consequence of these findings for one of the biggest B.C. mill firms—whose vice president had participated in the study group—was a reduction in the complexity and amount of written instructions altogether and the provision of some voluntary remedial adult education programs for employees.

Although much of the material and instruction at the workplace is, indeed, written in a language that is so technical or legalistic that it defies easy comprehension, the lack of easy readability is not the principal cause for widespread workplace illiteracy. Rather, it is the work settings themselves that lack opportunities or incentives for the workers to continue to learn or to use the whole gamut of skills that they have acquired during their school years and initial vocational training. The organization of the workplace, characterized by the strict division of labor, the concomitant disaggregation of work skills, and the complete lack of autonomy on the part of the workers, leads not only to alienation (a fact that was stressed by Karl Marx) and hence a lack of motivation, but also to a steady regression of knowledge and skills (as noted already by Adam Smith).

Thus, the remedy prescribed by the large B.C. mill employer neither deals with the cause of workplace illiteracy, nor will it efficiently cure the symptoms. In order to address the real cause of the problem, workplaces need to change to become an environment in which workers are motivated, incited, and rewarded to learn and to apply their skills, knowledge, and experience.

Furthermore, the whole area of education and training of the workforce needs to be addressed. It is the latter aspect that is the focus of this chapter. The traditional way of approaching the issue encourages instruction to be treated within a narrow learning-teaching focus. This leaves out broader contextual factors that influence who gets what kind of education and training under what conditions. However, there are several strong reasons not to approach the topic in the traditional way. More than 50 years of research in education has shown that not only is the same method not suitable for all groups, but more importantly, education and training of the workforce covers an enormous scope, from simple job task training to the most advanced education at the postgraduate level. What is necessary are broad principles that can inform strategies to address major problem, namely, how to engage a larger section of the workforce, particularly the undereducated, in effective forms of education and training.

First, a major criticism of research on instruction is that much of it has built on narrow behaviorist theories of learning and disregards the fact that instruction is a social as well as a psychological process. One has to take into account the broader context in which instruction and learning take place and not disregard the factors that frame and govern instruction (e.g., see Lundgren, 1977). Contrary to claims by some educational psychologists, learning and training are not two sides of the same coin. To neglect the teaching/training process as it exists in reality will, when combined with a narrow psychological approach, result in an inadequate conceptualization of the training phenomenon.

Second, recent developments in cognitive sciences are changing the way educational psychologists approach learning and instruction. Instead of a focus on how knowledge gets recorded, the interest is on how knowledge is constructed and the context in which learning/instruction take place. The essence of this is captured in concepts such as *situated cognition* or *situated learning* (Brown, Collins, & Duguid, 1989; Resnick, 1989). The change in theoretical perspectives has resulted in a questioning of traditional positions, for example, whether skill and knowledge exist independently of the situation in which they are acquired, or that knowledge is independent of context. Instead, researchers in various disciplines are now trying to shed light on the motivation to engage in learning, on what is learned, and how it is learned, as well as how the use of what is learned is situated in and mediated by the context.

In addition, in much of the discussion on training, how the effect of new technologies on skill structures is mediated by the way work is organized has been largely neglected. In the economic and sociological literature on future skill structure or changing modes of production, education and training are only mentioned in passing, although they are often hailed as an important part of the solution. In discussing training and instructional methods, it is important to try to unite the two perspectives, recognizing that training bridges two cultures—the culture of work on the one hand, and the culture of education on the other. Although not often mentioned in discussions about training, knowledge also has a value in itself and is the very basis of personal development of the individual and active community life.

The primary purpose of this chapter is to analyze and bring together the often separate discussions on changing skills demands, work organization, recent developments in the cognitive sciences, and experimentation with alternative methods of training. The first section analyzes the changing skill requirements in the workplace. The second section deals with work organization and workplaces as learning environments. The third section presents some recent developments in the learning and development literature that can bring together skills and work organization on the one hand, and training and instructional methods on the other. The conclusion draws a number of policy options and strategies that must be discussed when attempting to actively promote learning, education, and training at work, particularly for the illiterate and undereducated. The discussions are not restricted to training in formal and nonformal instructional settings, but on the contrary, pay close attention to the training potential of informal settings, such as the everyday work process.

REQUIREMENTS IN THE MODERN WORKPLACE

It is by now common knowledge that the workplace is undergoing pervasive change as a result of a number of factors. The three most important of
these are the introduction of new, sophisticated technologies in the workplace, new forms of work organization, and new trends in organizational
management. All three factors are changing the nature of work. They are
not isolated from each other, but are interconnected in different degrees of
intensity, and they have important consequences for the skills needed in
the workplace and, hence, for the way such skills are acquired.

Definitions of Skills

When discussing skill requirements in the context of training, it is useful
to start with some brief definitions:
    Training traditionally refers to learning focused on the present
job or professional activities, that is, training is aimed at improving the
skills or providing the knowledge currently required by the job. A training program, therefore, has a very specific objective: to focus on one or
more skills, areas of knowledge, or abilities. By contrast, *education* is seen
to be learning focused on a future job as it involves learning basic principles and constructs that can be applied to synthesize information, extract
relevant data, make judgments, and take action (London, 1989).
    Currently both terms are often replaced by the term *human
resources development* (HRD). Whereas *development* refers to non-job-relat-
ed, long-term personal growth, human resources development refers to
an organized learning experience provided or sponsored by the employer with the objective of enhancing the performance and professional
growth of an employee. Thus, HRD is more narrow than learning but
larger than training and consists of a variety of measures or courses,
some of which are work-related, whereas others are not, or only in a
very indirect way (London, 1989).
    This shift in terminology indicates a shift in awareness that skill
requirements in many modern workplace settings are, for the most part,
less technical than generic in nature. Therefore, skill training activities as
defined by the old understanding will no longer suffice to prepare workers for a job in a modern work setting. Rather, technical skill training
will have to be complemented by learning activities that might more
aptly be described as education rather than skill training.
    Skills are generally thought of as defined capacities, either embod-
ied in individuals or incorporated in jobs and expressed in terms of *job
requirements*. Such skills are produced through training and work experi-

ence and are applied through execution of work functions. This viewpoint assumes, at least implicitly, that the skills acquired are actually applied in work and that existing work situations represent either the only possible or the optimal *solution* at a given time. Furthermore, such a vision tends to consider the relationship between skills and work as a static one, as if skills were learned once and for all during a limited period of education and training and then applied steadily throughout working life.

Experience shows that this is not the case, and that reality is more dynamic. Instead of the term *skill*, which carries certain mechanistic and static biases, it may be preferable to use the term *qualification* (used in Germany as well as in France) which is broader, and includes background, orientation, and capacities, in addition to the mastery of a technique. *Qualification*, therefore, implies a broader concept expressing a state (Zustand état) as well as a process and takes into account the intimate interaction between the acquisition and the application of human capacities related to work.

Qualification Requirements

Some years ago there was disagreement among researchers as to the general effects of the far-reaching changes in the workplace with respect to workers' qualifications, yet there is ample evidence and general agreement now that at least for an important part of the workforce, broader knowledge and skills will be required than in the past. Hirschhorn (1984) has described the process by which work beyond mechanization transforms jobs, expands the range of workers' responsibilities, and requires from the worker both more integrated knowledge of technical systems and stronger communication skills. Microelectronic controls result in work processes that focus more on breakdown than routine and on irregular work intensity and partly unpredictable tasks; in other words, the technology and the way it is applied in the workplace defies the routinizing work organization and narrow definition of qualifications needed by workers to perform the tasks assigned.

What are the qualifications needed for the jobs that are affected by technological innovation? Given the rapidity of changes affecting the workplace, it is impossible to anticipate precisely future job contents and qualification requirements. Therefore, emphasis will have to be put more on generic skills, particularly the ability to adapt and learn, rather than on narrow occupation-specific training.

A survey commissioned by the European Community identified the general qualifications and dispositions that industry believes will be required from the workforce involved with computer-based systems or equipment (Sorge, 1981):

- The capability for analytic thinking applied to different processes of work
- A sense of quantitative appreciation of different processes
- The ability to conduct dialogue with equipment
- A sense of responsibility and a capacity for autonomous work
- The ability to link technical, economic, and social considerations in the appreciation of equipment and working methods
- A planned and methodical approach to work.

A list of competencies, drawn up recently by Levin and Rumberger (cited in Raizen, 1991) who are familiar with labor market developments and trends in job contents in the United States, reflects a similar group of cognitive competencies and dispositional attitudes. Besides more general competencies such as communication, reasoning, problem solving, and information processing skills, they include:

- The willingness to take initiative and perform independently
- The ability to cooperate and to work in groups
- Competence in planning and evaluating one's own work and that of others
- Understanding how to work with persons from different backgrounds and cultures
- The ability to make decisions.

It is important to note that despite the general cry for a better qualified workforce and worries about skill shortages, new technologies do not in and of themselves result in higher qualification demands or better possibilities for the employees to develop and broaden their skills. On the contrary, the research literature shows contradictory findings, with claims of deskilling, upskilling, polarization, and reskilling (not more but different qualifications needed). There are good reasons to be skeptical of the more optimistic as well as the more pessimistic positions. Both are expressions of technological determinism, that is, that the technology more or less automatically will result in positive or negative effects on skill demands and opportunities for the development of competencies (Ellström, 1992). A more plausible position, and one that has support in recent research (Löwstedt, 1989; Zuboff, 1988), is that the demand for and development of competencies depend on the interplay of the specific technology with implementation strategies of the work organization and the competencies of the workforce. Thus, it is the strategy of how to use the technology, not the technology itself, that determines what kinds of skills are needed and governs the employees' opportunities to develop their competencies. The unions have increasingly come to see the organization of work as the major obstacle for upskilling and reskilling (LO, 1991).

Roles

Whereas the analysis of workers' qualifications is mostly related to tasks, some authors have stressed that workers and managers in a modern work setting must learn primarily not new skills but new roles (Hirschhorn et al., 1989; see also, this volume). They see work holistically as a set of interrelated situations embedded in a role and relationship system, not as a set of individual competencies, and argue that by focusing on individual competencies and deficiencies rather than on holistic situations, training cannot help people learn the role to work effectively in a postindustrial economy (pp. 187-189).

Although this approach is very useful in stressing the social functions of jobs and the interrelationship with others working in the same work setting, it tends to neglect the fact that some of the qualifications needed for working with advanced technical systems are technical or rather domain-specific in nature and that such specific qualifications and knowledge are thought to be central to general tasks such as problem solving and interconnecting with other parts of the system (Raizen, 1991, pp. 8-9). The preparation for new roles is thus not the only purpose of job training; the ability to assume new roles and develop new relationships must be seen as part of a comprehensive set of qualifications, predispositions, and characteristics that are required by jobs in modern work settings.

WORK ORGANIZATION AS LEARNING ENVIRONMENT

Partly induced by the new technologies that have pervaded the workplace and partly occurring for other reasons, new models of work organization have been introduced in many enterprises. These have been accompanied, preceded, or sometimes caused by major transformations in management styles and labor relations. There is strong evidence that these far-reaching changes in work organization and management style are not transitory but structural in nature and that they are interconnected with other sweeping or gradual changes in economic (particularly in social and educational policies), international trade, and international developments (Boyer, 1989).

Changes in work organization have occurred suddenly, yet others have developed over time. Earlier stages included the application of scientific management, mostly in the manufacturing industry, but permeating to some tertiary sectors as well. The perfection of this Taylorist model of labor division and specialization by highly specialized equipment (*mechanization*), and the cheap mass production of standardized goods are the result of this model. The negative effects of the excessive rigidity of the system, worldwide competition, and the search for flexibility, greatly enhanced by the potential of the new technologies, have led to innovative ways of management and work organization that have been gradually developed during the 1970s and 1980s. A brief summary and overview of these changes is contained in Table 7.1.

With respect to the demand for and the utilization of workers' skills and knowledge, these changes in work organization and management style are far-reaching and most important. Whereas under the Taylorist forms of work organization, firms could rely mostly on unskilled labor, or when existing skills could be (and were) made redundant by such organization, today's work process requires more and broader qualifications than in the past. This is not limited to the industrial production process, but applies to a great variety of work settings, although the changes in manufacturing have been most visible. What firms need today are not just *functional* skills that can be put to use for a specific and well defined purpose, but qualifications as a generalized, polyvalent, and flexible resource that can be applied in many different work situations. Most important are what German labor economists have called *Schluesselqualifikationen* (key qualifications): fundamental qualifications that can be used as the base for acquiring more and new work-related competencies that might be required at a later stage. In addition, there is a need for extra-functional qualifications that are essentially of an attitudinal and behavioral nature and that include individual predispositions and characteristics such as diligence; attention to both overall process, context, and detail; willingness and ability to work in a team, and so on (Streeck, 1988).

It seems obvious that such broad and more general qualifications cannot be acquired in traditional training settings that have been designed and used for technical skills training, narrowly defined. Neither will the old methods of instruction and learning do. Many of the qualifications required by the modern workplace are of a nature that would be seen as falling under the auspices of education rather than in the range of training, as defined above. However, as has been pointed out by many authors, education that is largely equated with formal schooling has been proven or seen as problematic with respect to effective preparation for workplace qualifications (cf. Raizen, 1991, pp. 17-21). For a variety of reasons—motivational, cultural and cognitive—work qualifications seem to be best produced where they are used, that is, at the workplace.

Table 7.1. From Fordism to a New Model: A Synoptic Presentation

Fordist Principles	The Challenges of the 1970s and 1980s	The Principles of a New Model
F1: Rationalization of labor is the main target, mechanization is the means	C1: Underutilization of equipment large inventories of work in process	P1: Global optimization of the whole productive flow
F2: First design and then manufacture and organize work process	C2: Lags and large costs in passing from innovation to effective production	P2: Tentative full integration of research, development, and production
F3: Indirect and mediated links with consumers via marketing studies and strategies	C3: Losing touch with choosy consumers, failures in launching new products	P3: Close and long-lasting ties between producers and users, capture learning by using effects
F4: Low cost for standardized products is the first objective, quality the second one	C4: Ex-post quality controls cannot prevent a rising defect rate, consumers more selective about quality	P4: High quality at reasonable costs, via a zero defect objective at each stage of the production process
F5: Mass production for stable and rising demands, batch production for unstable demands	C5: Even mass consumer demand becomes uncertain and the Fordist production process appears as rigid	P5: Insert the market demand into the production process, in order to get fast responses
F6: Centralization of most decisions about production in a special division of a large firm	C6: Sluggish and inadequate reaction of headquarters to global and local shocks	P6: Decentralization as far as possible of production decision within smaller and less hierarchical units
F7: Vertical integration mitigated by circles of subcontractors	C7: Given radical innovations, even large firms can no more master the whole techniques needed for their core business	P7: Networking (and joint ventures), as a method for reaping both specialization and coordination gains
F8: Facing cyclical demand, subcontractors are	C8: During the 1970s, bankruptcies and/or loss of competence	P8: Long-run and cooperative subcontracting as far as

used as stabilizing device, in order to preserve large firms' employment

of subcontractors, now confronted with international competition

possible, in order to promote joint technical innovations

F9: Divide and specialize at most productive tasks, main source of productivity increases

C9: Excessive labor division might turn counterproductive: rising control and monitoring costs; built-in rigidity

P9: To recompose production, maintenance, quality control and some management tasks might be more efficient, technically and economically

F10: Minimize the required general education and on-the-job training of productive tasks, according to Babbage's and Taylor's principles

C10: New technical opportunities (IT), more competition and uncertain demands challenge most of the previous very specialized tasks

P10: A new alliance between a minimal general education and effective on-the-job training, in order to maximize individual and collective competence

F11: Hierarchical control and purely financial incentives to manufacture an implicit consent to poor job content

C11: Young generations better educated and with different expectations, reject authoritarian management styles. Too much control becomes counterproductive

P11: Human resources policies have to spur workers' competence and commitment and work out positive support for firms' strategy

F12: Adversarial industrial relations converge toward wage demands; collective agreements codify a provisional armistice

C12: Firms' employment might be hurt by the lack of cooperation and an exclusive concern for wages. A contrario, concession bargaining does not necessarily provide any advantage for wage earners

P12: An explicit and long-term compromise between managers and wage earners is needed to reap a general support to this model: commitment versus good working conditions and/or job tenures and/or a fair sharing of modernization dividends

Source: From *New Directions in Management Practices and Work Organization*, by R. Boyer, 1989, Paris: OECD. Reprinted by permission.

As in many other walks of working life, in recent developments with respect to work and learning for work tasks and roles, we are experiencing what has been called the limits of functional differentiation (Streeck, 1988). For some time it was considered that places of work and places of learning should be neatly kept apart and that in this way, both learning and work would be best served. This view has recently come to be criticized from a variety of different viewpoints. The growing attraction to other industrialized countries of the Japanese workplace-based system of skill training and the German *dual system* of apprenticeship training, which combines school-based theoretical instruction and hands-on learning by doing at the enterprise, is partly based on the conviction that the future may demand a reintegration of learning and work (Boyer, 1989; Streeck, 1988).

Besides this reemergence of more traditional patterns of integration, or rather mutual penetration of functions, roles, and social behavior, there are very interesting examples of new definitions and concepts integrating work and learning at the workplace. One of these is provided by the planning principles and process of Volvo's new car assembly plant in Uddevalla where holistic learning principles are being built into the production process as a matter of original work design and forward planning process (Ellegård et al., 1991).

COGNITIVE SCIENCE AND PERSPECTIVES ON TRAINING

The narrow focus that has dominated much of the literature on training can to a large extent be explained by the dominance of the behaviorist school and its way of equating learning with behavioral change. The interest in how cognitive skills are acquired and performed is a late phenomenon, spurred by increasing use of computers and changing modes of production. Recent insights in cognitive psychology, emphasizing the contextual influence on learning and training, provide new perspectives on methods of instruction. The purpose here is not to enter into a deeper discussion of these developments, but rather to try to arrive at some principles that can inform the education and training of the workforce, particularly as it involves educationally disadvantaged groups.

Toward a Contextualization of Learning

During the last 30 years, Piaget's stage theory has had a profound influence on cognitive psychology. According to the Piagetian equilibration model, the four stages of intellectual development are universal and occur in an invariant sequential order in all children (Flavell, 1963). Vygotsky, although sharing the concept of stages, differs in some crucial ways from Piaget (Sincoff & Sternberg, 1989). Whereas Piaget saw equilibration as the mechanism of cognitive growth, for Vygotsky the mechanism was internalization. Vygotsky maintained that development proceeds from the social context to the individual rather than the opposite. Consequently, he did not see the development stages as being universal because they reflect the dynamic relationships between individuals and their particular environment and culture, relationships that vary between individuals as well as within an individual over time. Cognitive development occurs through a process of internalizing concepts, values, and thought which are practiced in interaction with others. Sternberg (1985) stresses that different environments produce different adaptational requirements and ultimately different forms of mental activity. Similarly, in their review of recent theories Sincoff and Sternberg (1989) conclude that:

> Clearly, the development literature underscores the impact of environmental factors on children's thinking and development. Current theories on cognitive growth, however, must go beyond simply pointing out the necessity of considering contextual influences. They must pinpoint precisely the contextual factors affecting development and the way these factors alter mental activity. (p. 50)

This moves the focus to the social and cultural context in which the individual works, the setting in which education and training take place, and the relationship between the two. Demonstrating the importance of this relationship, Sticht, Armstrong, Hickey, and Caylor (1987) found that marginally literate adults in a job-related reading program made twice the gain in job-related reading than they did in general reading. By situating the learning in a meaningful context, such as, work, reading ability was enhanced. It is worth noting that several of the successful students had such a low initial literacy level that they were not expected to succeed in the training or the jobs they were trained for (see also Sticht & Hickey, 1991).

Language was central to Vygotsky's theory of development; thought comes into existence through language. This is recognized in current theories as *metacognitive* or, as it also is called, *executive processing*: those processes involved in the planning, monitoring, and evaluating of performance on intellectual tasks. *Non-executive processes* are those involved in performance such as actually solving tasks (Sincoff & Sternberg, 1989). According to Sternberg (1985), cognitive growth is closely dependent on the metacomponents that govern non-executive processes, which in turn allow the acquisition and reorganization of procedural and declarative knowledge. The ability to assemble increasingly sophisticated executive control structures underlies most of an individual's cognitive change. Those who are able to monitor their own effectiveness may learn from their failures and successes and through this refine their own functioning. Metacognition plays a central part in recent theories on transfer, which of course is the key in most training. Annett (1989) sees skill as a hierarchically organized control structure with general strategies at the top controlling the selection of subordinate routines. The difference between good and poor learners is found in both the knowledge and use of metacognitive strategies. The interesting point is that several studies have demonstrated the possibility of helping poor learners improve their underdeveloped strategies for gathering and analyzing information and in defining problems.

One aspect of metacognition is the degree to which people view themselves as having control of their own learning. There is increasing evidence that the willingness and ability to use strategies and knowledge to construct new knowledge depends on the level of perceived control (Resnick, 1989). In the tradition of Vygotsky, much of the interest focuses on the links among peoples' context, their conception of success and failure and themselves as learners, and on the kind of cognitive processes in which they are likely to engage.

The consequences of such theoretical considerations and approaches coincide to a large degree with the findings and recommendations for instruction and instructional research suggested by Raizen (1991, p. 24):

- It is not sufficient to teach knowledge and procedures; instruction must also focus on conditions of the application of the skills and knowledge and the skills being learned.
- Instruction must intermingle context specificity and generality, including the development of self-regulatory skills and performance control strategies.
- Instruction should take into account the learners' original ideas, stage discrepant or confirming experiences to stimulate questions, and encourage the generation of a range of responses with the opportunity to apply these in various situations.

It is interesting to note a similar discussion about humanization of the workplace between work organization and the principles for effective learning and instruction based on cognitive sciences. The *action regulation theory*, developed primarily by Hacker and Volpert, is relevant as it focuses in part on the impact of work conditions on peoples' socially constructed cognition and learning processes (e.g., see Hacker, 1985; Volpert, 1989) and implies a number of basic principles for work design and skill training.

Action Regulation Theory

The literature on action regulation theory is highly theoretical and complex (cf. Volpert, 1989, on which this section is based). It has had and continues to have a major impact on Nordic and German experiments to change the organization of work and modes of production toward a more participatory model which allows a wider scope for employees. Although the theory may not be well known in Japan, much of the main concept is very much a part of widespread practice in Japanese workplaces, as discussed below.

The theory provides a perspective on human development and more particularly on the impact of work conditions on personality characteristics, such as on individual learning processes, among others. It is constructed around two frames: (a) models of evolution and self-organizing systems, and (b) theories concerning society and the relations between individual and society.

A general assumption in the theory is that by striving for autonomy in action, a person tries to satisfy a basic control need. The action regulation theory provides an explanation of how a motivated and autonomous-oriented individual actor sets goals and reaches them. These processes are considered a psychological aspect of action and are referred to by the term *regulation*. The transformation of a general goal into a sequence of operations occurs through the hierarchical-sequential organization of action. There are various levels of action units differentiated by levels of regulation that determine the scope of action. Thus, autonomy, that is, the degree of freedom in the setting and reaching of goals, plays a crucial role. As long as the basic patterns are flexible, there is a broad scope for autonomous action which is an essential characteristic of personality development. According to such a perspective, regulation opportunities (the scope to act) are important determinants of the socialization process. They influence the way persons think about themselves, their aspirations, and their willingness to act, and they have far-reaching consequences for individual competencies. The implications for the qualifications of the workforce and the ways to acquire and use them are apparent. In hierarchical, inflexible work organization, restricted ability to act will result. As a result, individuals who are cut off from central processes of decisions and planning are incapable of learning more elaborate actions which, in turn, has negative effects on their motivation and competencies.

The negative impact of what Hacker and Volpert call *restrictive regulation requirements,* or lack of control of working conditions, on peoples' feeling, thinking, and acting is well documented in the research literature (Lennerlöf, 1986). There is also strong evidence that increased control has positive effects on well-being and motivation. In order to create working conditions that will enhance personal development and provide opportunities for workers to increase their motivation and learning, regulation requirements must be increased and regulation barriers removed. For this to happen workers need to be given room and responsibility to actively participate, and it is in this participative process that innovative qualifications decisive for development are learned. There are obvious similarities between such a view and the Japanese concept of inviting and promoting worker participation through various mechanisms and processes of which the quality circle is probably best known in other countries. Thus, task-oriented training in industry that stresses the connection between cognition and action must be seen as a crucial instrument in achieving changes in working conditions and in motivating workers to participate in these activities.

Volpert presents three principles that stress the connection of cognition and action that ought to guide training:

- The learning process must refer to different levels of regulations. It must not segregate them, for instance, by strict dissociation of the acquisition of knowledge from the acquisition of skill.
- To ensure and enhance the flexibility of action schemata, the adult learner needs to be confronted with varying situations and different action demands. Such variation should be systematic and cover the whole scope of possibilities. The same variation also applies to perceptual motor skills that can be the base of simpler operations only when they can be performed in different situations with the same high reliability.
- The learning process must be aligned to a high level of self-reliance of the learner. The learner must be respected from the beginning as an autonomous and reflecting person.

The opposite approach—segregated learning and training—is represented by all forms of drill. Methods of training should stress cognition, imagery, and action. Structure and learning research of perceptual motor-skills action demonstrates that the learning of movement patterns is not a simple chain of reactions. Imagination, cognition, and feedback play a great role. Empirical research shows that methods to acquire perceptual motor skills stress the role of speech, cognition, and imagination as highly effective. The most important methods are mental, observational, and verbal training; practice by mental rehearsal, by observation, and by verbalization of the motions.

A central issue in work organization and training is how to optimize cognitive regulation of work activity. Such optimization involves the same basic processes, but is applied to more complex work tasks, for example, in automated production. Several studies (Ellström, 1992; Engeström, 1987) have shown that it is important to develop abstract or imaginative knowledge about the production process, especially about the possibilities, necessities, and consequences of one's own intervention into the process. The best worker is someone who plans systematically, acts carefully, and seeks to prevent difficult situations.

According to Volpert (1989), three different groups of cognitive training must be distinguished:

- *Heuristic rules that help the person to internalize the rules as action guides.* It should be noted that very general rules of procedure (e.g., forming partial goals) have a positive effect because they present the possibilities for complex activities, while giving the learners scope for self-reliant design of the learning process.
- *Self-instruction that combines well-structured learning materials with forms of self-instruction.* Learners can be requested to record their own work activities and results or to observe coworkers. Research has shown that this kind of training leads to good learning results and increased motivation.
- *Task-oriented information exchange that allows a group of workers to discuss the problems of and solutions to complex work tasks.* The task may consist of developing a booklet depicting the difficulties and strategies in task mastering. In this case the concept of autonomous regulation is transferred to the group of workers.

Another way of distinguishing types of learning as a function of different scopes of action in the workplace is suggested by Ellström (1992, p. 58), building on Volpert (1989), Engeström (1987) and Rasmussen (1986) (see Table 7.2). This distinction explains the impact, in terms of qualifications, of the choices that are being made with respect to learning situations in the workplace.

Quality Circles as an Example for Applied Action Regulation Theory

Action regulation theory provides some insight into the workings of Japanese quality circles (QC) and their educative role. Quality refers to anything that can be controlled. It involves not only products and ser-

Table 7.2. Four Types of Learning as a Consequence of Autonomy of Action (after Ellström, 1992, p. 71)

	Type of Learning/Learning Hierarchies			
Aspects of Learning Situation	Reproduction Learning	Production Learning		Creative Learning
		rule-governed	goal governed	
Task/Goal	given	given	given	not given
Method	given	given	not given	not given
Result	given	not given	not given	not given

vices, but also the ways in which people work and how machines are operated, in short, all aspects of human workplace behavior and attitudes (Imai, 1986). In contrast to the tradition in Western countries, the QC aims not only at the execution of a given task in the production process, but also emphasizes improving existing products, methods, and systems (Watanabe, 1991). Justification is found in high regulation requirements and the lack of regulation barriers, that is, the wide scope of action that is open to Japanese workers. Watanabe explains that the difference in emphasis is found in Japanese job descriptions. Classification systems are not narrowly defined, task allocation is loose, and tasks are shared by many workers. This more holistic work process implies the prevention of a partialization of the learning process. Workers are constantly encouraged to make changes to the system, as long as they improve the quality and reliability of the products and processes. In Western countries such workplace behavior is often met with resistance, as it challenges the existing division of labor (e.g., see Oliver & Wilkinson, 1988). Applying Volpert's analysis, there is an indication of a higher level of development, that is, a level of action, among the Japanese workers. Such an analysis is documented in a study by Whitehill and Takezawa (cited in Watanabe, 1991). When workers were asked what they would do if they felt a change in their work method was unjustified and yet could not convince their supervisors, 25% of the Japanese, but only 7% of the Americans, stated that they would resist the order. The results show that although the Japanese culture may foster workers who are acquiescent on communal and social matters, generally they are not so when it comes to technical matters related to their own work. Watanabe also stresses the fact that, contrary to popular belief, it is not primarily the sociocultural system that promotes QC. Instead, the explanation is found in the life employment, egalitarian remuneration, and promotion systems, which tend to support a broadening of the regulation system.

QCs are a cornerstone in the Japanese strategy of improving both labor productivity and quality. The concept stresses the connection between cognition and action and contains many features discussed above that are not at the core of action regulation theory. Although not always apparent to Western observers, Japanese workers refer to QC as a mode of training that substantially contributes to greater problem awareness and better human relations, communication, and work motivation.

The action regulation theory has inspired much of the Swedish experiments with increased worker participation and new work organization (Dochery, 1991). The experiments in Sweden integrating cognition and action have focused on what has been called *everyday learning* at work. The research on everyday learning (Sköld, 1989) has concluded that:

- As a point of departure for problem-oriented learning, employees must be able to start from their own experiences at work.
- There must be evidence that their own contributions result in concrete changes and are dealt with by management.
- In order to increase the potential for an individual to act, it is important that collective but systematic discussions increase the individual's own world of experience (in the words of cognitive theory, metacognition).
- Collective analysis results in common positions and increases the workers' will to carry out the proposed changes.

The results from research on everyday learning are in accordance with action regulation theory and the findings of recent cognitive theory regarding the basic cognitive processes: perception, recognition, conceptualization, and motivation. According to these theories, activation and motivation presuppose a complete chain of cognitive processes (Leymann, 1989). Perception may suffer due to restricted possibilities for employees to develop an overall picture of the factors that influence their work.

The concept of everyday learning is closely associated with Kolb's concept of *experiential learning* that proceeds through four stages: (a) action based on conceptualization results in experiences (b) that are the subjects of reflection (c) resulting in analyses (d) that may lead to further action. According to the Swedish experience, a problem with everyday learning at work is that it often stops at the second step, and consequently skills and experiences are developed only within the original frame of reference. There is no base on which to question the existing system.

Learning becomes an issue only when a company or public administration is faced with major change. A key question is whether or not the changes will be regarded as a possibility for everyday learning, or if the administration will rely on traditional forms of education and training. A major problem is that everyday or experiential learning most often falls outside the responsibility of the educational department, whereas at the same time it may appear to be too common to be a concern for the production line supervisor. It is in this case that the Japanese QC provides an organizational focus for everyday learning and a mechanism by which such a form of experience develops into a higher order of learning and action.

A major conclusion from the Swedish experiments is that an effective way to organize learning at work is to organize work at all levels in such a way that all employees participate in the management process of the part of the operation in which they actually work. Experiments show that active design decisions aimed at support learning must be extended to at least five levels:

- setting of goals
- design of management systems
- design of policies and strategies
- design of work organization
- design of technical support.

What does this mean when translated into both general principles of training and concrete training programs? What, in particular, does it mean for the training of those workers who have a relatively low level of education and training to begin with and are thus reduced to simple, repetitive jobs, most of which are bound to disappear due to rationalization and further automation of the workplace?

For one, the workplace has to be (re)discovered as a crucial locus of learning. In order for the workplace to be conducive to learning, however, many workplaces will have to change.

To be conducive not only to applying but also acquiring and broadening qualifications, the organization of the workplace is an important factor in developing and maintaining a highly skilled and, in economic terms, efficient, competitive, and flexible workforce. The organization is important beyond the economic perspective and must also be seen as an essential element in the labor movement's struggle for humanization of work, workplace democracy, and, in general, the more equitable distribution of knowledge in society.

SUMMARY

The great majority of workplaces are undergoing pervasive change—due to a variety of factors, the most important of which is the introduction of modern technology—that change the nature of work, expand new forms of work organization, and advance innovative management principles. The changes have an important impact on qualifications needed in the workplace and how such necessary skills are being acquired.

Today's production process—not limited to manufacturing—requires from most workers more and broader skills than in the past. In addition to qualifications that are generic and polyvalent, there is a need for extrafunctional skills that are of an attitudinal and predispositional nature.

Due to their nature, most of the qualifications needed in the modern workplace cannot be acquired in training settings designed for specialized skill training or by traditional methods of skill training.

Many of the new key qualifications, by their nature and definition, fall in the broad range of educational activities rather than in skill training traditionally defined. However, education is most commonly equated with schooling, and schooling has generally proven, or been seen, to have serious shortcomings with respect to effective preparation for working life.

Many work qualifications seem to be best produced and acquired when they are used at the workplace. This points to the need for reintegration of learning and work at, or in close context with, the workplace.

In order to make such integrated learning possible and meaningful, work has to be organized in a way conducive to learning. Thus, the workplace has to be seen and organized as a learning environment in which qualifications are developed and applied and in which individual knowledge, experience, creativity, and sense of responsibility are incited and enhanced.

There is a close resemblance between the principles for humanization of work and the principles for effective learning. The latter can be both a result of organizational change and an instrument for such a change.

Informal learning (*everyday learning*) is the most important setting for continuous learning. This form of learning/instruction must be made visible. It is important for management and employees to develop routines for everyday learning in connection with traditional forms of training.

Learning situations that are located in the world of work increase the motivation, especially among the undereducated, to participate and engage in learning and facilitate the acquisition of content-specific as well as basic cognitive skills such as numeracy and literacy.

A major issue facing most OECD countries is how the low educational levels among the workforce can be raised. Based on the findings presented above, the efficiency of traditional remedial education programs administered solely through community colleges or municipal adult education must be questioned. Instead, it is advisable to develop programs in which the curriculum is a combination of workplace-specific and general content, and in which workplace based and institutional learning blend the cultures of both work and education.

8

Functional Context Education for Schoolplaces and Workplaces

Thomas G. Sticht

Applied Behavioral & Cognitive Sciences, Inc.

High-performance-high-wage workplaces engage employees in high skill-demand activities. Team work and customer-focused production and services demand communication skills for interacting with a diversity of people. Highly developed literacy and reasoning skills are needed for designing new work stations and carrying out multiple step procedures as customer demands change and old product lines give way to new ones. There is a need for increased workplace education and training that can help employees improve their fundamental learning skills to adapt to the more cognitively demanding workplaces. In turn, schools need to adopt new education methods that will provide graduates with the teamwork and individual thinking and reasoning skills needed to engage in high-performance work. However, much school- and work-based education and training is too abstract and decontextualized from real life. Too often learners cannot apply what they learn to real-world tasks. Contemporary cognitive science suggests that the teaching of basic literacy, reasoning, interpersonal communication skills, and subject matter (whether academic or work-related) is best accomplished when integrated into the functional contexts and tasks that engage people outside the school, including the world of work. Functional context education is discussed as an approach to education and training that is suitable for both schoolplaces and workplaces. From this point of view, learning both for and in the world of work is best accomplished following the same principles.

———

The changing nature of the organization of work influences learning incentives in both the workplace and the schools. In both cases it provides a greater incentive to learn in context rather than in the abstract. This chapter examines how both school learning and work learning need to fit into a functional context and how the two need to relate to each other.

Elsewhere in this volume, Rubenson and Schütze draw together perspectives on how sociotechnical changes influence the qualifications needed by workers in new organizations and the implications that such changes have for the instruction and training of workers. In this chapter I indicate the incentive value that these changes have for employers to initiate and employees to participate in education and training, expand on Rubenson and Schütze's idea of *contextualized learning*, and pursue their thesis that "education is most commonly equated with schooling, and schooling has generally proven or has been seen to have serious shortcomings with respect to effective preparation for working life."

I argue that both schooling and work are culturally constructed activities, and changes in one influence changes in the other. It is sometimes thought that childhood learning in school and adult learning at work follow different principles. I put forward the opposite view that, in fact, the same principles of functional context education are applicable in learning in school and at work.

THE CHANGING NATURE OF THE ORGANIZATION OF WORK

Briefly summarized, the argument made by Rubenson and Schütze is that old methods of production were developed around the time of the industrial revolution when most workers were uneducated. To utilize these workers, companies took complex production sequences and broke them up into hundreds or thousands of little acts, such as adjusting one bolt, and then assigned one worker to each act. Under this assembly line method of production, workers did not need to engage in complex cognitive activity, and the uneducated could be profitably employed. Decision making, planning, production scheduling, and inspection for quality were all handled by managers, supervisors, or inspectors. The supervisors reported to middle managers who in turn reported to executive managers who reported to *the boss* who made all the big decisions.

The *Tayloristic* production line was suitable for mass production runs in which supplies could be stockpiled, and endless thousands of the same product could be produced for a steadfast consumer, but times have changed. Today, consumers are worldwide. Large multinational corporations must compete to meet the demands of an extremely diverse consumer. International travel and telecommunications create rapid changes in consumer demands for a wide variety of products.

Under the new consumerism, plants need to be able to make short runs of products. They must therefore stockpile only the resources needed to meet immediate demands. Old production lines must be removed when demand for the product drops, and new production lines must be rapidly put into operation to meet customer needs.

As a consequence, many organizations are decentralizing decision making, planning, and production. Assembly lines with a thousand workers doing one act are being replaced by smaller production teams that take on the responsibility for an entire product. The team members meet with customers, take orders, arrange for the timely arrival of raw materials for the production process, and meet in their teams to plan their production schedules. Each team member must learn a variety of acts—how to operate three, four, or more machines—and must take responsibility for the quality of the work. In the new organization, quality is put in at the beginning and maintained by statistical quality control, not inspected at the end of production when it is costly to scrap products and start over. Finally, the team may package and deliver its own product to customers and provide a report of its overall activities to the greatly flattened management hierarchy (Sticht, 1991a, 1991b).

Implications of Sociotechnical Change for Job Requirements

Rubenson and Schütze note that within the new sociotechnical organizational structures, in which employees may have to be much more broadly accomplished, the terms *skills* and *job requirements* are too narrow. They use the term qualifications to connote the broader competence that the workers in the new production teams must possess.

A number of organizations and individuals have attempted to characterize the nature of the competence that workforce members should have. In the United States today, the most influential statement of this competence is the first report of the Secretary of Labor's Commission on Achieving Necessary Skills (SCANS, 1991). Based on an extensive analysis of present and future work in various businesses and industries, SCANS identified five *competencies* (knowledge and skill domains) that are needed for work in the high-performance organizations by the new sociotechnical structures:

1. Management of resources of time, money, people, material
2. Interpersonal competence for working with others
3. Information acquisition and use
4. Understanding complex systems
5. Work with various technologies.

These competencies are implemented by a three-part foundation of:

1. *Basic skills*: Reading, writing, arithmetic, oral language
2. *Thinking skills*: Decision making, problem solving, visualizing, reasoning
3. *Personal qualities*: Honesty, self-esteem, responsibility, sociability, self-management.

Over 110,000 of the SCANS reports have been distributed, and numerous schools and businesses are contemplating adopting or adapting the requirements described. Of particular importance is the fact that numerous high-performance organizations, such as Motorola and General Electric, are endorsing the SCANS competence statements as indicators of the broad qualifications that their workers need to stay personally competitive in their present and future jobs. Efforts are underway to develop certificates of competency tied to promotion as incentives for employees. Education and training programs are being designed in some companies to help employees attain the needed competence for certification.

Influence of Sociotechnical Changes on Worker Education and Training

In its research to identify the skills needed for work and to set standards for the successful transition from school into the world of work, SCANS (1991) addressed the problems of *decontextualized* instruction as discussed by Rubenson and Schütze:

> SCANS believes that teachers and schools must begin early to help students see the relationships between what they study and its applications in real-world context. . . . We know from the findings of cognitive science that the most effective way of teaching intellectual skills is in context, placing learning objectives within real environ-

ments rather than insisting that students first learn in the abstract what they will then be expected to apply. SCANS suggests three principles from cognitive science to guide real contextual learning in all our schools:

- Students do not need to learn basic skills before they learn problem-solving skills. The two go together. They are not sequential but mutually reinforcing.
- Learning should be reoriented away from mere mastery of information and toward encouraging students to recognize and solve problems.
- Real know-how . . . cannot be taught in isolation; students need practice in the application of these skills. (pp. 23-24)

Research in contemporary cognitive science provides an empirical base for functional context education, an approach to education in which the teaching of basic literacy skills and subject matter is integrated into the functional contexts that engage people outside the school, including the world of work. From this perspective, learning both for and in the world of work is best accomplished following the same principles.

Functional context education is based on theoretical constructs and research derived from action research in the military to develop more effective technical and literacy training programs for use in the world of work (Sticht, Armstrong, Hickey, & Caylor, 1987), experimental studies of the effects of contextualizing instruction in the schools (Duffy, 1992), and laboratory and field research aimed at understanding human cognitive development and its use in school and nonschool settings (Resnick, 1987). This practical and theoretical knowledge is currently being formulated into a functional context theory of cognitive development, learning, and instruction (Sticht & Hickey, 1991). The theory is being developed to meet a number of problems with education in school and at work. Some of these problems are discussed below.

THE CULTURAL CONSTRUCTION OF THE WORLD OF WORK

From the point of view of students in the schools or front-line employees in the workplace, the message is the same. If jobs are demanding more skills, then students and employees are going to have to learn more to get and keep a job. If, on the other hand, the pool of higher skilled, well-paying jobs is shrinking due to global competition, then students and employees are going to have to learn more to improve their personal competitiveness so that they can get and keep one of the scarce, well-paying jobs.

From the point of view of society, local, state, and federal governments must attend to the educational needs of individuals to prepare them to compete for work in well-paying jobs. To do this, governments must stimulate growth in the more highly skilled, well-paying businesses and industries to maintain their tax bases for infrastructure, social welfare, and quality of life services, including the provision of high-quality education to all. One of the critical ingredients needed to develop and attract such businesses is a workforce with the positive attitudes, extensive knowledge, and high skills needed to adapt to and perform well in high-performance workplaces (Commission on the Skills of the American Workforce, 1990). To provide this needed workforce, governments need to promote more and better learning in the schools for the world of work and more and better learning in the world of work to remain competitive in the world economy.

It is apparent that the supply of highly skilled workers and the supply of well-paying, high-performance jobs are interdependent, and both are generated by education and training. The world of work is an expression of the values and intellectual capacities of the individuals that constitute a society. As individuals organize themselves into a business or industry, they create within the larger culture a subculture organized by the particular products or services they provide; their understandings of their markets; and their beliefs, attitudes, and cognitive abilities, including the technological knowledge that permits them to use the various tools needed to accomplish the work of the business. They also develop social roles and status, with their own modes of dress, ways of behaving, special language, and knowledge and skill requirements.

To prepare students for high-productivity performance in the world of work, schools must provide a form of multicultural education in which students learn about the various subcultures of workplaces in the larger culture. To do this, business and industry must provide the schools with information about their cultures: who they are; what their people know and do in their various roles; how the organization fits into the economy and social system of the larger culture; what the particular beliefs in the organization are regarding work, modes of dress, and ways of relating among workers and supervisors; how they solve their internal problems; and how they train and retrain themselves to promote or keep abreast of changes in the marketplace.

THE SCHOOLS: TOPIC-ORIENTED VS. PERFORMANCE-ORIENTED LEARNING

The aim of workplace multicultural education is to permit learners to acquire the attitudes, knowledge, and skills needed to behave and perform well in the subcultures of various businesses or industries. Under this performance orientation, schools would organize learning around the world of work and teach students how to negotiate the cultures of manufacturing, retail trade, agriculture, government, and various other service industries.

Instead, however, the schools generally operate under a topic or subject matter orientation in which the goal is to acquire knowledge, not to perform in a specified social role or subcultural setting. The goal is to have students achieve some, generally unspecified, degree of understanding or knowledge of the *core* topics or subject matters of English, mathematics, science, history, and geography.

For the most part, because such subject matter is part of the general cultural heritage stored in books, when students enter school, education typically follows the prescription, "first you learn to read and then you read to learn." This means that reading, along with writing, is considered a *foundation* or *tool skill* which, after having been learned for its own technological utility in the early grades, is then applied, starting around the fourth grade, to learning the concepts, principles, facts, and so forth, of the various academic topics.

Interestingly, although mathematics is a subject matter, it is usually taught in the early grades as a foundation or tool skill. English, too, has aspects of both a tool skill in the early grades (writing, spelling, punctuation, grammar, and composition) and as a subject matter in the higher grades when focused on the study of literature.

Although science, history, and geography have their research methods and could be taught as tool skills for generating bodies of knowledge, they are mostly taught as facts and concepts about people, places, events, or things. This emphasis is particularly apparent in adult programs aimed at high school equivalency certification (e.g., the GED certificate). Such programs typically have neither laboratories to practice the scientific method nor assigned out-of-class research and writing projects (out-of-school time is scarce for adult learners). They typically focus on using reading, writing, and class discussion to learn the vocabulary, general facts, and concepts of the subject matter fields well enough to pass the GED test. (For an exception to this topic-oriented approach to adult education see the performance oriented approach of Nickse, 1980.)

DECONTEXTUALIZATION OF LEARNING IN SCHOOLS

According to instructional designers, one of the consequences of the topic-oriented approach to education is that the subject matter is removed from its context in the world outside the classroom, and this makes it difficult for learners to know how to apply what they have learned in school to the world of work (Duffy, 1992). In the schools, abstract thought takes precedence over action, symbols over actual objects and activities, and generalizable abstractions over contextualized applications (Resnick, 1987).

Such decontextualization can lead to a number of problems. First, it creates an artificial separation between the schools, where *book learning* takes place, and the rest of society, where *real* learning takes place. The separation can especially affect children whose parents hold no value for book learning and are unlikely to read to their preschool child or engage in learning activities themselves to serve as role models (Mason & Kerr, 1992).

Second, it may lead to the teaching of the basic skills before children fully understand the functional uses of written language and other graphic devices, perpetuating the belief that "first we learn to read and then we read to learn." Alternatively, content knowledge can be developed by field trips, oral language, drawing pictures, and carrying out experiments and demonstrations; then, when children are taught reading comprehension skills, they will have a richer body of knowledge to draw on for constructing understandings of what they are reading. Thus, reading comprehension can be improved even before students learn to read by teaching them important content through other means. As noted below, this idea is important in adult remedial reading (Duffy, 1992).

A third effect of the decontextualization of learning is that older students may not be motivated because they cannot see how what they are being asked to learn has any application in the world outside the school (Heath, 1983). Hence, they may not learn much of what the school has to offer. This does not mean that they will not learn quite a bit. Many students who are poorly motivated in school read and learn a lot about things they are interested in outside of school. For instance, a boy who is interested in motorcycles and automobiles may spend a lot of time reading magazines about them. Thus, although his academic work may suffer, he may show considerable aptitude for reading and learning about automobile mechanics (Sticht, 1975).

A fourth effect of decontextualization is that the knowledge gained in school can be used to pass paper-and-pencil tests of recall, but it cannot be used in the world outside school. A great student in the classroom may fail to see how his or her knowledge can be applied in different *real-world* settings. This may lead to distinctions between *academic intelligence* versus *practical intelligence* (Wagner, 1992).

DECONTEXTUALIZATION IN WORKPLACE
EDUCATION AND TRAINING

Decontextualized schooling may also affect workplace education and training. Students who enter the world of work, as human resources development staff, may inappropriately apply in corporate classrooms the practices they developed in school, such as teaching and learning topics rather than developing workplace approaches for improving performance (Resnick, 1987). One study found that writers of military manuals that were supposed to tell people how to do jobs approached the task as though they were to cover a topic exhaustively. Rather than asking for job and task analyses so that they could write procedures, they asked for bibliographic citations so they could cover the topic. Instead of targeting their manuals for the worker-users, they aimed them at a general reader with a fairly high reading level. Needless to say, users reported that the manuals did not tell them how to do their jobs and were difficult to read and comprehend (Kern, Sticht, Welty, & Hauke, 1975).

This process of transferring school-based experiences to workplaces also reveals itself in many workplace literacy projects of the sort discussed by Mikulecky (this volume). Many corporate managers with good intentions for helping employees achieve higher levels of literacy contract with vendors who offer traditional, school-based, decontextualized instruction in the basic skills just like they had received. This follows the school practice of seeing basic skills as abstract, content-free information processing techniques that one first *gets* and then *applies.*

However, consistent with the SCANS position, Rubenson and Schütze note that the development of reading skills by workers may be accelerated by situating the learning in a meaningful, work-related context. Furthermore, it is frequently possible to improve general literacy as much or more in job-related literacy programs as in outside literacy programs (Sticht et al., 1987). This suggests there is value in the advice of Rubenson and Schütze "to develop programs in which the curriculum would be a combination of workplace specific and general content integrating the cultures of work and education."

INVESTING IN THE EDUCATION OF ADULTS TO
IMPROVE THE EDUCABILITY OF CHILDREN

As I have argued earlier (Sticht, 1983), if adult education and training are pursued with greater zeal in the workplace, not only may companies influence the productivity of their current workforce, but the intergenerational transfer of educational outcomes from parents to their children may also improve the productivity of the schools and a more competent future workforce will be available (Van Fossen & Sticht, 1991).

In short, the best way that business and industry might help to reform schools and improve the qualifications of the future workforce is to reorganize themselves into high-performance organizations, thereby creating an opportunity for employees to engage in jobs demanding high levels of cognition. Then employers should provide meaningful, contextualized educational opportunities so that employees can efficiently develop new competence and the improved self-esteem and self-confidence that generally attends the acquisition of competence. Such a provision may provide double-duty dollars; both the productivity of the workplace and the productivity of schools may be improved. The investment return should be incentive enough for both employers and employees to value and engage in lifelong learning.

SECTION V:
Literacy and Basic Skills

9

Workplace Literacy Programs: Organization and Incentives

Larry Mikulecky
Indiana University

Organization and quality of workplace literacy programs vary a great deal between nations, between industries, and between large and small employers within the same industry. Workplace literacy programs range from well-established government training programs to union-organized programs to less clear-cut partnerships funded by federal, state, and local governments in conjunction with employers.

Incentives for participation in workplace literacy programs are also diverse. The most direct incentives involve various forms of financial support for students. A key form of this support is employer-paid time while training at the work site. Other less common incentives for recruiting and retaining employees in programs include cash bonuses, potential and guaranteed promotions, and job retention. Program features and benefits include career counseling, child care, transportation, and program flexibility as well as improved self-esteem and family relations. Barriers such as past educational failure, schedule conflicts, and fear of job dismissal are among the disincentives for continued employee participation. Employer incentives for initiating programs include significant funding from outside sources; potential improvements in productivi-

ty, quality, and employee loyalty; and a decreasing need to recruit, screen, and train inexperienced replacements.

A problem central to providing programs and incentives is determining who is to receive training. There are often several different groups in the workplace (e.g., very low literates, nonnative English speakers, high school graduates with only moderate literacy skills) who need different sorts of literacy training. Some of the more effective programs provide multiple strands of education, that is, different instruction for different groups.

Although a growing body of research has identified principles and elements associated with effective workplace literacy programs, few programs are able to incorporate all elements. This chapter briefly recounts the nature of effective workplace literacy programs, more thoroughly examines the organization of current programs, and focuses a good deal of attention on incentives for participation.

WORKPLACE LITERACY PROBLEMS AND EFFECTIVE PROGRAMS

Workplace literacy programs need to address a number of problems. They need to be able to distinguish the differing needs of different groups. They must also respond to severe limitations in available learning time. There are also indications that the transfer of general literacy education to specific workplace applications is low and that learning gains tend to revert if practice is not continued (Mikulecky, 1990; Philippi, 1989; Sticht, 1982, 1989). In a survey of the relatively few U.S. and Canadian workplace literacy programs that have been rigorously evaluated, Mikulecky and d'Adamo-Weinstein (1991) report:

1. Effective programs require significant resources in terms of learner time on task (i.e., 50-100 hours of instruction per average 1 year of learner gain).
2. Effective private programs report learner cost figures more than double those of average public programs (i.e., $7,000 vs. $2,800).
3. Effective programs integrate basic skills training with workplace technical training. This usually involves counseling as well as on-the-job training linkage and analysis of the basic skills needed on learner jobs.

These findings are supplemented by a recently released study of 37 workplace literacy programs funded by the U.S. Department of Education (Kutner, Sherman, Webb, & Fisher, 1991). The study identifies four key components of effective programs: (a) active involvement by project partners, (b) active involvement by employees in determining literacy needs, (c) systematic analysis of on-the-job literacy requirements, and (d) instructional materials directly related to the job.

No single class or course seems able to meet the demands of diverse populations within a single workplace or to provide a sufficient amount of instruction to move very low-level literates to the functional literacy levels called for in developed nations' workplaces. In fact, programs with a single approach for all are, almost by definition, ineffective.

Multistrand approaches that provide several different types of courses and strings of educational experiences and that address long-term training goals for specific groups appear to offer the highest probability of success. For very low-level literates this may mean providing long-term (several hundred hours over several years) tutoring or small group instruction that later leads to other courses and instruction. Employees who read well enough to understand simple newspaper stories may benefit from middle-size classes that integrate basic-skills instruction with technical training. Classes for nonnative English speakers are most beneficial when they integrate oral and written English and provide direct instruction in language usage in the workplace.

Many programs currently do not address these learner differences other than to hope that an overworked instructor in a drop-in center will be able to meet their variety of needs. In usual practice, this guarantees that few needs are really met. The recognition that there are truly different groups with literacy assistance needs brings with it new issues. For example, few programs have the resources to meet the needs of all.

The recognition that different groups exist and that these groups need different degrees and types of instruction initiates discussions about who receives training first and how much training they should receive. Equal access to underfunded drop-in centers is one approach, but it has been criticized as providing equal access to ineffective education. Furthermore, some learners need much more time and individual attention than others. Resources can be expended to help one low-level literate develop to a functional level, or the same resources can be used to help several mid-level literates to brush up and master new technical literacy skills. Different sets of priorities may take precedence according to whether program funding is primarily from the employer, unions, or the state.

In remarks made at the roundtable from whence this volume was produced, Sticht pointed out that simple-minded approaches to categorizing people have not worked effectively. Literacy is only one aspect of personal skills that influence job performance. Results from literacy programs provided by the U.S. military in the 1970s suggest that some low-level literates perform on the job as effectively as middle-level literates.

The recognition that different groups require different responses extends also to incentive programs for recruiting and retaining learners. Effective incentives for low level literates are likely to differ from those effective with mid-level literates. Indeed, effective incentives may depend on the nature of the program developed for each different learning group. For example, guaranteeing anonymity and privacy in one-on-one tutoring may be more important for a low-level group, whereas providing clear access to upward career paths may be more important to other groups.

ORGANIZATION OF CURRENT WORKPLACE LITERACY PROGRAMS

Although it is desirable to know something about the organizational arrangements associated with current workplace literacy programs, it is a daunting task to make sense of the myriad of available program descriptions, funding arrangements, and national frameworks for delivering training. The task is complicated by the lack of consensus about terms such as *basic skills* and disagreements about whether technical training with basic-skills support or language training with a literacy component for nonnative speakers constitute workplace literacy training.

Inadequate information and definitional problems make international comparisons difficult, but some key elements of program organization can be addressed:

- Program funding sources
- Degrees to which programs are joint ventures
- Program format.

Program Funding Sources

For many nations, especially many Organisation for Economic Co-operation and Development (OECD) members, workplace literacy funding is subsumed under funding for general vocational training. Employers often contribute to employee training through a periodically assessed tax or levy. In Germany, corporations contribute a total of nearly 3.5% of annual payroll to public training and employment schemes through joint employer/employee-financed ventures and mandatory contributions to local Chambers of Commerce; literacy and basic-skills instruction is a small part of a national plan. Similar plans are in operation in Sweden and Denmark. In Ireland, large companies are required to contribute from 1-2.5% of payroll annually to a renewal fund that returns 90% of the money to approved company training programs (National Center on Education and the Economy, 1990). In France, vocational training (of which workplace basic skills is a part) is financed 58.6% by state expenditure, 35.4% by private expenditure, and 6% by the contributions of various public and other organizations (Kenawaty & Castro, 1990). In Australia, past support has come from a mixture of government funding, union funding, and corporate funding through negotiated settlements. Recently, however, Australia has taken the route of taxing employers 2% of corporate profits to be used in a training fund, although the details of this arrangement are still being worked out. A Canadian survey of 110 workplace literacy programs indicates that only 4% are funded totally by corporate funding; the remainder are, to a large degree, funded through federal or provincial taxes (Johnston, 1991).

No comprehensive study of funding sources for U.S. workplace literacy programs exists. In its survey of 20,000 U.S. employers with more than 100 employees, the American Society for Training and Development (ASTD) estimates that American businesses spent more than $44.4 billion for training in 1989 (Oberle, Gerber, & Gordon, 1989). A small fraction (less than 10%) went to remedial education. Not all workplace literacy programs were conceived of as remedial training, however. Thus, it is not possible to determine what proportion of workplace literacy training is subsumed under categories such as communication skills, technical skills, clerical skills, team building, problem solving, and several other categories.

Bussert (1991) attempted to discern the outlines of funding sources for U.S. workplace literacy programs through an examination of published program descriptions. Of 107 workplace literacy program descriptions analyzed by Bussert, 33 discussed funding sources. Of these 33 programs, 33% were funded by single providers, with businesses (21%) the largest single source followed by state and local funders (6% each). The majority of programs had multiple source funding, including 27% from federal sources, 48% from state/local governments, 67% from businesses, 9% from unions, and 12% from other organizations such as libraries and area literacy councils. The degree to which funding from these organizations might include taxpayer money is not clear.

Degree to Which Workplace Literacy Programs are Joint Ventures

Bussert (1991) found that 92% of the 107 U.S. workplace literacy programs involved joint ventures of two or more partners, including multiple unions, multiple businesses, a school and a business, or a government agency with a business and a union. The most common types of partnerships among analyzed programs were:

Type of Partnerships

- Employers working with others   88% of partnerships
- Schools (public school, community
  college, and university) working in
  partnership with others   51%

- Unions working with others   34%

In their discussion of Canadian workplace literacy programs, Taylor, Lewe, and Draper (1991) noted the high degree of Canadian government funding and the urgency for real partnerships among businesses, industry, and education. No analysis of the present degree of partnerships among Canadian programs was mentioned, however.

As discussed earlier, program priorities and goals are influenced by the nature of the partners involved. Some union-supported programs define literacy programs as an employee benefit and place a premium on programs that are voluntary and focus on learner-identified goals. Programs in which the employer is a predominant partner may focus more closely on preparation for future technical training or other corporate goals. Because most programs are joint ventures, goals are often multiple, and these differing goals directly influence the nature of incentives for learner involvement.

Program Format

Wide variations in program format are a direct result of the multiple groups served by literacy instruction in the workplace and the fact that programs are often developed by partners with differing goals. In a review of program descriptions, Bussert (1991) identified 53 programs that were described in enough detail to allow for format categorization. Open entry/exit programs were reported by 17% of the programs, whereas 32% reported flexible hours (ranging from drop-in centers to scheduled classes available during inconvenient shifts and lunch hours to home study). Flexible location (i.e., tutoring on and off site at churches, libraries or homes of tutors) was reported by 5.6% of the programs. The vast majority (74%) offered a multiple strand curriculum (i.e., two or more of the following: Adult Basic Education (ABE), General Equivalency Diploma (GED), English as a Second Language (ESL), a selection of basic skills/technical courses), whereas 13% reported self-pacing of learning (i.e., home study, PLATO computerized learning, or learning modules).

INCENTIVES

For workplace literacy programs to succeed, there must be convincing reasons and incentives for participation on the part of employees, employers, and whomever else is asked for support. To a large degree, the incentives available are dictated by the organizational aspects of programs, as discussed in previous sections (i.e., format, funding, and goals of partners). These incentives can come in the forms of release time from work, tangible financial rewards, increased opportunities, flexibility, support services, and in terms of such intangibles as increased self-esteem and recognition.

In addition to incentives, workplace literacy programs and participants must contend with a range of disincentives. These can range from the past negative educational experiences of low literates to present child care or schedule conflicts to fear of losing one's job for revealing literacy difficulties to one's employer.

On a group-by-group and sometimes individual-by-individual basis, effective program planners weigh the countervailing pressures of incentives and disincentives. For example, counseling or nurturing and anonymous tutoring can help alleviate fears while increasing scheduling flexibility. The key, at the program level, is regular monitoring of why potential program clients do not participate.

A discussion and analysis of the types of incentives employed in workplace literacy programs follow below.

Employee Incentives: Tuition and Course Support

In the studies reviewed, the most commonly reported incentive for employee participation in workplace literacy programs is full payment of tuition, book, and material costs. No workplace basic-skills program expected individual workers to pay for their own tuition. Sometimes programs were paid for with taxpayer funds, sometimes union funds, and sometimes employer funds, but never with funds directly from individual workers. (The case can be made, of course, that union funds and taxpayer funds are actually worker funds available indirectly.) In cases of extreme literacy difficulties, the incentive of free tuition may not outweigh fears of job loss if problems become known. Although the fear is not often justified, some programs make every effort to maintain individual learner anonymity.

Government-funded course support. Newcombe et al. (1989) discussed several examples of government-funded tuition in Australia. Department of Labor funding provided support for programs with General

Motors Holden, Williamston Naval, and Melbourne's Werribee Farms. These job literacy programs were fully funded for workers of the three companies except for lost productivity time of the enrolled participants.

European governments also support employees' efforts to improve basic education skills (Luttringer & Pasquier, 1980). For example, in Belgium, employees can take time off from work to attend general education or vocational courses with continued payment of their normal wages by employer and government matching funds. The same is true in Italy, where priority is given to remedial education. In France, the government pays for employees' educational leave for medium length and long courses.

Over 95% of Canadian workplace literacy programs are completely or partially government funded (Johnston, 1991). In the United States, there are indications that nearly three-fourths of the programs are partially supported by federal, state, or local governments (Bussert, 1991).

Employer-sponsored course support. In some workplace literacy programs, support comes entirely from employers. Earlier information from the American Society for Training and Development (ASTD) survey (Oberle et al., 1989) of large U.S. businesses discussed previously provides a sense of the extent of this support. Howden (1990) discussed one such program started by the *West Palm Beach Post* newspaper in 1990 for employees with basic skills or English language problems. The program provided tuition and release time to attend either ABE, ESL, or GED classes. Bussert's (1991) survey of 107 workplace literacy programs indicated that 67% of programs received some employer economic support, but it did not report the percentage funded solely by employers. Johnston (1991) indicated that only 4% of programs in Canada are funded completely by employers. It is more difficult to define employer support in Europe and Australia. When a company is taxed directly to provide training, can that company be described as supporting training? If so, a very high percentage of European and Australian employers may be supporting some sort of basic skills training.

Union-sponsored course support. Unions also play a role in providing the incentive of paid educational leave, although the magnitude of this role differs from nation to nation. In the United States, several major unions (United Auto Workers, and member unions of the AFL-CIO) have negotiated agreements that an amount from $.05 to $.20 per hour, per worker, go to training that is of benefit to employees. For UAW/Ford, these funds amounted to over $80 million in a single year (B. Elrod, Director, Math or Enrichment Program, UAW/Ford, personal communication, May, 1989).

In Australia, unions have supported basic skills courses for at least two decades. Some have negotiated fully paid tuition leave for English language training. In 1987, the Western Australian Industrial Relations Commission incorporated such tuition leave into the Government Water Supply, Sewerage and Drainage Employees award (Singh, 1989). Strong union backing led to the agreement of several other companies and unions to grant time off without loss of pay to union employees in health, metal, rail, public transport, and other industries who attended recognized English language or numeracy classes (Matheson, 1989a, 1989b).

Italian, German, and Swedish unions are the principal organizers of workplace basic skills programs (Luttringer & Pasquier, 1980), and the International Laborers Union of Canada is also active in conducting courses (Patterson, 1989).

Employee Incentives: Continued Educational Advancement

Some employer sponsored workplace literacy programs provide tuition support which begins with basic skills and continues through college courses (Cooper, Van Dexter, & Williams, 1988). Continued educational advancement is a key incentive for many employees who recognize the need for more education. Workplace literacy support as the first step in a longer educational journey is an incentive in its own right. Employees see their efforts leading to an improved personal future through further educational attainment. Liston (1986) reported a cooperative venture between General Dynamics' Electric Boat Division and Rhode Island Community College. Nearly 40% of the employees started with basic-skills classes before pursuing an associate's degree and journeyman's certificate. Course support was provided by the employer. Rhode Island Community College created a new associate's degree program for these employees and provided the basic-skills support needed to attain the degree.

Another example of a program that begins with basic skills but continues onward to higher educational goals is reported at A. C. Rochester, a division of General Motors which manufactures fuel injectors for cars (National Center on Education and the Economy, 1990). At this plant, the United Auto Workers and New York State jointly funded a workplace literacy and college credit program. Twenty percent of the division's employees enrolled in the job-specific basic-skills program, and 50% enrolled in the college courses, often after having started in the basic-skills program.

Employee Incentives: Cash Bonuses, Promotions, and Job Retention

Personal gain in the form of cash bonuses or increased chances for promotion is sometimes offered to employees who take part in workplace literacy programs. In addition, several programs report job retention or stability as an incentive. Many workers legitimately fear that without increased basic skills they will not be able to retain their jobs.

Cash bonuses. Howden (1990) discussed a cash incentive plan in place at the *West Palm Beach Post* in Florida. Employees who improved four grade levels in the *Post's* ESL and workplace literacy programs received $100 bonuses, and those who advanced from ESL to ABE/GED classes received an additional $100; any *Post* employee who passed the GED received a $250 bonus. The newspaper paid these bonuses from its own funds.

Grimes and Renner (1988) described several similar cash incentive programs. For example, Revere Ware, Inc., a maker of cooking utensils, offered employees $100 savings bonds as an incentive for completing a GED course and a $25 gift certificate to be used at a local restaurant just for taking the GED test. Landscaping employees at Synnestvedt Nursery received $150 upon successful completion of the work-oriented vocabulary course for nonnative English speakers. Success was determined by attendance and measurable improvement in speaking and understanding English.

Promotions. In developed nations, basic-skills levels are increasingly an issue in job promotion. Henry and Raymond (1982) reported that over 65% of U.S. businesses surveyed about basic skills deficiencies indicated that such deficiencies limited the job advancement of their high school graduate employees, and 73% responded that deficiencies limit the promotability of non-high school graduates.

The same concern is voiced in other developed nations. In Australia, English competency is now considered an important factor in job mobility (Matheson, 1989a). It is likely to become more so because national award restructuring drastically reduced the number of job descriptions in each occupational area by consolidating the duties and skills required of workers. To be promoted, and sometimes even retained, employees must have higher levels of basic skills (Matheson, 1989b).

In many cases, higher levels of basic skills and degrees or certification credentials are clearly defined in new employer promotion policies. Liston (1986) reported that at General Dynamics Electric Boat Company, employees who did not master basic skills and complete an associate's degree could not advance in the company. Promotion after completion of a workplace literacy class is also seen in the hotel industry. The University of Hawaii (1990) reported that Sheraton Hotel employees who participated in ESL and workplace literacy courses were considered more promotable by supervisors.

Philippi (1989) evaluated a workplace literacy program at Peavy

Electronics, a Mississippi electronics firm. The program involved matching computerized basic-skills lessons to skills demands on jobs. Learners were diagnosed for skill deficiencies, and they received an average of nearly 40 hours of computer-based, job-specific basic-skills instruction. Supervisors reported that they would recommend 60% of the 63 participants for promotion and 57% for pay increases. During the short period of the pilot test, over 20% of the participants inquired about openings in jobs requiring higher basic skills and/or computer operation. This was an important finding because a major promotion problem in the firm was that many experienced workers previously lacked the skill levels and confidence to even consider advancement to new positions.

Basic-skills improvement is not a guaranteed pathway to promotion, however. An independent evaluation of Working Smart, a federally funded program based in Los Angeles, found that only 15% of randomly selected employees responded that Working Smart helped them get a job or promotion (Los Angeles Unified School District, 1990). Thirty percent of the interviewees were unemployed at the time of the random sample. It is difficult to determine the degree to which Working Smart program results can be attributed to program problems and the degree to which results were influenced by other factors (i.e., the economy, personal characteristics, etc.). The independent program evaluator felt low program quality was a factor; there were little or no measured gains in student learning on pre- and post-CASAS (competency) tests. Teachers also complained of irrelevant material, students being overloaded with content, slow pace, and poor on-site classes.

Job retention and stability. In developed nations, job stability is far from guaranteed. It appears that a significant proportion of low-skilled jobs are lost each year to technical advances in the workplace or to Third World competitors who can do low-skilled work for lower cost. Even jobs that retain the same title often increase in responsibilities and basic-skills demands. An incentive for some workers to take workplace literacy training is fear of job loss.

Westberry (1990) reported that three of nine plants in Tennessee offered workplace literacy classes to employees who had nonsecure jobs. These companies stressed quality control and numeracy in the basic-skills training. Grimes and Renner (1988) reported that 19% of Kelly-Springfield Tire's 1,200 employees read below the sixth-grade level. The plant manager was concerned about the effect of high technology on these 232 low-literate employees and thus urged workers to enroll in adult literacy courses during lunch breaks.

Low literacy skills has also caused alarm for some independent or self-employed workers. For example, truck drivers in the United

States are now required to pass a series of tests to be certified for a variety of hauling jobs. In Pennsylvania, truckers must pass a written test on hazardous waste (Bethlehem Area Chamber of Commerce, 1990). Because a high percentage of the truckers have difficulty with written licensing tests, the Bethlehem Chamber of Commerce started free classes to increase literacy skills of commercial truck drivers in the area. Similar conditions exist in each of the 50 states in the United States.

The need for employees to keep up with technological change is international. Taw (1990) reported that some British workers at the North Middlesex Hospital felt nervous about proposed changes in food technology (such as chill-cook procedures) and contemplated leaving the hospital, despite 18-25 years of service. After workers participated in a job-specific literacy program, their hospital supervisor noticed improvement in work quality and attitudes. Taw also reported that Britain faces increasing basic-skills demands from the European Community (EC). For example, EC pesticides regulations involve complex calibrations.

There is not much hard evidence on the effectiveness of workplace literacy programs in maintaining employee jobs. Norris and Breen (1990) cited an interesting example, however. At Alpha Semiconductor, a manufacturer of electronic devices in Massachusetts, 25% of the company's 400 workers did not speak English as their native language, and most had problems communicating. Special English language classes were developed, and only three participants were let go during a recent lay-off of 60 employees. Supervisors reported improved productivity and quality of work on the part of participants and attributed it to decreased translation time and the fact that students had fewer inhibitions about asking questions before beginning unfamiliar tasks.

Employee Incentives: Related Support Services

Workplace literacy classes do not always provide sufficient incentive to overcome obstacles to employee participation. Additional support services such as transportation, child care, or career counseling of some sort are sometimes needed to secure employee participation and retention.

Transportation and child care. Transportation and child care are relatively rare in workplace literacy program descriptions, and there is no firm evidence of the effectiveness of these services in securing employee participation. One such program, reported by Stein (1989), is the Fraen Corporation's basic-skills program which provided free transportation to employees who attended ESL and numeracy classes outside their regular shifts. Transportation and child care were free of charge to employees enrolled in the POWER workplace literacy and ESL classes

(Triton College, 1990). The Working Smart hotel and foods literacy projects in Los Angeles also offered free transportation and referrals for child care (Los Angeles Unified School District, 1990).

Counseling. Counseling of some sort is a more common support service/incentive for employee participation in workplace literacy programs. Often counseling takes the form of personal support for those with previous failures and low self-concept. Sometimes counseling takes the form of career guidance so that employees can see the relevance of their efforts to future occupational choices.

The previously described Hawaii Sheraton workplace literacy program was well designed, but it lacked a counseling component. Program directors reported 29% attrition of participants in the job-specific and general literacy classes (University of Hawaii, 1990). Directors attributed part of this attrition to the need for educational counseling. The program evaluation reports:

> A certain number of participants failed to develop a personal commitment to the program and maintain progress for themselves. Some participants were not able to see the long-term rewards of their hard work, but instead expected to be rewarded after a short period of participation. In response to this problem, the program. . . [needed]. . . more educational counseling and goal setting. (pp. 81-82)

Levine and Pansar (1990) described a cooperative program with a strong counseling component, the Boston Workplace Education Collaborative, a partnership set up by the AFL-CIO, Roxbury Community College, and the Boston Private Industry Counsel. At least 81% of the students' folders contained extensive Individual Education Plans, usually reflecting the support of an Education Counselor who helped participants monitor progress toward their goals. The counselor's hours were flexible to allow maximal student interactions, and a translator was provided to students who were not proficient in English. For similar counseling incentives see also Triton College (1990), Stein (1989), Bethlehem Area Chamber of Commerce (1990), Continuing Education Institute (1990), and Gross, Lee, and Zuss (1988).

Sometimes successful programs add counseling in order to increase learner retention. An example is the award-winning Jefferson County Adult Literacy Program in Kentucky (Balmuth, 1988). As a deterrent to program attrition during January, the providers scheduled individual student conferences and were successful in cutting drop-out rates.

Counseling is a positive incentive only when it is well planned. The International Masonry Institute and the International Union of Bricklayers and Allied Craftsmen (Bricklayers and Allied Craftsmen,

1990) reported that career counselors were underutilized in a workplace literacy program because they were located in community colleges and not at the site of the literacy classes; consequently, the counselors were viewed by students as detached from the blue-collar world. Lack of organizational planning also decreased the utility of career counselors for the REEP/Hotel Workplace Literacy Project (Arlington County Public Schools, 1990). In this job-related ESL literacy program, career counseling as an incentive was not used to advantage because workers had to rush back to their jobs right after the literacy classes, and the teacher/counselors had little opportunity to answer questions or direct students.

Employee Incentives: Program Flexibility

Program flexibility is viewed by many learners as an incentive for participation in workplace literacy programs. Flexibility in curriculum, location, and scheduling helps provide learners with exactly what they want, when they want it, and where they want it.

Bluff (1989) described Australia's Trade Union Postal Course, a program with a high degree of flexibility. This correspondence-by-mail program had flexible scheduling, location, and curriculum. Students were offered a number of courses to choose from, and they worked at their own pace. If they had problems, a tutor came to their homes free of charge. In a compilation of learner evaluation comments, Bluff recorded repeated high praise for aspects of flexibility such as self-selection, self-pacing, and learning in a location where privacy can be maintained. Cooper et al. (1988) described a similar home-study program in the eastern United States supported by Bell Atlantic Corporation.

Home study is not the only way to provide a flexible schedule. Though on site, the Hawaii Sheraton job skills and ESL programs (University of Hawaii, 1990) scheduled classes at several times, and the learning center and its computer lab were open Monday–Saturday, 8 a.m. to 6 p.m. Drop-in learning centers of this sort are fairly common. Holmes (1989) described two in England—the Drop-in Skills Center in Nelson, Lancashire, England, and the literacy and numeracy job training program of Simon Engineering in Stockport, which had no classes but instead provided a tutor to answer trainee questions about technical drawings and measurements. Unemployed adults came three days a week to identify their skills.

Variations on flexibility were reported by Gross et al. (1988), who discussed flexibility of location and time (such as on- and off-site tutorials during the week or on Saturdays). Another variation comes from the UAW/Ford who devised a basic skills enrichment course in module format that allowed learners to work with an instructor individually in the learning center, in small scheduled classes, or alone at home (Philippi, Mikulecky, & Kloosterman, 1991). The module approach allows workers to study away from class and increases the amount of time learners spend with the materials.

Employee Incentives: Intangible Benefits

Learners remain in programs when they perceive themselves to be deriving benefit. Improved literacy often brings benefits of an intangible sort—increased self-esteem, recognition from supervisors and peers, and increased benefits for family members. This analysis of employee incentives would be remiss if it did not include these less tangible, but important, incentives.

Positive changes in employees' self-esteem after participation in workplace literacy programs are noted in several program evaluations and descriptions (Coffey, Eoff, Mayo, & McDaniel, 1990; Gross et al., 1988; Westberry, 1990; and University of Hawaii, 1990). Although assessments of self-esteem are usually not planned as part of program evaluations, evaluators typically remark on increases in learner self-esteem in compilations of anecdotes from interviews with supervisors, instructors, and sometimes learners themselves. Westberry (1990) reported that many programs attempt to foster increased self-esteem through recognition dinners, congratulations in newsletters, and special certificates.

Most workplace literacy programs do not set out to improve relations among family members, but this benefit is reported as a side effect by a few programs. Jones and Medley (1987) assessed employee family relations before and after a workplace literacy program and indicated that improved family relations occurred, even though the curriculum focused on improving job-related reading skills. The authors speculated that social skills learned as a result of instructional methods (e.g., students sharing ideas, listening to the concerns of others, and learning to attack problems with open minds) may have transferred to uses at home. In another program (Coffey et al., 1990), reasons for employee enrollment in a hospital literacy project included helping with children's homework. Gross et al. (1988) provided learner-reported examples of how better reading and writing skills improved family relations for participants of Project REACH in New York City. One workplace literacy student described being able to help her 8-year-old son with homework and leave handwritten messages for her children. Another student was able to write to his father for the first time to express his feelings toward him.

Employee Incentives: Dealing with Real and Perceived Barriers

In addition to positive incentives, workplace literacy programs must also contend with disincentives for employee participation. A typical and concrete example of a barrier to continued participation is that changing work schedules can frustrate ongoing participation in programs. Less concrete disincentives relate to employees' fears of supervisor reprisal for revealing literacy difficulty or of repeating school failure.

Studies of why adult learners leave both adult basic education programs and workplace literacy programs reveal a pattern. A survey of 192 learners who left adult literacy programs found the most common cause to be work schedule conflicts (Bean, Partanen, Wright, & Aaronson, 1989). Grimes and Renner (1988) reported similar findings in their study of eight workplace literacy programs in Illinois. Program coordinators noted a trend of limited participation among employees unless the class or tutoring was held on site or at a local union hall. Many employees, especially those with families, found it difficult to take the extra time to attend a class if it was scheduled outside of working hours or interfered with family and working schedules.

Strong negative feelings related to education are a disincentive for many adult learners. Van Tilburg and DuBois (1989) interviewed 28 ABE participants in London and in Columbus, OH, and found a common trend. They reported that emotions appeared in the interview when "barriers and encouragers" to the decision to return to school were discussed. Issues of family/friend support, embarrassment, fear of failure, feelings of "being dumb," and frustration with one's position in life all surfaced as factors related to the initial decision to return. This unease over continued education on the part of many adult learners is corroborated in Bean et al. (1989).

Fear of supervisor punishment is a disincentive in a number of programs. Jones and Kaye (1984) examined incentives and demotivating factors for 161 employees to participate in training at a long-term rehabilitative care facility. They found that fear of punishment by the supervisor correlated significantly ($r = -.26$) with involvement in training. This correlation was stronger than correlations with more formal (tangible) factors. Grimes and Renner (1988) corroborated the significant role of fear as a disincentive in their report on eight Illinois workplace literacy programs. They reported that some employees, especially those reading at the lowest levels, would not go to on-site classes unless mandated because they were embarrassed or fearful of losing their jobs. The authors suggested that off-site classes should be made available and that union contacts can help dispel fears of dismissals in unionized companies.

Employer Incentives: Government Funding

One of the most widespread external incentives for employers to be involved in workplace basic-skills programs is funding from governments. The earlier discussion of funding sources for workplace literacy programs outlines the degree of government support from one country to another.

The degree of government funding for workplace basic-skills and literacy programs is large and growing in most developed nations. All significant Australian programs appear to receive some level of funding from government agencies. In addition, Australia's recent award restructuring plan makes 2% of corporate profits available for training. Given the clear demand for ESL and adult literacy training in Australia (Matheson, 1989a), it seems likely that a significant proportion of these funds will be allocated to workplace literacy programs.

United States federal monies for workplace literacy programs have been available through the Jobs Training Partnership Act, as well as special funding initiatives of the Departments of Education and Labor. In addition, some regularly funded ABE programs are delivered in workplace settings without being labeled as *workplace literacy* funds. For each year since 1987, dollar amounts allocated for demonstration projects in workplace literacy have increased at the federal level. In 1991, the Department of Education awarded $19.3 million in National Workplace Literacy grants (U.S. Department of Education, 1991). In that same year, $242 million was allocated, mainly for basic-skills education, through the U.S. Adult Education Act. That amount was planned to increase to $260 million in 1992 ("Literacy law," 1991). However, no thorough computation of the total amounts of federal monies allocated to workplace literacy programs in the United States has been made. Simply considering funds for ABE programs offered in workplace settings and funds for federal workplace literacy demonstration projects, an estimate of $50 million in U.S. federal funds spent in 1990 would not be inappropriate.

At the same time that U.S. federal monies have been increasing for workplace literacy programs, state and local government funds have also been growing. West Virginia, South Carolina, and North Carolina provide 100% in matching funds for workplace literacy projects (Askov, Aderman, & Hemmelstein, 1989). Massachusetts has matching funds for workplace education (Stein, 1989). Florida, Idaho, Michigan, Tennessee, Utah, Virginia, and Missouri are heavily involved in funding and organizing workplace literacy initiatives, although dollar figures are not always available (Chynoweth, 1989). Among these states, Virginia appropriated $4.25 million for the enhancement of literacy services. As a result, states have gone from providing no funds for local literacy programs to providing 51% of the state-federal total. Indeed, states may become the driving force in the implementation of literacy projects.

The total of national and local government support for workplace literacy programs appears to be rapidly growing in most developed nations. In some countries the growth is so rapid and diverse that no clear accounting of available funds has been made. For employers, the incentive of available taxpayer money for workplace literacy programs is clear. In many European countries and Australia, such programs are a way to retrieve tax monies paid out.

Employer Incentives: Retention of Employees

In many industries, companies are finding it difficult to find employees with required skills from the existing workforce. Experienced workers who are unable to adjust to technology may have to be released, leaving the employer with the cost of searching for new employees with higher skills and possibly having to train them further if they lack relevant experience. Other industries lose workers who quit rather than face jobs with skill demands that they cannot meet. Screening, identifying, hiring, and training new workers is a growing business cost that many employers would like to reduce.

A Burger King franchise in Detroit, MI, for example, was experiencing a turnover rate of 160%, resulting in high training costs for new employees. The franchise established a prepaid tuition assistance plan ranging from basic skills to college support, paying employees' educational expenses based on the hours worked per week. It was able to reduce turnover to 38% and to increase productivity as well (Bethlehem Area Chamber of Commerce, 1990). Cooper et al. (1988) reported a similar success story for A. J. Heinz of Pennsylvania, a food manufacturer. The author credited workplace literacy classes with playing a part in reducing the number of low literates and ESL employees who would have been released in the face of new technological demands.

American employers must help the state pay unemployment benefits for laid-off workers. Grimes and Renner (1988) reported that Illinois businesses helped the state pay close to $840 million in unemployment insurance in 1987. Cutting these unemployment costs and reducing the costs for finding and training new workers are incentives for employers to participate in workplace literacy programs.

Hargroves (1989) reported on a particularly extensive long-term study of the impact of a Federal Reserve Bank basic-skills program on job performance, earnings, and retention. Results indicated that several months of formal basic-skills training combined with on-the-job experience and counseling can enable undereducated youth catch up with typical entry-level workers. Two-thirds of the Bank trainees (who would not otherwise have been eligible for employment) were placed in jobs.

The trainees stayed longer on the average than their entry-level peers, despite a low unemployment rate and ample job opportunities outside the bank in the late 1980s. The majority of graduates earned as much as their entry-level peers who were more educated and experienced. "In summary, the program produced a supply of employees who were trained as well or better than other new entry-level employees and understood the Bank's employment practices" (p. 67).

Employer Incentives: Increased Productivity and Quality

Testifying before the U.S. Senate and Labor Relations Committee in 1989, Lee Iacocca, the Chief Executive Officer of Chrysler Motors, indicated concern about employee low-literacy levels affecting the quality of Chrysler products (Congress of the United States, 1989). The corporation was investing 10% of its $117 million training budget in basic-skills training. A survey of 391 U.S. banks revealed that 20% of employees in entry-level jobs were seen by supervisors as having basic-skills problems (Mikulecky, 1989). The American Bankers Association reported that in 1988, U.S. banks spent $32 million on basic-skills training (an increase of 50% since 1985). Concern about employee productivity, quality of products and customer service, and the ability of employees to benefit from subsequent training were among the reasons and incentives cited for such significant investments.

There is some evidence that workplace literacy programs increase worker productivity. Coffey et al. (1990) used supervisors' handwritten evaluations of participants in a job-specific literacy program at the Medical Center of Memphis to monitor productivity gains. They reported improved productivity, quality, enthusiasm, alertness, punctuality, and ability to follow instructions. Participants in workplace literacy and job-specific ESL classes in the hotel industry in Hawaii and California were reported by evaluators to have improved in quality of work and customer relations (Los Angeles Unified School District, 1990; University of Hawaii, 1990). In a sample of the 61 participating employers in the Hawaii program, supervisors said participants improved 71% in work attitude, 64% in attendance, 56% in work efficiency, 59% in productivity, and 61% in quality of work.

Philippi (1989) reported on a military Job Skills Education Program adaptation in Mississippi involving the National Alliance of Business, Meridian Community College, and employees of Peavy Electronics. Although no control group was available for comparison, postprogram interviews with supervisors indicated varying degrees of program effectiveness. Supervisors noted job performance improvement in 33% of the participants, an increase attributed to improved ability to read gauges and schematics, to do calculations, and to work in teams. Nearly half of the supervisors felt their jobs had become easier as a result of the JSEP program.

An Australian ESL study estimated that improved language skills saved at least 150 hours in lost time per worker, per year, at an approximate value of $2,920 per worker (Singh, 1989). Projected on a national level, this estimate places the value of Australian ESL programs at $3.2 billion.

Employer Incentives: Increased Safety

Henry and Raymond (1982) reported safety concerns to be an important literacy related issue with employers. Costs in health care, human lives, liability suits, lost reputation, and lost profits are all related to potential mistakes made as a result of low employee literacy levels. In some cases, these concerns motivate employers to introduce workplace literacy programs.

There is some evidence that workplace literacy programs can have a positive effect on workplace safety. Norris and Breen (1990) noted that after the job-specific literacy training at Alpha Industries, inappropriately reported accidents and spills were reduced by approximately 20%. In addition, because safety was a part of the curriculum, 80% of program participants knew the safety procedures and vocabulary associated with their department. Safety was also part of Sheraton's workplace literacy curriculum (University of Hawaii, 1990), and feedback from managers and supervisors of the participants indicated a 49% improvement in safety practices.

Employer Incentives: Improved Employee Relations

There is some indication that workplace literacy programs can help increase employee morale and loyalty toward an employer. McMahon (1990) suggested that the workplace literacy program at GMA of Pennsylvania, initiated by workers and management, played a role in an employee vote against a union shop. In the Hawaii Sheraton Hotel study, supervisor ratings indicated that the corporate loyalty of employees involved in workplace literacy programs improved 54%, and work relations with co-workers improved 62% (University of Hawaii, 1990). The Hershey company also reported stronger employee loyalty to the company after it sponsored GED classes (Cooper et al., 1988).

CONCLUSION

The incentives that prove most effective for workplace literacy programs have a good deal to do with how programs are organized. Program organization, in turn, is heavily dependent on:

- Client groups served by the program (i.e., low literates, mid-level literates, ESL learners, etc.)
- Key program partners and funders (i.e., employers, unions, governments), and the sometimes overlapping and sometimes conflicting goals of various learners and partners associated with a particular program.

There is a wide variety of both tangible and intangible incentives in use to recruit and retain learners in workplace literacy programs. These incentives often are not enough for success, however, unless programs also actively address such disincentives as learner fears, schedule conflicts, and mistaken beliefs.

Balancing these different incentives and disincentives for particular learning populations is likely to create a wide variety of incentive plans with limited generalizability. For example, low-literate parents who cannot be released from production during work hours might best be recruited and retained by a program providing child care, anonymity, one-on-one tutoring, and meeting in a union hall where learners would not be likely to encounter supervisors. Bonus payments for learning gains and internal awards for accomplishments could also be part of the mix. The best incentive mix for mid-level literates whose skills are not up to new training demands might be a technical preparation basic skills course offered at the work site by a community college that includes the possibility of further training to move learners upward on a career ladder. The goals of instruction for both groups might differ depending on funders and priorities of the program. These goals usually reside somewhere along a spectrum with *learner goals* at one end and *employer goals* or *state goals* at the other end. Programs that retain learners tend to address a mixture of learner goals and goals of other program partners.

Yet, the most powerful incentives are probably employer incentives. An employer can assign training during work time. Successful completion of training can be linked to promotion and income. In other words, employers who are themselves committed to workplace literacy have the ability to create a strong incentive to employees to participate in programs. Other incentives to individuals are important, but not likely to be as strong as these.

10

Workplace Basic Skills Programs in the United Kingdom: Why so Few?

Alan Wells
Adult Literacy and Basic Skills Unit London, UK

The development of basic skills programs at U.K. workplaces has been slow in relation to the rapid changes that are taking place in industry and the labor market. It also appears to be slow in relation to parallel developments in the United States (see Mikulecky, this volume). However, comparisons between the two countries are instructive, and give some hints about the background factors favorable to the spread of work-based basic education. This study compares U.K. and U.S. workplaces from an historical and projective perspective by examining terms, perceptions, and attitudes in both cultures. The purpose of such an analysis is to examine a pattern found in the relationship between basic skills program development and the labor market and to offer the challenge of extending this pattern to other cultures for consideration as well.

THE CHANGING INDUSTRIAL SCENE IN THE UNITED KINGDOM

As in most industrialized countries, industry and employment are changing in the United Kingdom. Traditional industries have declined, particularly in the manufacturing sector; unemployment has risen rapidly, and the employment pattern is becoming very different from the pattern as recent as a generation ago. The major reduction in employment opportunities in the past 20 years has been in unskilled and semi-skilled jobs.

The coming decade presents additional challenges for British industry. Increased competition through the Single European Market after 1992, greater labor mobility in Europe, particularly at higher skill levels, and greater access to Eastern European markets make it more crucial than ever to have a well-trained, flexible workforce.

Traditionally, the United Kingdom has concentrated on developing the skills of young workers entering employment for the first time. Often even this has not been done very well; however, a substantial number of unskilled and low-skilled jobs, and full employment, traditionally meant that many young people could go directly into work from school. Compared to their German and French contemporaries, a far higher proportion of U.K. 16-year-olds go directly into employment rather than undertaking further education and training.

In the future, even an improved youth training system will not be sufficient. Although the total working population is likely to grow in the 1990s, there will be far fewer 16- to 19-year-olds in the workforce in 1994 than in 1984. The average age of workers will grow during the 1990s; therefore, a training strategy cannot depend mainly on the new entrants to the labor market. Regular training and updating of existing older workers, as well as the attraction of marginalized groups back into work, will be essential.

Such a change in the U.K. workforce needs to be seen in the context of other trends in the labor market. Much job growth will be in the service sector (matched by a continued decline in the number of manufacturing jobs). There will be a rise in the number of people working in higher skilled employment, an increase in self-employment, and a growth in the number of small businesses. Part-time work will also become more common.

However, it is dangerous to be too precise about these trends. Prospects are, at the time of this writing, confused by a rise in unemployment that most commentators see as cyclical. The evidence suggests that U.K. employers are less interested in training when business is bad and rarely plan or think of the longer term. Often when an upturn comes, there is a cry of skill shortages from those employers who have done little to develop the skills of employees in the past.

SKILL SHORTAGES AND GAPS

Skill shortages and skill gaps are a problem in British industry, and it is not clear whether the present training strategy will do much to improve the position. A recent survey of employers suggests that skill shortages exist in a wide range of employment areas, from relatively high-level engineering to lower level sales and service occupations. Recruitment offers an alternative to training existing staff, but even this appears to present problems. Studies show the cost of retraining existing staff compares favorably with the cost of recruiting new staff. Furthermore, the studies of the skills of unemployed people in the United Kingdom indicate that a large number of those available for work are likely to have relatively poor skills. Many of the recruitment difficulties for low-level occupations are caused by high turnover and the low skill level of applicants. It also seems that employers recognize that skill shortages and gaps have an impact on business performance.

The same survey describes how employers have tried to deal with skill shortages and gaps. The largest number questioned spent more on recruitment or used more expensive channels than normal. It is encouraging that over 40% of the employers had been prepared to provide more training to less qualified people, although less than 30% had been prepared to retrain existing staff.

The scarcity of higher level skills is likely to become more pronounced in the next few years as unskilled and low-skilled jobs disappear. New requirements such as statistical process control and knowledge of new technology will be matched by greater employer responsibility for health and safety and performance standards for employees.

Such dynamics should be convincing evidence to persuade employers that basic skills is important and investment worthy. So why does so little exist? Of course, as Mikulecky points out, a major problem is caused by isolating basic skills training from more general training. Although changes in industry and the labor market are convincing reasons for training of some kind, this does not automatically lead to a recognition of the importance of investing in basic skills.

CLARIFYING TERMS AND TYPES OF PROGRAMS

There is a need at this stage to clarify some of the terms being used. Different types of workplace training need to be distinguished because the attitudes of potential participants are likely to be different and the terms used might affect their participation. The stigma and embarrassment of poor reading and writing skills usually seem to be far more significant, for example, than any stigma felt by someone who was never taught English. Thus, basic skills courses for native English speakers often have to be marketed as *Improve your Communications Skills* or *Personal Effectiveness at Work*, whereas language training has always been described in more direct terms.

Employers in the United Kingdom also appear to have different attitudes about basic skills courses for those who failed in school. Many continue to expect applicants for jobs to be literate and able to numerate, and the view is taken that it is the fault of the individual or of the education system if this is not the case. Few see it as their responsibility to train or educate at this level, and if individual employers were left to their own devices, there would probably be little workplace basic skills provisions. Such a deep-seated attitude may also be one of the reasons why there is so little business sponsorship of literacy programs in the United Kingdom. There are recent indications, however, that employers identify basic skills training as their responsibility more readily when seeking to upgrade existing staff.

There is a need to distinguish between basic skills training for unemployed people, usually provided as part of or alongside other vocational training, and basic skills training in the workplace for existing employees. The distinction is often not made clear, yet it is crucial. Basic skills training for unemployed people may take place in a workplace as part of government programs, but employers have little stake in it. It does not cost them money, and because they do not provide a job guarantee for the unemployed people on placement, they have little responsibility for outcomes. There is also some tendency to confuse basic skills training at work and basic skills training for workers that is not necessarily at the work site.

As mentioned earlier, a particular category of basic skills training that needs separate analysis is that aimed at people with a native language other than English. Often referred to as English Language Training, this began as part of the United Kingdom's approach to the assimilation of a substantial number of immigrants in the 1960s and 1970s, many of whom were from the Indian subcontinent. Non-English-speaking immigrants were from diverse backgrounds ranging from highly qualified graduates from Indian universities to peasants who had not had any formal education and were therefore often illiterate in their own language. Both informal and formal programs were established, and targeted funding from the national government was made available in 1966 and still exists today. To some extent the programs won universal support from employers; it did not cost them anything, and it was obvious that employers needed to share responsibility for helping nonnative-speaking employees learn English. Industrial Language Training Units (ILTU) were set up in most areas, and a National Center for Industrial Language Training flourished in the mid-1970s.

The movement floundered with a new government in 1979, largely because by then the work of ILTUs had moved from language training for Asian workers to anti-racist training in industry. Whatever the rationale for the switch in focus, many employers found it threatening, and government funding was withdrawn in the mid-1980s. Some language training continues to exist in industry, although reduced immigration has taken the pressure off, particularly as the non-English-speaking population is an aging group. The situation could change with the freer movement of people between member countries of the European Community.

Finally, when discussing basic skills training in the context of work, it is important to have a rough definition of which basic skills are being included. At the Adult Literacy and Basic Skills Unit (ALBSU), *basic skills* is used to refer to literacy, numeracy, and, in some cases, language, rather than wider personal skills or, for example, computer competence. The narrower definition may exclude training that has elements of basic skills but is, in fact, much wider. One function of a narrow definition is that it prevents governments from claiming far more *basic skills training* than actually exists. Wider definitions may account for higher reported official levels of basic skills training in France, Belgium, and Germany, for example.

WORKBASE

The history of workplace basic skills provisions for native English speakers in the United Kingdom is fairly short. Little existed before the mid-1970s, and attempts at that time to establish a provision in connection with the national adult literacy campaign failed. The establishment of a national organization, *Workbase*, in the late 1970s gave an impetus to a workplace basic skills provision. The organization arose out of the trade union movement, and its early initiatives were with public sector service industries. It had a clear approach: to publicize the need, conduct a survey of the workforce or part of the workforce, present the result to management and trade unions, and offer to provide specific courses for all or most of those who expressed interest. Courses were offered during work time and were designed to try to meet the needs of the individual employees as well as the employer. Basic skills training was seen as similar to other training, and the importance of release rather than after-work study was constantly emphasized.

Courses were very much work-related, although health and safety and employee communication were almost always included. ALBSU funding (and other local government funding) meant that much of the work, at least initially, was subsidized by the taxpayer, and *Workbase* became one of the major providers of workplace basic skills training. Much of what was developed was in the public sector, and sometimes provision within committed socialist local authorities was relatively easy to get established. The private sector proved more difficult, as did the establishment of paid release for basic skills training through trade union collective bargaining.

The difficulty of demonstrating the effectiveness of basic skills training on performance, productivity, and employee self-improvement proved problematic. The first major private sector employer involved was visited in a blaze of publicity by the Minister of Education, but a few months later the factory had to close, for entirely separate reasons. Such events did not help publicity for basic skills training.

More recently, *Workbase*, with ALBSU support, has concentrated on becoming a national advisory service, developing skills in basic education scheme staff so that they can provide such training locally. Mikulecky makes the important point that effective workplace basic skills provision cannot consist of general literacy and numeracy teaching with no connection to the world of work. In the United Kingdom many basic education teachers do not have the knowledge and skill needed to adapt their approaches to an industrial setting, so advice and training for trainers has been essential. This has led to increased activity, particularly through the almost 70 Basic Skills Open Learning Centers established in the past few years, but the pace of development still appears to be slow compared to the situation in the United States described by Mikulecky (this volume). Why is this?

WHY IS THERE SO LITTLE PROVISION?

The lack of workplace basic skills provision in the United Kingdom is attributed to a number of factors. Some claim that the effect of the recession on British industry makes basic skills training difficult to sell. If this were the case, however, we should have noticed a decline in provision from a peak of a few years ago. Rather, it appears that opportunities have increased, and slow progress is due rather to more deep-seated factors.

The welfare state in the United Kingdom and the *perceived* state responsibility for education and welfare means that employers have been little involved in education until recent years. Industry/school links have in the past been poor, and many employers have seen an involvement with education as unusual. Industry/higher education links, particularly concerning research, have also been limited. Trade unions have been averse to admitting that some of their members could have less-than-perfect basic skills, and pay bargaining has usually been just that: about pay rather than other conditions of employment.

There has also been little funding available. Much of the funding for workplace basic skills described by Mikulecky comes from national or local government rather than from individual employers. In the United Kingdom, employers have also found it difficult, however committed, to find the resources necessary to provide basic skills training during work time; but there is little public subsidy available to make up the difference. Nor are there tax advantages in providing skills training, or a payroll levy as in some other industrialized countries.

There are further differences between the United Kingdom and some other countries. There is no equivalent of the American general equivalency diploma (GED), a generally recognized certificate of basic education that is an important incentive to individual employees. (A recently launched competence-based skills qualification related to National Vocational Qualifications, however, is helping to motivate some workers.) The major constraint is not employee incentives—all the evidence is that workers are likely to want to take up opportunities—but rather with the attitude of employers and, most importantly, public funding.

There are, however, positive signs. ALBSU's new *Basic Skills at Work* program will provide surveys of need—and the first results of these surveys indicate greater employer awareness of the need for better basic skills—as well as pilot projects aimed at improving the basic skills of both unemployed and employed adults. ALBSU also intends to concentrate its development funding on the provision of workplace basic skills training. Such concentration is likely to be a small effort compared to those described in the United States by Mikulecky, but at least it is a start.

SECTION VI:
Comparing Industrialized and Developing Nations

11

Incentives for Adult Learning in Developing Countries: Lessons and Comparisons

Laurel Puchner
National Center on Adult Literacy
University of Pennsylvania

This chapter analyzes Third World adult education experiences with an eye toward lessons that can be applied in industrialized nations. Arguing that to increase participation in adult learning, effort must be put toward the creation of a context that is favorable to adult learning rather than focusing on isolated program features, the chapter discusses features of a "favorable" context, ways to create such a context, and the particular case of female participation and motivation. The chapter also outlines ways in which the knowledge taken from developing countries may be utilized in industrialized country settings, listing general characteristics that lead to increased motivation for and participation in adult learning.

Adult education programs in developing countries have used a wide variety of techniques to encourage participation in adult literacy and basic education programs and have considerable experience in the area of nonformal adult education in general. Examination of these experiences reveals valuable information concerning the relationship between individual motivation and the factors involved in the adult learning process. Because the usual direction for flow of information is from North to South, the South's experience remains little known and under-exploited by the North's industrialized countries.

Analysis of Third World adult education experiences is useful for industrialized countries for several reasons. First, although industrialized and developing countries share many factors influencing motivation to participate in adult education, these factors often exist in a more subtle form in industrialized nations as compared to the Third World. Therefore, looking at developing countries can bring added attention to certain factors, such as barriers to women's participation, or the importance of knowing the culture of the target population, which are often less obvious and thus ignored in industrialized societies. Second, it is sometimes assumed that putting more money into adult education is the key to success in industrialized countries. In the Third World, however, one finds successful adult education programs and campaigns that were carried out under conditions of extreme scarcity of resources, both human and financial. Although resources are important, and more money is needed for adult education in industrialized nations, looking at the factors contributing to success under poor economic conditions can be helpful in determining where best to apply resources that exist.

Finally, there exists in the industrialized world a growing recognition of the existence of marginalized and underserved populations whose needs are not being met by current programs. Many similarities exist between the situations of these *Fourth World* groups in industrialized countries and circumstances in the Third World, such as generally low educational levels, poor economic and living conditions, and seemingly few opportunities for improvement of either one. Such similarities render examination of developing country adult education experiences useful, especially in view of the lack of attention often given these marginalized groups in discussions of adult education in industrialized countries. In discussions of how improved workplace education might improve the quality of the workforce, there is a tendency to forget the untapped human resources that exist in marginalized populations who are barred from participation due to various social and economic forces.

This chapter reviews factors related to incentives and participation in adult education in the Third World. From these experiences, certain lessons can be derived that may be relevant to industrialized and developing settings more generally. In particular, the chapter attempts to show that effort must be put toward the creation of a context that is favorable to adult learning for a given target population rather than focusing attention uniquely on program features and on specific situational factors.

Traditional attempts to increase motivation have focused on either removing situational barriers to participation or making programs more attractive. Third World experiences seem to indicate that such an approach is insufficient, and that motivation is influenced by a myriad of forces that interact to form an entire context in which an individual lives that will be more or less favorable to adult education participation for an individual or a population. To influence motivation, I argue, one must begin with an assessment of all the various components of which the context is composed, including opportunity structure for using knowledge gained from education, individual perceptions, community attitudes toward participation, and political forces. Once such an assessment has been made, educators must then act at each of these levels in order to bring about a change at the contextual level, which in turn may influence motivation and hence participation.

The chapter begins by introducing factors that influence participation, with a stress on the importance of the overall context in terms of adult learning. The following is a presentation of different ways of creating a favorable adult learning context within a community, with particular consideration of the specific case of women. Finally, I offer several conclusions concerning applications of Third World lessons in industrialized countries, and some ideas for further research.

THE ADULT LEARNING CONTEXT

An incentive is something that has a tendency to move to action or to spur on. In the case of adult education, it means something that drives or motivates an individual to participate. One reason for interest in incentives in adult education is the problem of dropout, which commonly occurs in programs in developing and industrialized countries alike. We are thus not concerned uniquely with the drive to initiate the activity, but also with the drive to maintain the activity for a certain length of time (which will vary depending on the circumstances).

Stromquist (this volume) points out that using "lack of motivation" as a reason for nonparticipation or dropout can be problematic, as it may lead to a tendency to blame the individual for not participating rather than the enabling or disabling conditions surrounding him or her. It must be made clear, then, that use of the term *motivation* in this chapter is not meant to imply that individuals actually make a choice based on personal preference about whether or not to participate. Indeed, a major goal of this chapter is to show that the individual condition of "being motivated" depends most on the contextual conditions surrounding the individual.

One of the reasons for past failure to increase motivation and hence participation in adult education has been the tendency to try to isolate specific incentives which, it is hoped, will provide the necessary motivation. The factors looked at in such attempts usually lie in two main groups. The first group consists of what could be called *situational factors* and comprises practical aspects of the personal situation of the individual in question that might influence participation (Cross, 1981). These factors are relatively uncontrollable demographic features, such as the age, gender, income, or number of children of an individual, as well as the amount of prior schooling or position in the societal structure.

The second group comprises what can be called *institutional factors* (Cross, 1981) and includes the features of a particular adult learning program. Examples from this group would include class location, program content, quality and gender of instructor, and the cost of the class. Other examples would be the presence of child care provision, the holding of workplace classes as a part of the paid workday, or the provision of transport to and from class.

In his survey of adult education programs, Mikulecky (this volume) notes that simply providing a certain incentive as a part of a program was not sufficient to enhance participation in the programs he examined. Mikulecky's finding supports the more general observation that although it is the situational and institutional factors that are most often addressed in efforts to improve the success of adult education, they are relatively minor components of an overall adult education context that determines motivation for and hence participation in adult education.

The importance of overall contextual factors has been recognized by certain Third World researchers dating back to the early 1970s (Ahmed, 1975; Kassam, 1982; Unesco, 1976). Ahmed (1975) notes that although literacy programs in developing countries pay considerable attention to technical aspects of the program, such as teaching methodology and content, what organizers rarely question is the major assumption that literacy is relevant and necessary in the lives of the target group. When certain predisposing conditions favorable to the acquisition of literacy skills exist a "motivated learner who perceives the value of literacy in his life can go a long way to overcome the methodological and pedagogical barriers" (p. 7). Other researchers, recognizing the importance of noninstitutional factors, have emphasized the necessity of regarding the teaching of literacy skills and the mobilization of people to learn the skills as two separate tasks (Kempfer, 1973).

Looking at the overall adult education context implies a comprehensive consideration of the various factors influencing learning and using what is learned in a particular community. Crucial factors that go beyond situational and institutional factors include the opportunities available for an individual to benefit from the learning offered, the social or community support an individual receives, and the ability to perceive benefits that exist, all of which interact to form a motivational force influencing an individual's life.

FEATURES OF THE ADULT LEARNING CONTEXT

The contextual conditions necessary to create sufficient motivation for adult learning appear to differ greatly in developing as compared to industrialized countries. The problems that result from attempts to provide literacy without the right environmental conditions have been made especially clear in the Third World by examples of glaringly inappropriate attempts to provide adult education, examples that range from teaching reading and writing in communities in which there exist absolutely no reading materials, to attempts to get the main female actor in a family to attend literacy classes when: (a) her husband is opposed to it, and (b) there already exists in the family a delegated literate person who can accomplish the needed literacy tasks. However, even though such instances are not as likely to occur in industrialized countries, the dynamics behind the existence of opportunities and the psychological aspects of the perception of these benefits remain basically the same despite changes in context and in the types of learning involved. Furthermore, the same dynamics are involved in the process of creating and sustaining motivation throughout the learning process. An important aspect of such a context is that the movement from mobilization provided by a favorable climate to the motivation that results from it is a cyclical process, as problems of motivation are turned into actions of mobilization that then lead to further motivation and further involvement (Mbakile, 1980).

Opportunities to Use Adult Learning

The most important component of an adult learning context appears to be a structure that permits and encourages the use of the knowledge to be gained in the adult learning process. Evidence that motivation comes easiest when it is in direct fulfillment of priority needs abounds in Third World adult education literature. During a tour of the Rajasthan State in India, one Indian adult educator came upon two or three villages running women's literacy classes, each with a full classroom of 30 to 35 women (Kumari, 1979). Upon asking how it was possible for these villages to enlist the participation of so many women, she found that a large number of the men of the villages had been recruited into the military, and letter-written correspondence was the only means of communication for these mothers, wives, and daughters (Kumari, 1979). In another example, results from a study of a cooperative and adult learning program in Gabon showed that the secretaries of the cooperatives at the local level had the best attendance and obtained the highest level of literacy; the only difference between the secretaries and other members of the cooperative such as treasurers or presidents was that they used reading and writing skills the most in cooperative activities (Galy, 1981). Finally, in a Mozambican case study (Lind, 1988), literacy program organizers found that the most important individual background factor behind variations in literacy learning was the amount of contact an individual had outside of his or her own home village; variables such as prior Portuguese language experience, age, gender, profession, or membership in political organizations were not found to be significant. Findings such as these are consistent with the growing realization in industrialized nations, as pointed out by Rubenson and Schütze (this volume), that learning and its uses need to be linked in order for effective learning to take place.

Money can be an important incentive for participation in adult education, so a structure that allows economic gain may be an important contextual feature. In a study carried out in Tunisia and Ecuador (Kahler, 1982), literacy programs motivated individuals when the individuals believed there would be increased economic opportunities or welfare as a result. These findings led to several hypotheses concerning adult learning and economics, put forth by the researchers: (a) individuals value literacy skills when the skills provide economic rewards from employment or production; (b) individuals value literacy when opportunities for self-improvement exist within their context; and (c) individuals value literacy when social and economic mobility is high (Kahler, 1982, pp. 71-72). Ryan's (this volume) findings that in the U.K. the main incentive to adults to undertake learning is an expectation of increased job rewards show the potential relevance of these hypotheses to industrialized settings.

The purpose of the Tunisia and Ecuador projects was to examine how economic improvement serves as an incentive for adults to participate in practical skills training programs in order to achieve higher literacy skills. In both the Ecuador and Tunisia sites, questionnaire results showed that the initial motivation to participate in the programs was largely economic (i.e., participants hoped to make more money; Kahler, 1982). Two further findings, however, demonstrate that even when economic incentives were present and visible to the learner, the results desired by organizers were not easily achieved.

In Tunisia, at the end of the program, business owners were

asked to rate the program exercises learned in terms of usefulness. Although the learners rated cashbook and inventory sheet presentation exercises as most the useful and claimed that they helped them to realize economic benefits, follow up visits two weeks later showed that very few of the participants had in fact modified their accounting practices (Kahler, 1982). In terms of accomplishing developmental goals in adult education, this finding seems to indicate that although economic or other incentives were enough to keep the participants in the program, the program did not motivate learners to subsequently apply the new information.

A second finding showed the potential danger of providing promises of quick economic gain. Business owner participants had been told by staff members that they could qualify for loans if they demonstrated their net worth with an inventory of current merchandise and projected use for each loan. Access to credit was thus a major motivation for the majority of participants, who had no accounting system or inventory procedures prior to the program, and this incentive to acquire the necessary knowledge was strong enough so that attendance at the first four workshops was quite high. Between the fourth and fifth workshops, however, the business owners learned that it would be another two to three months before the first loans would arrive, resulting in very low attendance at the fifth workshop (Kahler, 1982).

Individual Perception

A favorable opportunity structure is not only difficult to attain or to provide, it is also only one step in the direction toward the provision of a context favorable for adult learning. The existence of visible, tangible, and realistic rewards may be of little value if the individual is not aware of these opportunities and desires them. As has been suggested above, to be motivated to participate, an individual needs to see the benefits and to perceive these benefits as a possibility for him- or herself. The proposed relationship between the environment and an individual's perception of it is clear in Rubenson's Expectancy-Valence Model (Cross, 1981), according to which the strength of motivation is determined by combining positive and negative forces in the individual and in the environment. The expectancy part of the model has two components: the expectation of personal success in the education activity, and the expectation that being successful will lead to positive circumstances. The valence part of the formula is concerned with affect, which depends on the anticipated consequences of participation. An individual's perception of the situation, then, is as important as the actual external circumstances.

In a given community, the price and wage signals that the economic context gives to the individual may be an important factor determining economic incentives to participate in adult education (Kahler, 1982). If an individual is not integrated into production processes, then he or she will not see these signals. In developing countries, this observation could apply to subsistence farmers and other rural workers, an issue similar to the situations of many homeless persons, those on welfare, and others who may be cut off from production processes in industrialized societies. This situation is especially likely to affect women, who have been historically marginalized in terms of their contribution to market activities of society.

Community Support

Another important feature of a favorable adult learning context is support for, or at least acceptance of, adult education by the community within which a person lives. Normative social pressure is an important factor in motivation, and a context favorable for adult learning is one in which this pressure condones or even demands it. A related and interesting factor is the association between learning and desire for change. Although the relationship between education and innovation is not clear, it is evident that societies in which much change is taking place are ones in which demand for education is higher (Kahler, 1982). This finding supports the notion that rather than trying to implement innovative changes related to adult education alone in order to influence participation within a community, organizers need to look at and act on the community as a whole in order to be effective. In industrialized countries, as opposed to developing nations, it is relatively easier to overlook this need for a more holistic view as it is sometimes assumed that the rapid societal changes that are occurring in the industrialized world affect all individuals and communities equally. Obviously, they do not, and assessment of the effects of these changes on individuals' lives should precede intervention efforts.

Community support, sometimes spurred by political forces, can create a general mobilizational force capable of initiating and maintaining participation in adult learning. This mobilizational force can be powerful, and major campaigns have been launched and sustained for periods of time as a result of such forces and, interestingly, in the absence of other favorable components such as observable opportunities to use the knowledge and a clear vision of potential benefits. Motivation for such campaigns apparently does not last long, however, and whatever short-term effects have resulted from them may fade away rapidly (Galy, 1981; Indian Ministry of Education and Social Welfare, 1978a; Von Freyhold, 1982). In Tanzania, one volunteer adult education teacher in Dar es Salaam described how 60 to 80 persons signed up for courses as a result of party pressure, but only 10 or 15 came to class (Von Freyhold, 1982).

When combined with the other necessary contextual factors, however, this general mobilization becomes an essential component of a successful adult literacy program. Impressive Third World examples of such mobilization are the mass literacy campaigns carried out as a result of revolutionary sociopolitical forces in Cuba and Tanzania. Conditions leading to the popular drive for literacy present in these campaigns may not exist in industrialized countries; what needs to be recognized is the potential value of such mass mobilization toward the success of adult education programs.

Situational and Institutional Factors

As components that influence and form a part of the general adult education context, situational and institutional factors are significant and affect participation in many ways. When discussing potential situational and institutional factors, a fine line exists between motivation and accessibility. If it is difficult or impossible for an individual to attend a class, he or she may not attend. In the Third World, survival needs generally come before other needs, such as education. It is understandable, therefore, that during the rainy season an individual may miss class to cultivate his or her field in order to eat that year, no matter what the probability might be that the adult education classes would lead to desirable economic opportunities in the years to come. The risk the person takes in putting the fate of the whole family in the hands of adult education would be too great in this case. In industrialized countries, the same general principle would apply when a woman cannot attend class because she must look after her children. In this case, the risk she might take in using her savings to pay for child care in hopes of the benefits that will accrue from her participation in education would be too great.

A further reason why institutional and situational factors ought to be considered is that they tend to disfavor certain societal groups more than others. For example, lack of child care provision has more of an effect on women than men in most communities, and amount of prior schooling experience or income level is often related to gender, age, or ethnic group as well. Similarly, holding classes at a distance from the community, or charging a fee for classes, will affect the poorer members of a community more than members who are relatively well off.

Institutional and situational factors also interact closely with other contextual factors. The importance of pedagogy, for instance, which is discussed in more detail later, must not be underestimated as a force influencing a person's self-perception and hence affective attitude toward education; it can also bring to light certain opportunities previously unknown to the learner. Factors such as the timing and location of a workplace class can have an influence on general worker attitude toward a program and thus on the amount of social pressure condoning or disapproving of adult education.

Unfavorable situational and institutional conditions are relatively easy to identify and to change. The identification of problems can be accomplished by asking learners themselves, by observation, or by simple experiments and can reveal factors that are not obvious or that appear counterproductive at first glance. In India, although an overall societal goal is integration of castes, it has been found preferable in certain cases to hold separate classes for each caste in order to assure equal participation among castes (Indian Ministry of Education and Social Welfare, 1978b). In Somalia, although the alphabetic and drill-based teaching methods used during literacy campaigns there may not be the best method according to some specialists, they were, however, culturally familiar in a society accustomed to Koranic schooling (Bhola, 1984). In certain contexts, charging a small fee for adult education may increase motivation for participation by raising the perceived value of the class (Kahler, 1982).

CREATING A "FAVORABLE" CONTEXT

Some Third World educators who have recognized the importance of contextual factors for adult education have gone further to point out the possibility and the desirability of deliberately creating such factors (Ahmed, 1975; Bhola, 1989). In some situations, organizers must make the needed plans and provisions for adult learning in order to enable individuals to benefit from it. Because motivation is rarely spontaneous, an environment conducive for adult learning needs to be and can be created by building the rewards and incentives into the social, economic, and political structures which exist in a community (Bhola, 1983).

The methods possible for creating a context favorable for adult learning vary greatly from situation to situation and from target group to target group. Attempts to broaden the definition of literacy and to take context into account have led program planners in the recent past to use functional literacy as the desired goal. In developing and industrialized countries alike, however, the functional literacy goal has led to a tendency to forget that *functional*, because it means the ability to use literacy in everyday life, takes on a different meaning for each individual, depending on his or her lifestyle, activities, and desires. An agriculture program that provides functional literacy to certain individuals may not be beneficial for others who have no desire or need to farm because it is not tied to skills valued by the learners. Motivating learners is often difficult for organizers of adult education in industrialized countries, partly because discussion of adult education often centers on economic arguments placed in terms of the supply and demand of the global marketplace. Such concerns are often not shared by the individual learner or at least are often not understandable to the learner when looked at within this global frame of reference.

Knowing the Population

A first step toward the creation of the correct climate is knowledge of the population in question. Because cultural differences between adult education organizers and learners are often relatively evident in developing countries, Third World adult educators have long recognized the need to study the culture of the target population before determining the structure and content of adult education programs. Third World educators also traditionally work from the basic assumption that one ought to adapt the program to the people because experience has shown that it is usually undesirable and inefficient to try to do the reverse. The *étude de milieu* approach, however, is rarely applied in industrialized countries, despite often large differences in background and culture between those who decide to implement programs and those who are supposed to participate, whether they be members of ethnic minority or majority groups.

Gathering information about the population to be served is helpful in determining the cultural relevancy of content and the structure of adult education programs, in determining what types of opportunity structures can and should be made available, and in enabling organizers to tap into ethnic or local indigenous systems of support and communication. For immigrant populations and minority ethnic groups, this last type of information is becoming increasingly valuable as it becomes more and more evident that state goals of integration are not to be easily or rapidly realized, and that ethnic structures, including learning styles and communication systems, are not in the process of dying out. Rather, in light of recent nationalistic movements, they could be said to be gaining strength.

The study of community structures in the United States and in developing countries has led to the recent development of family approaches to literacy and/or development in general. Looking at the family unit rather than at the individual can provide important clues to problems surrounding the motivation to acquire skills. In developing countries it has been found that certain families may decide that only one or two members need be literate in order to satisfy the family's literacy demands (Lind & Johnston, 1990). Similarly, a father may refuse to let his daughter attend class because it is more difficult to find a husband for an educated girl (Giere, Ouane, & Ranaweera, 1990). In developing and industrialized settings alike, the potential importance of a family approach can be seen by looking at individuals' concerns surrounding adult education. For example, a mother's felt need for further education may stem from a desire to help her children with their schoolwork, and it is not uncommon, in either developing or industrialized countries, for a wife to drop out of a program at her husband's command.

Studying the target population may also provide knowledge of local community groups that can serve as liaisons between adult education organizers and the target population. The advantages of using existing community structures to organize adult education programs have long been recognized in the Third World. Examples come from Senegal, where adult education is linked to all branches of social activity, from artisan's guilds to women's groups to fishermen (Fougeyrollas, Sow, & Valladon, 1967); and from China, which depended largely on mass organizations, such as the National Federation of Women and the Communist Youth League, as the catalyzing agents of adult education for its mass literacy campaign (Coletta, 1982).

Knowledge of existing local community structures can also help raise the target group's awareness of existing opportunity structures and the possible benefits of adult education programs. In addition to more common forms of publicity and awareness raising, one sort of prelearning experience or sensibilization that has been used in the Third World is small, short-term programs whose goal is not to create a citizen who will contribute more effectively to the current workforce, but to create a general positive atmosphere and feeling toward adult education in a given target group. In developing countries, those who have had prior experience in adult education tend to be more motivated to participate in the future (Lind & Johnston, 1990). By accustoming individuals or communities to the concept of adult education, these programs may raise the chances of future participation. This approach been undertaken in developing countries in populations with little exposure to written language, with the goal of developing preliteracy and perhaps preeconomic skills (Kahler, 1982).

Instructional Methods

Another vital tool in creating and especially in maintaining a favorable context for adult education is the content and pedagogy of the program itself. The right pedagogy can aid individuals to develop a positive self-image and a positive perception of their ability to succeed in a program. Pedagogy can also reinforce the benefits of learning and demonstrate the connection between the knowledge and opportunities to benefit from it. Rubenson and Schütze (this volume) discuss the need for curricula to be both context-specific and general and for a close integration of learning and work. One pedagogical method that is being developed and used in several Third World situations is participatory development, in which learners are involved in the planning, management, and governance of the program itself (Shaeffer, 1991). By giving people control over the learning situation, this type of program enhances self-perception and gives people a chance to use immediately whatever skills they are obtaining.

For example, in a Community Publishing Program in Zimbabwe, learners create educational materials as part of their training, with the aim of building practical and analytical skills, confidence, and creativity (Zimbabwe Ministry of Community and Cooperative Development). Seeing such products in the early stages of the program may provide motivation to continue until the more long-term and ultimately more important benefits of the learning manifest themselves, and, adapted to a given setting, this type of approach could be useful in industrialized settings as well. Another method for showing quick results to learners is the use of frequent auto-administered tests. Tests are not appropriate for all situations, but they can be helpful in increasing or maintaining motivation (Indian Ministry of Human Resources Development, 1988).

Language is a critical aspect of pedagogical importance, both in developing countries and in the education of nonmajority language speakers in industrialized countries. In reference to the latter, for example, Wells (this volume) stresses the large difference between teaching reading and writing to native English speakers versus non-English speakers in basic skills programs in the U.K. Although research on mother tongue and second language literacy among adults is limited, combined with the results of research done on children, it tends to support the teaching of literacy in the first language before moving on to the second or majority language (International Development Research Centre, 1979; Okedara, in press). Many language specialists now believe that there exists an underlying cognitive/academic proficiency common across languages (Cummins, 1987). Support for this theory comes from research done in Morocco, where similar processes have been found to play a role in the acquisition and retention of literacy skills in Arabic and French (Wagner, 1990). Under this theory, learning a language at any point in one's life is based to a certain extent on the structures of the first language, meaning that learning skills in a second language will be easier if they are already mastered in the first language. Learning to read and write in the native language may also have positive effects on motivation because the individual will see faster results.

However, the national language policy of a country, and the contexts in which a given language is used are also important factors to consider (Wagner, 1990). If one language is associated with higher esteem in a community, or if the situations in which a person wishes to use the knowledge acquired in adult education require only the nonnative language, individuals may be more motivated to participate in a program using that language.

Politics

One important and final factor to be invoked in a general discussion on creating a favorable context for adult education is the role of the state. Many Third World researchers have pointed out the necessity of political will and government support in bringing about the conditions necessary for successful adult education ventures (Bhola, 1984; Lind & Johnston, 1990). Governments clearly can provide a positive influence through legislation, fiscal support, and the creation of general mobilizational forces (see chapters by Luttringer and Noyelle, this volume, for a discussion of legislative incentives for participation in adult education).

Many examples of Third World legislation, such as Iraq's Compulsory Literacy Law of 1978, which imposed fines or imprisonment on all illiterates who did not regularly attend literacy classes (Bhola, 1983), can be cited. Unfortunately, they are better used to show what ought not be done. Luttringer (this volume) warns against too much government control and stresses the need for flexible measures that can be adapted to individual situations. However, legislation passed in industrialized and developing countries that acts to promote adult education specifically (such as allowing workers a certain number of days per year for continuing education) or to eliminate inequalities in the workplace (such as measures toward elimination of unequal hiring practices) are positive steps. Noyelle (this volume) emphasizes the need for legislation to create needed links between the workplace and the unemployed, and legislation that acts to create work opportunities (such as setting aside jobs for a particular target group) may be necessary in many situations. Developing country examples of positive steps include laws passed in Niger (in 1979) and Tanzania (in 1973) claiming that all enterprises must provide education at the worksite and during work hours for all workers (Galy, 1981; Shengena, 1982), and legislation passed in Brazil in the 1970s allowing companies to deduct 2% of their taxable income as a voluntary contribution to the Brazilian national literacy campaign (Bhola, 1984).

One important responsibility of governments is the promotion of the teaching profession and in particular the adult teaching profession. Learner motivation is closely tied to teacher and program planner motivation, so government incentives to teachers, such as adequate salaries, have important implications for participation. In some Third World countries, such as Botswana and Nigeria, programs for training adult educators hold established positions in university education departments. In most industrialized countries, on the other hand, the teaching of adults is hardly recognized as a legitimate profession.

Governments can also play a role in providing resources for the physical materials necessary for classes, for research, and for media publicity and campaigning in support of adult education. As has been mentioned before, although conditions such as those leading to the strong political mobilization characteristic of some Third World mass literacy campaigns are rare, governments can still play an important role in the general sensibilization and mobilization of a population toward adult education.

THE CASE OF WOMEN

Women constitute an important component of adult education efforts. However, because of the common but erroneous assumption that the variables involved in participation are the same for both men and women, women's needs are sometimes ignored. Some of the differences are relatively straightforward, such as the fact that the lack of child care is more likely to affect women than men. Others are less evident, however, such as the finding in some Third World communities that the distance between a school and a village has entirely different consequences for participation depending on the sex of the child, as parents will let their boy children travel further from home than they will their girl children (Stromquist, 1989).

Women often have more situational constraints on participation than men, such as more child care and domestic responsibilities and lower average income, all of which have a negative impact on participation. In addition, institutional factors are often more suited to the situation of men in society than women. For example, although in some Third World areas 80% to 90% of women are involved in agricultural production, the messages promoted in adult education programs for women tend to exclusively address housework, cooking, and child care (Stromquist, 1989). In industrialized countries programs may be more likely to offer relevant skills for income generation and employment in male-dominated as opposed to female-dominated occupations. Inequalities in program structure may be due in part to a lack of female involvement in the top-level planning and administration of such programs (Odunga, 1988; Stromquist, in press).

For several reasons, the overall learning context is more likely to favor motivation and participation for men in adult education than for women. First, opportunity structures are more likely to favor men, manifested, for example, by the higher wages received on average by men than women (i.e., they have more potential benefit from the same learning experience), the relative ease with which men enter into typically female professions compared to the inverse, and promotion and hiring practices that tend to favor men. Second, men are more likely to be aware of existing opportunities because they are traditionally more involved in production processes than women. Because men are the traditional breadwinners in most societies, they are also more likely to have a positive self-perception as far as their future success is concerned. Finally, women have less community support in many situations, also due to the traditional female role of homemaker (Stromquist, 1989).

In planning for adult education, the differing situations of men and women have several implications. First, because of the existence of gender-related differences in constraints, opportunity structure, and the overall learning context, investigation into situational and institutional constraints on participation should be done separately for men and women, even when dealing with topics with no obvious relation to gender. Looking at all aspects of the situation is especially important when dealing with immigrant and minority ethnic groups because differences may exist among these populations that are not present in the majority population. Second, when designing programs aimed specifically for women, organizers should be careful not to reinforce negative stereotypes in attempts to present female-oriented subject matter. Literacy programs aimed at women sometimes work to fix existing social roles of female dependence more firmly (Stromquist, 1992b). It is also important to recognize, however, that what constitutes negative or positive subject matter may have very different meanings depending on the community. Thus, the content of educational curricula must be very carefully adapted to each milieu.

Last, when taking steps toward creating a context favorable to adult learning, it must be ascertained that all of the relevant factors work in favor of women as well as men. Only by realizing that there exists a fundamentally different set of criteria for maximizing motivation and hence participation of women than for men will one be able to create an environment equally favorable for both sexes.

COMPARING INDUSTRIALIZED AND DEVELOPING COUNTRIES

In industrialized countries, the factors leading toward a favorable climate are often manifested differently than in the Third World, but the principles behind them may be the same. There are four general characteristics to what I term a "favorable" context for adult learning in developing countries.

1. Existence of an opportunity or benefit structure linked to the knowledge to be acquired. In developing countries creation of such a structure may mean forming better commercial and communicative links between a rural town and an urban area, whereas in industrialized countries it may mean shifting to a high-performance work organization in a given work setting or setting aside jobs for a female homeless population.
2. Awareness on the part of the target population that these opportunities exist. In developing countries rural farmers may not be aware of marketing opportunities; in industrialized settings, as mentioned before, many homeless and those on welfare may not be attuned to the marketplace and therefore are not likely to know about jobs. For this awareness to be of benefit to the individual, however, it must be accompanied by the perception that the benefits to come from the learning experience are desirable and attainable.
3. Support of the community and/or peers of an individual for the activity. In developing countries, if adult education is seen as a negative force in a given community, it may be unlikely that an individual would break away from the norm to participate. In some industrialized nations, such as France, workers have the right to take a certain number of days out of the work year for additional training activities. However, if the general opinion among workers does not support such activities, workers are unlikely to participate. Furthermore, Hirschhorn (this volume) provides convincing evidence of how strongly the group nature of the work environment shapes learning, so that not only do opinions of other workers effect participation, but the social organization of the workplace may effect what type of learning takes place.
4. Sustainability, such that the usefulness and benefits of the knowledge being learned are continually demonstrated and reinforced. In developing and industrialized countries alike, appropriate pedagogy, in particular one that attempts to show the usefulness of the knowledge being learned throughout the process, is often a key component in the maintenance of motivation for individuals. Rubenson and Schütze (this volume), for example, point out the need for learning to take place in a meaningful context and for learners to view themselves as having control over their own learning as two essential components of a successful learning situation. Mikulecky (this volume) includes such aspects in his list of identified major components of good programs.

In an industrialized society, the opportunities and needs to use knowledge gained in an adult education program might range from a young immigrant mother wanting to help her children with their school work to a middle-aged worker for whom a technological change necessitates the use of new skills to perform her current job. In the former case, it may seem unlikely that the arrival of her children at preschool age would suddenly motivate an illiterate woman to participate in a literacy program, but if community pressure to push children to succeed in the new country is high, the combination of factors may create a sufficient mobilizing force. For the worker, it is possible that the promise of a raise in salary following the completion of the program is an appropriate and necessary motivation; but if the program is part of a general company movement supported by workers and administrators, the salary incentive may not be necessary. In both examples the learners must have enough confidence so that they will be able to succeed in the program, and the relationship between the learning process and the desired outcome must be continually maintained.

In industrialized countries, because they are relatively highly literate, societal structures may appear more likely to have certain incentives for adult education built in. The incentives that exist, however, are sometimes most obvious and most real to those who already have the opportunity to benefit from a certain amount of education and not to members of the too often forgotten underserved and marginalized populations. Because a society has a relatively large number of literate persons already, and because much of the functioning of society depends on the use of literacy, it does not mean that participation in adult education by an individual will lead to a better life for that individual. A major phenomenon hindering the success of adult education programs in industrialized countries is the assumption that because individuals live in a literate world, links between knowledge to be acquired and the life work of an individual are automatic. In most cases they are not, and more attention must be given to creation of these links, especially among marginalized groups.

CONCLUSION

Types and results of adult education efforts vary from North to South and from country to country, but experience has shown dropout rates from adult literacy programs to be a persistent phenomenon in developing and industrialized countries alike. Looking at Third World experiences seems to indicate that motivation depends on several interrelated factors, the most important of which is the overall context surrounding adult education for a particular individual or a particular target group. Attempts to increase participation generally fail to take into account all of the necessary components, mainly due to a lack of knowledge of the dynamics involved.

Further research is needed on the subject of motivation and incentives in both developing and industrialized countries. One area of particular note is the relationship between further education and empowerment. How empowering—in both economic and noneconomic terms—is literacy or functional literacy? Although the feeling is that current members of the workforce need to upgrade their skills for nations to be competitive in a global marketplace, alternative theories claim that in some industries and in some countries the trend may be toward the reverse. If in a particular nation the trend is toward a deskilling rather than an upskilling of the workforce, then it is important to know what types of noneconomic reward structures for adult education may be exploited; and even if higher skills are needed, economic rewards do not appeal equally to all individuals, and such alternative opportunities based on the general theme of empowerment may be used to reinforce economic ones.

Further research is also necessary to determine the forces that are most important for creating a perceived need for adult education by members of a community. The general claim made in this chapter is that the forces influencing participation are numerous and complex and that often the most important factors do not have the most obvious or direct relation to adult education. However, much research is needed to single out which factors are most influential under which conditions and for which types of populations or individuals.

Even if one is capable of clearly identifying them, taking into account all of the necessary factors involved in assessing and creating a favorable adult education context will require a certain amount of effort on the part of interested parties and, as has been pointed out earlier, a certain amount of political support. Even if all conditions cannot be met in any given situation, increased understanding of the factors influencing motivation allows a maximization of participation as well as better knowledge of how and where to concentrate research efforts. It is increasingly clear that only the combination of these two aspects—properly applied research and more focused efforts to take the necessary factors into account—will lead to the desired goal of increased motivation and hence increased participation in adult education in developing and industrialized countries.

12

Adult Learning Under Conditions of Hardship: Evidence from Developing and Developed Countries

Nelly P. Stromquist
University of Southern California

This chapter reviews briefly how frequently invoked notions of context, community, and motivation embody tensions in definition and use. Although they must be taken into account when designing strategies to enhance adult participation in work-related programs, attention must also be paid to the fact that considering these notions should not mean accepting them as givens. In the case of context and community, measures might have to be taken to modify cultural norms or the local basis of power that constrain individual choice. This would be particularly relevant regarding women, who tend to occupy subordinate positions in society. In the case of motivation, often structural and situational forces may preclude an individual's desire to enter an adult education program. Incentives and rewards will have to be provided that not only address the specific needs of program participants, but also fit the various stages of the adult education program. Most incentives concentrate on the enrollment and retention phases, even though women students seldom receive the support services (e.g., child care, transportation) to facilitate participation. Missing in most programs are incentives after program

completion, the most important of which is a salary that permits a reasonable exis-
tence. Other important incentives are jobs with decent schedules and the possibili-
ty for promotion. The chapter presents a number of specific recommendations to
improve participation in work-related training. It concludes by noting that politi-
cal forces, that is, the condition of powerlessness of many of the adults who become
targeted for work-related training, shape the form and content of these training
programs. Therefore, "incentives" do not simply emerge as forms of curriculum
design, but are rather the result of significant compromises.

Work-related adult education programs assume two basic forms: those
designed to compensate for the lack of basic education of individuals
who have not participated in or benefited from formal education, and
those treating the needs of people whose occupational training must be
upgraded or modified. Students in basic literacy or training programs
tend to have very low levels of education and to be afflicted by a number of constraints typical of poor and marginal populations. Students in
more specialized, technical programs represent a heterogeneous group
in terms of socioeconomic status and cognitive level.

One must recognize from the outset that adult education programs are quite diverse. They can range from basic literacy programs to
training in the use of sophisticated automotive equipment, and from
training in business skills such as accounting to techniques for building
latrines. As the types of adult education vary, so do their clienteles.
Literacy programs are attended by poor and socially marginal individuals or immigrants with limited knowledge of the culture and language
of their host countries. Those in specialized technical programs tend to
be high school graduates in low- and middle-class families with less
severe financial problems. Obviously, the incentives that are effective for
the successful participation of these different groups in adult education
programs will also differ. In addition, incentives applicable to urban
areas may be less relevant in rural settings.

Adult programs focusing on the provision of basic skills,
whether literacy or job training, are notoriously difficult to implement.
Enrollment rates are commonly lower than anticipated, and low rates of
retention affect overall successful completion figures. These problems
emerge in part from the population being served: low-income and
minority individuals, many of whose lives are dominated by short-term
goals in which efforts to make ends meet and constraints regarding
everyday life, particularly in the case of women, prevail. Problems also
arise because adult education programs are conceived as slight modifi-
cations of *schooled* forms of training and because programs are not clearly linked to job opportunities for successful program completers.

It could be asserted with a reasonable degree of confidence that adult education programs are usually developed with a limited knowledge of the population they are to serve. Program designers tend to assume that educational offerings will be perceived as important by those who need them; they also tend to assume that adults are easily available for participation.

Although important lessons can be gleaned from experiences with adult education in developing countries, few experiences have been systematically explored in the Third World. Rich ethnographic studies, which are the most appropriate to produce knowledge about social dynamics regarding participation and the education-work link, are expensive to conduct and are thus rare in developing countries. The absence of adult education programs within universities in the Third World is a common condition. Puchner (this volume) finds that few universities in Africa have adult education programs. In Brazil, the country with the largest number of illiterates in Latin America, only one university (Paraiba) offers advanced training (an M.A. degree) in adult education. Even though Brazil is the home of Paulo Freire, the well-known educator whose ideas have revolutionized adult education, only one university (Espirito Santo) offers a course to train teachers in his literacy methods (Haddad, 1989).

Research from developed countries, which is more extensive and qualitative in nature, offers a number of useful insights. Another reason for considering such research is that even within advanced industrial countries in North America, one can find sizable pockets of populations that are poor and destitute; these are increasingly referred to in the literature as the *Fourth World.*

However, the adult education literature originating in and concerning developing countries, although limited, has contributions to make. It is more open in its treatment of the differential distribution of power in society and how this distribution causes various social groups to face structural obstacles beyond individual motivation.

Puchner is correct in her distinction among the situational, institutional, and contextual factors that affect participation in adult education programs. She is also correct in her assertion that the creation of a favorable context is perhaps more important than an exclusive focus on program features. Situational factors are particularly important in the case of women, in which sociocultural norms and beliefs seriously restrict their freedom of action and movement from the home. This chapter first examines three notions often found in the literature on incentives for participation in education programs and adult education in particular: context, community, and motivation. Second, it offers specific incentives for participation in adult education programs pertinent to both developed and developing countries.

INCENTIVES FOR PARTICIPATION

An individual's participation in a work-related training program may be fostered by external factors as well as personal reasons. A particular configuration of family, economic, and historic forces creates a context that may be favorable or not to participation. The social dynamics that operate at the community level between the family and the society at large also affect participation. Finally, psychological factors play a role in their own right and may lead individuals to seek participation in spite of unfavorable contextual and community conditions.

The Notion of Context

Context is a product of both cultural and political forces. Thus, a context might be all-encompassing and diffuse, but it is not neutral. Knowledge of community structures is useful insofar as it enables us to identify power structures and sources of potential support and conflict. Knowledge of the community cannot be interpreted, however, to mean that educational programs will be developed only with community consent. When community structures and leadership are unequal and unfair—as seems to be the case in many developing countries—they will need to be questioned and challenged. Tensions may also emerge in the interplay within local family structures. One may learn, for example, that fathers prefer to send sons rather than daughters for further training and that parents prefer to marry off their daughters young. The question is: Should these traditional and oppressive practices be challenged?

An understanding of a given situation is a prerequisite to changing it. People are not always less skilled because of their own inability or lack of desire to attain skills; they often face obstacles of a macrolevel nature. If a context supports ideologies that maintain the inferiority of certain groups, such as minorities and women, then the context has to be questioned, not merely worked around.

The Notion of Community

The concept of community is critical, yet it may be more relevant to rural than to urban areas. In rural areas, the size and spatial arrangement of villages and small towns foster social environments in which various beliefs and norms are closely shared and monitored. Rural adult education programs, therefore, need to be attuned to the characteristics and needs of groups that live in close proximity. In large metropolitan areas, programs of adult education, especially those dealing with learning the use of technical equipment, tend to draw students from several neighborhoods. The commonality among students may not be their sharing of a single spatial location, but rather their similar origins in a social class characterized by such features as economic hardship, frequent illness, local violence, transportation difficulties, and vulnerability to unemployment. It would seem that to the extent that cities contain a more heterogeneous population, programs may enjoy greater freedom from community constraints.

Working with agencies familiar with the communities they serve, as Puchner notes, is essential. Broadly defined, effective community support is that which is provided through some sort of organization. In a few cases, the organization might be a sensitive local governmental agency. Most often it is a nongovernmental organization (NGO) because such groups have been much more eager to develop community support than local governmental agencies. The growth of NGOs in Asia, Africa, and particularly Latin America is evidence that their work in adult education has been seen as useful and therefore worth supporting.

An understanding of the community should also mean an understanding of the individuals within their environment. Who are the persons for whom the skills are being offered? Were the programs designed for their needs or for the needs of third parties, mostly employers? In what families do these persons live? Do they have children of their own? Are the women unwed mothers? What means of transportation are available, and what are the difficulties of physical access to training sites and to jobs? Also, an understanding of their cognitive skills is important. What levels of education do they have? Are they high school dropouts or high school graduates?

There is increasing awareness in the United States that the urban underclass (characterized by persistent poverty, prolonged welfare dependency, more out-of-wedlock births, and high dropout rates) need a multifaceted approach involving economic development, criminal justice, health, education, job training, social service, housing, and transportation programs (U.S. General Accounting Office, 1990). This realization has led to the design of more encompassing policies, as reflected in the Carl D. Perkins Vocational Act and Applied Technology Education Act of 1990. The act, which continues work initiated in 1976, represents a new generation of legislation in which the individuals targeted for assistance are identified with precision (e.g., single parents, displaced homemakers, single pregnant women). The legislation requires that comprehensive services be offered to provide, subsidize, and reimburse preparatory services associated with academic and vocational skills and to assist with dependent care, transportation services, special services, and supplies, including career counseling. In Britain, although it has not yet been enacted into law, progressive groups have advocated the use of maintenance grants for students in aged 16-19 and a system of paid leave for adult learners, with priority given to those who left school at the minimum age and without qualifications. These grants would be accompanied by the provision of child care and nursery education (Socialist Movement, 1990, p. 31).

The frequent admonition to know the population prior to program design is well taken. The suggestion that *études de milieu* take place is appropriate, but actual efforts should go much farther. Not only is a *knowledge* of the background and culture of the individuals in adult education classes necessary, but so is the *utilization* of the background and culture. Experienced personnel is required to translate needs and preferences into effective educational strategies. Unfortunately, as noted earlier, we still know little about the design and implementation of effective adult education programs.

The Notion of Motivation

In discussing participation in the literature of adult education programs, motivation receives considerable attention. The notion of motivation has been found to be useful to program designers and administrators in their efforts to explain the low rates of retention that characterize adult education programs (and particularly literacy programs, in which average completion rates rarely surpass 50% of the initial enrollment). If the dropout problem is defined as one of motivation, the issue may be misdiagnosed from the start. Motivation, as such, has a tautological sense: "If you are motivated, you participate. If you don't participate, it is because you're not motivated."

The burden of participation is placed on the individual as though he or she is able to make a choice based entirely on personal preferences. Such a definition is unwise because it takes attention away from enabling (in this case disabling) conditions for participation. Rockhill, after a series of in-depth interviews analyzing the problems of women in sustaining attendance in literacy classes, concludes:

> I have difficulty with the idea that lack of motivation is Maria's problem—or the problem of most of the women we interviewed. Time and again, we have heard stories of incredibly strong desire countered by opposition in their living situations, an opposition that often comes directly from their husbands. (1986, p. 5)

Although Rockhill's study concentrated on women, obstacles of a structural and situational nature also affect poor men.

Motivation is better used to refer to the initial decision to enroll. One might say that people are motivated to participate in a program and signal their willingness by signing up. Once a program begins, participants must confront their everyday life and the tension it presents vis-à-vis the demands for regular and fixed-time attendance of most educational programs. This is an area that needs much more research. Data of women involved in a literacy program in Sao Paulo showed that attendance was characterized by frequent absences and tardiness. Taking care of children, returning home from work late due to the nature of their work or public transportation problems, waiting on a tired husband, traveling to pay bills on the first of the month (the poor do not have checking accounts), and falling ill (a common occurrence among poor people) all contributed to make attendance in class sporadic (Stromquist, 1992b). Some learners persist; many others simply stop. Is motivation at work here? Only a tremendous and immediate reward could persuade most people to continue under these circumstances.

Puchner identifies three sets of factors that affect motivation: situational (those affecting the personal circumstances of individuals), institutional (those pertaining to the features of the training program), and contextual (those including opportunity structures for using the newly acquired skills, the individuals' perceptions of the usefulness of the adult education program, community attitudes toward the program, and political forces).

The situational factors are also described as including "relatively uncontrollable demographic features such as age, gender, income, . . . as well as amount of prior schooling, or position in the societal structure" (Puchner, 1991, p. 4). One observation that should be made about this statement is that the impact of those "demographic features" may be concrete and may materialize in specific individual circumstances; nonetheless, many individual situations are culturally determined. They are societal products, inasmuch as they involve social constructions of what being a "woman," a "60-year old person," an "Indian," or a "minimum-wage earner" means. Furthermore, these are social constructions that can be changed via policies, and therefore they are not "uncontrollable."

CONTENT AND INSTRUCTIONAL METHODS

Content and instructional methods of adult education programs are essential in creating a favorable program context. Both content and method are inherently political, and it would be a mistake to see them only under the purview of program designers. The selection of what is covered in adult education programs (and education in general) is eminently political in that it serves a conscious interest. Funders of programs, either governmental agencies or employers, play a substantial role in shaping curriculum content. Furthermore, it must be remarked that a curriculum is political by virtue of what it covers as well as what it leaves out.

The decision to select and compensate teachers is also a political act. It determines who teaches and the quality of teaching. Usually in nonformal education programs the staff consist of primary teachers (for literacy programs) or semiskilled individuals in search of supplementary salaries. The staff in nonformal education programs seldom receive training to deal with adult students. Although some teachers develop pertinent competencies through trial and error in adult education classes, the high turnover of staff in these programs prevents the accumulation of knowledge among teachers. The decision to remunerate adult educators with low wages is not accidental. Rather, it represents a political interest in ignoring the needs of certain groups in society and, at worst, in maintaining the disadvantage. (For an insightful analytical framework of adult education policies, see Torres, 1990.)

Staff training is important to improve programs. But if "equal opportunities" are to be a serious objective of the program, this training will also require instruction in and access to information about the population being served. Stafford (1991), in her five-month study of participants in youth-training programs focusing on welding, painting, and knitting skills, found that program implementors knew little about youth culture (what interests them, how they see the world of work, how they value peers and friends of the opposite sex, what their job expectations are). As a result, the programs were only marginally integrated into the lives of young people.

THE PROVISION AND TIMING OF INCENTIVES AND REWARDS

The strategic provision of incentives and rewards can occur at three different moments: enrollment in the program, participation in it, and job placement. It is important to recognize that different moments call for different types of incentives, and that different implementors of adult education (governments, NGOs, and private firms) may not be able to provide all of them.

Salaries are a crucial reward. In some cases the incentive indeed may not be there. Salaries may be too low to encourage people to gain skills for employment that will pay very little. Or, incentives during the training programs of young people may be so small that they are left with no possibility of leaving their parents' home or marrying, or material consumption. In reaction to this, Finn observed that, "In place of a traditional passage to adulthood there is a period of extended dependence on the state and on a sometimes unwilling family" (cited in

Stafford, 1991, p. 116). From her own research, Stafford concludes that, "poverty and declining material standards must be the worst position of all from which to build good-quality youth training" (p. 116).

Are we considering learning at the workplace or in-training programs before employment? The former is normally provided by employers; the second more likely by the state. Developed countries exhibit variation in the way they treat their low-skill population. In the United States, only 1% of the employers' payroll goes to support the training of workers, in contrast with 3.5% in Germany, 2.5% in Singapore, and 1.2% in France. In the case of the United States, moreover, it is estimated that only 7% of the $30 million spent annually reaches front-line workers (California Workforce Literacy Force, 1990, p. 48). In addition, unlike Germany, Japan, and Sweden, the United States has no national strategy for noncollege youth (Nothdurft, 1989).

The poor treatment of low-skill populations, juxtaposed to the strong shift toward a service-dominated economy (as the service sector now accounts for 71% of employment; OECD, 1991c), augurs a tremendous social challenge for the United States. The service sector is well known for the bimodal working force it engenders: people with high levels of skills to assume the professional positions in the service sector, and a much larger number of people with low skills in menial occupations. Although a division of labor is certainly inevitable, the problematic situation resides in that individuals in the low-skilled segment are increasingly confronting wages at the minimum level or slightly above it, wages unable to support individual workers—rent alone is estimated to cost between 60% and 75% of their income. These remuneration levels do not promote an enthusiastic labor force; in turn, worker apathy and high turnover generate employers' responses of minimum training. Thus, a cohesive vicious circle is created.

Support for workplace training will also need an understanding of the workplace. Gustafsson notes that, "Trends towards more hierarchical and unequal relations at the workplace will adversely affect the conditions for learning" and asserts that, "It is likely that more emphasis on cooperative and self-ruling units of production (including schools) will promote learning" (1988, p. 228). In this regard, Gustafsson makes a critical observation regarding developing countries, particularly those facing a substantial external debt, such as those in Africa and Latin America: The structural adjustment policies imposed by the International Monetary Fund and the World Bank will result in fundamental changes in work and work organization; and yet, "insufficient attention has been paid to the implications that these may have for learning" (p. 229).

As Puchner notes, women require special attention. This attention is necessary not only because of their needs regarding children and family responsibilities, but also because of their needs as individuals in their own right. In this regard, it constitutes a positive step to recommend that adult education programs remove sex stereotypes. It will also be necessary, however, to provide women with content that is emancipatory in nature. This, in turn, suggests the need to give more attention to organizations capable of creating and sustaining a favorable environment for women, such as those fostered by women-run NGOs.

Correctly, the attention of program designers is moving from mere enrollment in adult educational programs to retention and successful completion. It is important, however, to move even farther to the actual attainment of employment by those trained in the programs. Evidence is only beginning to be obtained. Here again the developed countries are ahead of the developing countries. A three-year study of an adult education program in banking and finance in the United States presents clear evidence that men and women face different problems in retaining their newly acquired jobs. Through careful ethnographic methods, the study found that few women were able to retain their jobs after successful program completion. Problems posed by long distances from home to workplace, part-time employment with use of late shifts, and difficulties finding suitable child care made it unsafe and expensive to continue employment. The distance to the women's place of employment (as proof operators verifying bank receipts in one large building downtown) made it necessary for them to make several bus connections, thus sometimes causing them to arrive late. Employers were not sensitive to the logistical difficulties of women with these problems and fired them (Hull, 1991). An interesting observation made by the author of this ethnographic study is that "contrary to much popular literature a lack of *basic skills* wasn't a sufficient explanation for the difficulties that students experienced in succeeding at and holding their jobs as proof operators" (p. 77, emphasis in original).

Hull presents a rich set of recommendations to improve adult participation in work-related training (pp. 82-87). Those that seem more relevant to our discussion are the following:

- Provide substantial incentives. The best incentive will be living salaries.
- Provide accessible and low-cost transportation.
- Provide assistance not only for job placement, but also for job retention. Newly employed individuals should receive assistance while on the job.
- Provide other skills that will make it possible for employees to advance in their jobs. Do not give too narrow a set of skills, but broaden literacy instruction.

- Provide longer programs rather than short-term training.
- Offer child care facilities for women with children.
- Create opportunities for full-time employment.
- Fund research in the worksite and training programs.

To these should be added one more which is especially critical:

- Include the participation of labor unions in the identification of adult education programs for both individuals in the workforce and those outside it.

CONCLUSIONS

To the extent that effective incentives need to be comprehensive and address a marginalized population, solutions to the problem of low participation and success in adult education programs will be complex, costly, and conflictual. The understanding of how context operates to affect individual choice and institutional features is crucial. Yet, to fully appreciate the analytical advantages of this concept, it is necessary to realize that it unavoidably combines power and interest, class and gender, and the dilemmas of continuity and change. Additional research is needed to understand more fully the social dynamics affecting those in need of further education. Concepts such as motivation have limited usefulness when problems of an economic, social, and political nature arise.

In the case of developed countries, important challenges to participation in adult education programs stem from the combination of the limited understanding of the target populations and the accelerated growth of the service sector of the economy, which is generating a low-skilled population treated as disposable by most employers. In the case of developing countries, the challenges emerge from a global economic recession that in promoting the role of the free market is also casting aside interventions that may not be convenient to employers, but which carry important social returns. Given the political forces underlying many adult education programs, the provision of incentives for learning may be best considered as gradual political compromises on the road to a more democratic society.

References

Ahmed, M. (1975). *On literacy strategies for rural development*. Persepolis: International Symposium for Literacy.

Annett, J. (1989). Training skilled performance. In M.A. Colley & J.R. Beech (Eds.), *Acquisition and performance of cognitive skills*. New York: Wiley.

Arlington County Public Schools. (1990). *REEP/hotel workplace literacy final performance*. Washington, DC: Office of Vocational and Adult Education. (ERIC Document Reproduction Service No. ED 322 290)

Askov, E., Aderman, B., & Hemmelstein, N. (1989). *Upgrading basic skills for the workplace*. State College: Pennsylvania State University. (ERIC Document Reproduction Service No. ED 309 297)

Balmuth, M. (1988). Recruitment and retention in adult basic education: What does the research say? *Journal of Reading, 31*(7), 620-623.

Bassi, L.J., & Ashenfelter, O. (1986). The effects of direct job creation and training programs on low skilled workers. In S.H. Danziger & D.H. Weinberg (Eds.), *Fighting poverty: What works and what does not*. Cambridge, MA: Harvard.

B.C. Council of Forest Industries/IWA Canada. (1991). *A preliminary study of job-related communication skills in B.C. sawmills*. Vancouver: Author.

Bean, R., Partanen, J., Wright, F., & Aaronson, J. (1989). *Attrition in urban basic literacy programs and strategies to increase retention*. Pittsburgh, PA. (ERIC Document Reproduction Service No. ED 317 797)

Becker, G. (1962). Investment in human capital: A theoretical analysis. *Journal of Political Economy, 70*(5), 9-50.

Becker, G.S. (1975). *Human capital* (2nd ed.). Chicago: University of Chicago Press.

Benton, L., & Noyelle, T. (1992). *Adult illiteracy and economic performance*. Paris: OECD.

Bertrand, O., & Noyelle, T. (1988). *Human resources and corporate strategy: Technological change in banks and insurance companies.* Paris: OECD.

Best, M. (1990). *The new competition: Institutions of industrial restructuring.* Cambridge, MA: Harvard University Press.

Bethlehem Area Chamber of Commerce. (1990). *Bethlehem Area Chamber of Commerce literacy project, 1989-1990.* Harrisburg: Pennsylvania State Department of Education. (ERIC Document Reproduction Service No. ED 324 468)

Bhola, H.S. (1983). *The promise of literacy.* Baden-Baden, Germany: DSE, Nomos Verlagsgesellschaft.

Bhola, H.S. (1984). *Campaigning for literacy: Eight national experiences of the 20th Century, with a memorandum to decision-makers.* Paris: Unesco.

Bhola, H.S. (1989). *World trends and issues in adult education.* London: Jessica Kingsley Publishers.

Bishop, J.H. (1990). Job performance, turnover and wage growth. *Journal of Labor Economics, 8*(3), 363-386.

Bishop, J. (1991). On-the-job training of new hires. In D. Stern & J. Ritzen (Eds.), *Market failure in training.* New York: Springer Verlag.

Bishop, J. (1994). The impact of training in school on on-the-job productivity, wages and turnover of new hires. In L. Lynch (Ed.), *The private market for training.* Chicago: University of Chicago Press.

Bishop, J., & Kang, S. (1988). *A signaling/bonding model of employer finance of general training.* Ithaca, NY: Center for Advanced Human Resource Studies, Cornell University.

Bishop, J., & Kang, S. (1994). *On-the-job training/sorting: Theory and evidence.* Columbus: National Center for Research in Vocational Education, The Ohio State University.

Bluff, L. (1989). *The trade union postal course scheme.* Australia: World Perspective Case Descriptions on Educational Programs for Adults. Sydney: Australia: New South Wales Board of Education. (ERIC Document Reproduction Service No. ED311 160)

Boyer, R. (1989). *New directions in management practices and work organization.* (Discussion Paper). Paris: OECD.

Bricklayers and Allied Craftsmen. (1990). *Literacy of trowel trades project: Evaluation report.* Washington, DC: Office of Vocational and Adult Education. (ERIC Document Reproduction Service No. ED 324 442)

Brown, C. (1991, September). *An institutional model of training.* Paper presented to Conference on Economics of Training, Cardiff Business School.

Brown, J.S., Collins, A., & Duguid, P. (1989). Situated cognition and the culture of learning. *Educational Researcher, 18*(1), 32-42.

Brown, W. (1973). *Piecework bargaining.* London: Heinemann.

Brown, W. (1990). Managing remuneration. In K. Sisson (Ed.), *Personnel management in Britain.* Oxford: Blackwell.

Bussert, K. (1991). *Organizational characteristics of 107 workplace literacy programs.* Unpublished manuscript, Indiana University, Bloomington, IN.

California Workforce Literacy Force. (1990, November). *California's workforce for the year 2000.* Sacramento: Senate Publications.

Chynoweth, J.K. (1989). *Enhancing literacy for jobs and productivity, Academy final report*. Washington, DC: Council of State Policy and Planning Agencies. (ERIC Document Reproduction Service No. ED 313 583)

Clement, W., Drake, K., Fong, P., & Wurzburg, G. (1991). *Further education and training of the labor force: A comparative analysis of national strategies for industry training: Australia, Sweden and the U.S.* (OECD working paper SME/MAS/ED/WD(91)3). Paris: OECD.

Coffey, P., Eoff, J., Mayo, R., & McDaniel, G. (1990). *Skills enhancement program, Tennessee. Regional Medical Center at Memphis*. Memphis, TN: Literacy Foundation Memphis, Inc. (ERIC Documentation Reproduction Service No. ED 324 459)

Colardyn, D. (1990). *Assessment and recognition of skills and competencies: Developments in France* (OCDE/GD(90)6). Paris: OECD.

Coletta, N. (1982). *Worker-peasant education in the People's Republic of China* (World Bank Staff Working Papers No. 527). Washington, DC: World Bank.

Commission on the Skills of the American Workforce. (1990). *America's choice: High skills or low wages*. Rochester, NY: National Center on Education and the Economy.

Congress of the United States. (1989). *Eliminating illiteracy: Hearings on examining proposed legislation*. Washington, DC: Senate Committee on Labor and Human Resources. (ERIC Document Reproduction Service No. ED 313 528)

Continuing Education Institute. (1990). *Workplace literacy participation for nursing home employees, Final report*. Washington, DC: Office of Vocational and Adult Education. (ERIC Document Reproduction Service ED 324 497)

Cooper, E., Van Dexter, R., & Williams, A. (1988). *Improving basic skills in the workplace: Workplace literacy programs in region III*. Harrisburg: Pennsylvania Department of Labor, Employment and Training Administration. (ERIC Document Reproduction Service No. ED 308 392)

Cross, K.P. (1981). *Adults as learners*. San Francisco: Jossey-Bass.

Crozier, M. (1987). *Etat modest, état moderne: Stratégie pour un autre changement*. Paris: Fayard.

Cummins, J. (1987). Theory and policy in bilingual education. In Organisation for Economic Co-operation and Development (Ed.), *Multicultural education*. Paris: OECD.

DeFreitas, G. (1991). *Inequality at work: Hispanics in the U.S. labor force*. New York: Oxford University Press.

Dochery, P. (1991). *Lärande i arbete* [Learning at work]. Report to the Swedish Work Environment Fund. Stockholm: Sweden.

Doeringer, P.B., & Piore, M.J. (1971). *Internal labor markets and manpower analysis*. Lexington: D.C. Heath.

Dolton, P.J., Makepeace, G.H., & Treble, J.G. (1991, December). *Measuring the effects of training in the Youth Cohort Study*. Paper presented to NBER/Center for Economic Performance Conference on International Comparisons of Private Sector Training, London School of Economics.

Dore, R., & Sako, M. (1989). *How the Japanese learn to work*. London: Routledge Kegan and Paul.

Duffy, T. M. (1992). What makes a difference in instruction? In T. Sticht, M. Beeler, & B. McDonald (Eds.), *The intergenerational transfer of cognitive skills: Volume I. Programs, policies, and research issues*. Norwood, NJ: Ablex.

Elias, P. (1991, September). *Labor mobility and individual heterogeneity: A study of the effects of training, unions and employment status on labor turnover*. Paper presented to Conference on the Economics of Training, Cardiff Business School.

Ellegård, K., et al. (1991). *Reforming industrial work: Principles and realities*. Stockholm: The Swedish Work Environment Fund.

Ellström, P.E. (1992) *Kvalifikation, utbildning och lärande i arbetslivet* [Qualification, education and learning at work]. Linköping, Sweden: University of Linköping.

Engeström, Y. (1987). *Learning by expanding: An activity theoretical approach to developmental research*. Helsinki, Finland: Oriental Konsultit Oy.

Feuer, M., Glick, H., & Desai, A. (1987). Is firm-sponsored education viable? *Journal of Economic Behavior and Organization, 8*(1),

Full Employment UK. (1989). *The next rung up: Training, enterprise and unskilled workers*. London: Full Employment UK.

Finegold, D. (1991). Institutional incentives and skill creation: Preconditions for a high skill equilibrium. In P. Ryan (Ed.), *Information costs, training quality and trainee exploitation*. Presented to Project on Vocational Education and Training, Center for Economic Performance, London School of Economics.

Finegold, D., & Soskice, D. (1988). The failure of training in Britain: Analysis and prescription. *Oxford Review of Economic Policy, 4*(3), 51-53.

Flamholtz, E.G. (1985). *Human resource accounting*. San Francisco: Jossey Bass.

Flavell, J.H. (1963). *The developmental psychology of Jean Piaget*. New York: D. Van Nostrand.

Fougeyrollas, P., Sow, F., & Valladon, F. (1967). *L'education des adultes au Senegal*. Paris: Unesco, IIEP.

Friedman, T., & Williams, E.B. (1982). Current use of tests for employment. In A.K. Wigdor & W.R. Gardner (Eds.), *Ability testing: Uses, consequences, and controversies* (Part II, pp. 999-1069). Washington, DC: National Academy Press.

Friend, I., & Blume, M. (1975). The demand for risky assets. *American Economic Review, 65*, 900-922.

Galy, K.A.K. (1981). *Alphabetisation des adultes et developpement economique et social au Niger: Contribution a l'identification des problemes de l'alphabetisation*. [Adult literacy and social and economic development in Niger: Contribution to the identification of literacy problems.] Doctoral thesis, Universite de Paris V, Paris.

Garonna, P., & Ryan, P. (1991). The problems facing youth. In P. Ryan, P. Garonna, & Edwards (Eds.), *The problem of youth: The regulation of youth employment and training in advanced economies*. London: Macmillan.

Glick, H.A., & Feuer, M.J. (1984). Employer-sponsored training and the governance of specific human capital investments. *Quarterly Review of Economics and Business, 24*(2).

Great Britain, Department of Employment. (1988). *Career development loans information booklet*. London: Department of Employment.

Great Britain, Department of Employment. (1991). 1990 labor force survey preliminary results. *Employment Gazette, 99*(4), 175-96.

Great Britain Training Agency. (1989a). *Training in Britain: Employers' perspectives on human resources*. Sheffield: Training Agency.

Great Britain Training Agency. (1989b). *Training in Britain: Individuals' perspectives*. Sheffield: Training Agency.

Great Britain Training Agency. (1989c). *Training in Britain: Employers' perspectives on human resources*. Sheffield: Training Agency.

Great Britain Training Commission. (1988). *Training Commission, Annual Report 1987/88*. Sheffield: Training Commission.

Giere, U., Ouane, A., & Ranaweera, A.M. (1990). *Literacy in developing countries: An analytical bibliography* (Bulletin of the International Bureau of Education No. 254-257). Paris: Unesco.

Green, F. (1991, September). *The determinants of training of male and female employees in Britain*. Paper presented to Conference on the Economics of Training, Cardiff Business School.

Greenhalgh, C., & Mavrotos, G. (1992). *The role of career aspirations and financial constraints in individual access to vocational training* (University of Oxford Discussion Paper 136). Oxford: University of Oxford.

Greenhalgh, C., & Stewart, M.B. (1987). The effects and determinants of training. *Oxford Bulletin of Economics and Statistics, 49*(2) 171-190.

Grimes, J., & Renner, R. (1988). *Toward a more literate workforce: The emergence of workplace literacy programs in Illinois*. Springfield, IL: Illinois State Library. (ERIC Documentation Reproduction Service No. ED 313 530)

Gross, A., Lee, M., & Zuss, M. (1988). *Project REACH Final Evaluation Report*. New York: City University of New York. (ERIC Documentation Reproduction Service No. ED 314 602)

Gupta, N. (1988). *Exploratory investigations of pay for knowledge systems*. Bureau of Labor-Management Relations, U.S. Department of Labor. Washington DC: GPO.

Gustafsson, I. (Ed.). (1988). Creating conditions for learning. In *Recovery in Africa. A challenge for development cooperation in the 90s* (pp. 223-229). Stockholm: Swedish Ministry for Foreign Affairs.

Hacker, W. (1985). Activity: A fruitful concept in industrial psychology. In M. Frese & J. Sabini (Eds.), *Goal-directed behavior*. Hillsdale, NJ: Erlbaum.

Haddad, S. (1989, September). *Promoting literacy programs: The link between post-literacy and adult education and higher education institutions in Brazil*. [Promocao de programas de alfabetizacao: Pos alfabetizacao e educacao de adultos com a vinculacao das Institucoes de Ensino Superior no Brasil]. Sao Paulo: Centro Ecumenico de Documentacao e Informacao.

Hall, R. (1988). Intertemporal substitution in consumption. *Journal of Political Economy, 96*(2), 339-357.

Ham, J.C., & LaLonde, R. (1991, September). *Estimating the effect of training on the incidence and duration of unemployment*. Paper presented to Conference on the Economics of Training, Cardiff Business School.

Hargroves, J. (1989). The basic skills crisis: One bank looks at its training investment. *New England Economic Review*, pp. 58-68.

Hashimoto, M. (1982). Minimum wage effects on training on the job. *American Economic Review, 72*(5), 1070-1087.

Haveman, R., & Wolfe, B. (1984). Education and economic well-being: The role of non-market effects. In E. Dean (Ed.), *Education and economic productivity*. Cambridge, MA: Ballinger.

Hawaii University. (1990). *The skills enhancement literacy projects of Hawaii, final project model*. Manoa: Office of Vocational and Adult Education. (ERIC Documentation Reproduction Service No. ED 324 449)

Heath, S.B. (1983). *Ways with words: Language, life and work in communities and classrooms*. Cambridge, UK: Cambridge University Press.

Henry, J.F., & Raymond, S.U. (1982). *Basic skills in the U.S. workforce: The contrasting perceptions of business, labor, and public education*. New York: Center for Public Resources.

Hersch, J. (1991). Equal employment opportunity law and firm profitability. *Journal of Human Resources*, 139-153.

Hirsch, D. (1991). Overcoming adult illiteracy. *OECD Observer, 171*, 21-24.

Hirschhorn, L. (1984). *Beyond mechanization: Work and technology in a postindustrial age*. Cambridge, MA: MIT Press.

Hirschhorn, L. (1989, October). *Training factory workers: Three case studies*. Wharton Center on Applied Research, University of Pennsylvania.

Hirschhorn, L., Gilmore, T., & Newell, T. (1989). Training and learning in a post industrial world. In H. Leymann & H. Kornbluh (Eds.), *Socialization and learning at work*. Aldershot, England: Avebury.

Hollenbeck, K., & Smith, B. (1984). *The influence of applicants' education and skills on employability assessment by employers*. Columbus: The National Center for Research in Vocational Education, The Ohio State University.

Holmes, B. (1989). Literacy and numeracy: What cause for concern? (London: British Government, Department of Employment). *Employment Gazette, 97*(3), 133-139.

Howden, G. (1990). *Workplace literacy*. Paper presented at the ANPA Foundation Literacy Conference, Washington, DC. (ERIC Documentation Reproduction Service No. ED 323 364)

Hubbard, R.G., & Judd, K.L. (1986). Liquidity constraints, fiscal policy and consumption. *Brookings Papers on Economic Activity, 1*, 1-60.

Hull, G. (1991). *Examining the relations of literacy to vocational education and work. An ethnography of a vocational program in banking and finance*. Unpublished report to the National Center for Research in Vocational Education, University of California, Berkeley.

Imai, M. (1986). *Kaizen: The key to Japan's competitive success*. New York: Random House.

Indian Ministry of Education and Social Welfare. (1978a). *Fifty years of adult education in India: Some experiences*. New Delhi: Author.

Indian Ministry of Education and Social Welfare. (1978b). *Summary of the report of the working group on adult education for the medium-term plan 1978-1983*. New Delhi: Author.

Indian Ministry of Human Resources Development. (1988). *National literacy mission*. New Delhi: Author.

International Development Research Centre. (1979). *The world of literacy: Policy, research and action*. Ottawa: IDRC.

James, R. (1987, January). *The excess cost of training*. Clothing World.

Jarvis, V., & Prais, S.J. (1989). Two nations of shopkeepers: Training for retailing in France and Britain. *National Institute Economic Review, 128*, 58-74.

Jessup, G. (1991). *Outcomes: NVQs and the emerging model of education and training*. Lewes, England: Falmer Press.

Johnston, W. (1991). *An inventory of Canadian workplace activity*. Halifax: A.B.C.

Jones, A., & Kaye, D.F. (1984, August). *Demotivating and disincentive influences in the health care organization*. Paper presented at the annual Conference of the American Psychological Association, Toronto, Canada. (ERIC Documentation Reproduction Service No. ED 258 065)

Jones, I.S. (1986). Apprentice training costs in British manufacturing establishments: Some new evidence. *British Journal of Industrial Relations, 24*(3), 333-362.

Jones, P.L., & Medley, V. (1987, November). *Teaching reading in the workplace*. Paper presented at the annual meeting of the Mid-South Educational Research Association, Mobile, AL. (ERIC Documentation Reproduction Service No. ED 288 002)

Kahler, D.W. (Ed.). (1982). *Literacy at work: Linking literacy to business management skills*. Washington, DC: Creative Associates, Inc.

Kassam, Y.O. (1982). Literacy and development: What is missing from the jigsaw puzzle? In H. Hinzen & V.H. Hundsdorfer (Eds.), *Education for liberation and development: The Tanzanian experience*. Hamburg: Unesco Institute for Education.

Katz, E., & Ziderman, A. (1990). Investment in general training: The role of information and labor mobility. *Economic Journal, 100*, 1147-1158.

Kempfer, H. (1973). Guidelines for an attack on literacy. In A. Bordia, J. R. Kidd, & J.A. Draper (Eds.), *Adult education in India: A book of readings*. Bombay: Nachiketa Publications Limited.

Kenawaty, G., & Castro, C.M. (1990). New directions for training: An agenda for action. *International Labour Review, 129*(6), 751-771.

Kern, R.P., Sticht, T.G., Welty, D., & Hauke, R.N. (1975). *Guidebook for the development of Army training literature*. Alexandria, VA: U.S. Army Research Institute for the Behavioral and Social Sciences.

Kirsch, I., Jungeblut, A., Jenkins, L., & Kolstad, A. (1993). *Adult literacy in America: A first look at the results of the National Adult Literacy survey*. Washington, DC: National Center for Education Statistics.

Kumari, S. (1979). Problems of motivation of women for literacy. In G.S. Rao (Ed.), *Problems of women's literacy*. Mysore, India: Central Institute of Indian Languages.

Kutner, M., Sherman, R., Webb, L., & Fisher, C. (1991). *A review of the national workplace literacy program.* Washington, DC: U.S. Department of Education, Office of Planning, Budget, and Evaluation.

Lalonde, R. (1986, September). Evaluating the econometric evaluations of training programs with experimental data. *American Economic Review, 76*(4), 604-620.

Lee, D., Marsden, D., Rickman, P., & Duncombe, J. (1990). *Scheming for youth: A study of YTS in the enterprise culture.* Milton Keynes: Open University Press.

Leighton, L., & Mincer, J. (1981). Effects of minimum wages on human capital formation. In S. Rottenberg (Ed.), *The economics of legal minimum wages.* Washington, DC: American Enterprise Institute.

Lennerlöf, L. (1986). *Kompetens eller hjälplöshet? Om lärande i arbete. En forskningsöverskrift.* [Competence or helplessness? Learning at work: A review of research]. Stockholm: Arbetarskyddsstyrelsen.

Levine, M.L., & Pansar, E. (1990). *Boston workplace education collaborative: Final external evaluation.* Roxbury, MA: Roxbury Community College. (ERIC Documentation Reproduction Service No. ED 322 393)

Leymann, H. (1989). Learning of theories. In H. Leymann & H. Kornbluh (Eds.), *Socialization and learning at work.* Aldershot, England: Avebury.

Lind, A. (1988). *Adult literacy lessons and promises: Mozambican literacy campaigns 1978-1982.* Stockholm: Institute of International Education, University of Stockholm.

Lind, A., & Johnston, A. (1990). *Adult literacy in the Third World: A review of objectives and strategies.* Stockholm: Swedish International Development Agency.

Liston, E.J. (1986). *The CCRI electric boat project: A partnership for progress in economic development.* Paper presented at the annual conference of the National Council for Occupational Education, San Diego, CA. (ERIC Documentation Reproduction Service No. ED 275 373)

Literacy law estimated to cost states more than $5 million. (1991). *Education Daily, 24*(157), 2.

LO. (1991). *Det Urechlande arbetet.* Stockholm: LO.

London, M. (1989). *Managing the training enterprise—High quality, cost-effective employee training in organizations.* San Francisco: Jossey Bass.

Los Angeles Unified School District. (1990). *Working smart: The Los Angeles workplace literacy project final report.* (ERIC Documentation Reproduction Service No. ED 322 341)

Löwstedt, J. (Ed.). (1989). *Organisation och teknikförändring* [Organization and Technological Change]. Lund: Studentlitteratur.

Lundgren, U. (1977). *Model analysis of pedagogical processes.* Lund: Liber.

Luttringer, J.M., & Pasquier, B. (1980). Paid educational leave in five European countries. *International Labour Review, 119*(4), 407-423.

Lynch, L. (1992, March). Private sector training and the earnings of young workers. *American Economic Review, 82,* 299-312.

Madigan, K. (1990). *Further education and training and collective bargaining: The experience of five countries.* Unpublished working paper. Paris: OECD.

Main, B., & Shelley, M.A. (1988). Does it pay young people to go on YTS? In D. Raffe (Ed.), *Education and the youth labor market*. Lewes, UK: Falmer.

Marsden, D.W. (1986). *The end of economic man? Custom and competition in the labor market*. Brighton: Wheatsheaf.

Marsden, D.W., & Ryan, P. (1990, November). Institutional aspects of youth employment and training policy in Britain. *British Journal of Industrial Relations, 28*, 351-369.

Marsden, D.W., & Ryan, P. (1991a). Institutional aspects of youth employment and training policy: Reply. *British Journal of Industrial Relations, 29*, 497-505.

Marsden, D.W., & Ryan, P. (1991b). Initial training, labor market structure and public policy: Intermediate skills in British and German industry. In P. Ryan (Ed.), *International comparisons of vocational education and training for intermediate skills*. Lewes, England: Falmer.

Martin, J., & Roberts, C. (1984). *Women and employment: A lifetime perspective* (Social Survey Report SS1143). London: HMSO.

Mason, J., & Kerr, B. (1992). Literacy transfer from parents to children in the preschool years. In T. Sticht, M. Beeler, & B. McDonald (Eds.), *The intergenerational transfer of cognitive skills: Vol. II. Theory and research in cognitive science*. Norwood, NJ: Ablex.

Matheson, A. (1989a). *English on the job*. Sydney, Australia: Australian Council of Trade Unions.

Matheson, A. (1989b). *Rail industry award restructuring*. Sydney, Australia: Australian Council of Trade Unions.

Maynard, R. (1991, September). *Evaluating employment and training programs: Lessons from the U.S. experience*. Paper presented to Conference on the Economics of Training, Cardiff Business School.

Mbakile, E.P.R. (1980). Literacy and post-literacy programmes: The Tanzanian experience. In Commonwealth Secretariat (Ed.), *Participation, learning, and change*. Dar Es Salaam: Author.

McCormick, K. (1991). Japanese engineers, lifetime employment and in-company training. In P. Ryan (Ed.), *Information costs, training quality and trainee exploitation*. Presented to Project on Vocational Education and Training, Center for Economic Performance, London School of Economics.

McMahon, J.L. (1990). *Math/measurement for upgrading basic skills of industrial hourly workers: Final report*. Harrisburgh: Pennsylvania State Department of Education. (ERIC Documentation Reproduction Service No. ED 324 479)

Mehaut, P., & Clement, Y. (1989). *Formation continue et negotiation collective en France* (Adult training and collective bargaining in France Report). Paris: OECD.

Mikulecky, L. (1989, June). *Developing basic skills programs for banking*. Paper presented at the annual conference of the American Institute of Banking, Chicago, IL.

Mikulecky, L. (1990). National adult literacy and life-long learning goals. *Phi Delta Kappan, 72*(4), 304-309.

Mikulecky, L., & d'Adamo-Weinstein, L. (1991). Evaluating workplace literacy programs. In M. Taylor, G. Lewe, & J. Draper (Eds.), *Basic skills in the workplace* (pp. 481-499). Toronto, Canada: Culture Concepts, Inc.

Milward, N., & Stevens, M. (1986). *Workplace industrial relations 1980-1984.* Aldershot, England: Gower.

National Center on Education and the Economy. (1990). *America's choice: High skills or low wages, the report of the Commission on the Skills of the American workforce.* New York: National Center on Education and the Economy. (ERIC Documentation Reproduction Service No. ED 323 297)

Newcombe, J., et al. (1989). *Workplace basic education program* (World perspective case descriptions on educational programs for adults: Australia). Battle Creek, MI: Kellogg Foundation. (ERIC Documentation Reproduction Service No. ED 311 160)

Nickell, S. (1982, January). The determinants of occupational success in Britain. *Review of Economic Studies, 49,* 43-53.

Nickse, R. S. (1980). *Assessing life-skills competence.* Belmont, CA: Fearon Education.

Nolan, P. (1990). Restructuring and the politics of industrial renewal: The limits of post-Fordism. In A. Pollert (Ed.), *Farewell to flexibility? Questions of restructuring work and employment.* Oxford: Blackwell.

Norris, C.Z., & Breen, P.K. (1990). *Lower Merrimack Valley workplace education project: Final report.* Haverhill, MA: Alpha Industries, Inc. and Community Action, Inc. (ERIC Documentation Reproduction Service No. ED 322 796)

Nothdurft, W. (1989). *School works: Reinventing public schools to create the workforce of the future.* Washington, DC: The Brookings Institution.

Oberle, J., Gerber, P., & Gordon, J. (1989). *Industry report: Training* (Vol. 26). Minneapolis, MN: Lakewood Publications.

Odunga, J.N. (1988). Causes of dropouts among adults attending literacy classes: A case study of Tarime District, Tanzania. In Institute of Adult Education, Tanzania (Ed.), *Studies in Adult Education No. 49.* Dar Es Salaam: Author.

Okedara, J.T. (1992). *Mother tongue literacy in Nigeria.* Ibudan, Nigeria: University of Ibudan.

Oliver, N., & Wilkinson, B. (1988). *The Japanization of British industry.* Oxford: Basil Blackwell.

Organisation for Economic Co-operation and Development (OECD). (1973). In *Recurrent Education: A strategy for lifelong learning.* Paris: OECD.

Organisation for Economic Co-operation and Development (OECD). (1988). *New technologies in the 1990s: A socioeconomic appraisal.* Paris: OECD.

Organisation for Economic Co-operation and Development (OECD). (1990). *OECD economic surveys: Australia.* Paris: OECD.

Organisation for Economic Co-operation and Development (OECD). (1991a). *Further education and training of the labor force in OECD countries: Evidence and issues* (Working paper. SME/MAS/ED/WD(91)5). Paris: OECD

Organisation for Economic Co-operation and Development (OECD). (1991b). Enterprise-related training. In *OECD employment outlook 1991.* Paris: OECD.

Organisation for Economic Co-operation and Development (OECD). (1991c). *OECD in figures: Statistics on the member countries.* Paris: OECD.

Organisation for Economic Co-operation and Development (OECD). (1992a). *Adult illiteracy and economic performance.* Paris: OECD.

Organisation for Economic Co-operation and Development (OECD). (1992b). *High-quality education and training for all.* Paris: OECD.

Parsons, D. (1972). Specific human capital: An application to quit rates and layoff rates. *Journal of Political Economy, 80*(6), 1120-1141.

Patterson, M. (1989). *Workplace literacy: A review of the literature.* New Brunswick, Canada: New Brunswick Department of Advanced Education and Training. (ERIC Document Reproduction Service No. ED 314 142)

Payne, J. (1990). *Adult off-the-job skills training: An evaluation study.* Sheffield, UK: Policy Studies Institute, Great Britain Training Agency.

Payne, J. (1991, September). *Women's training needs: The British policy gap.* Paper presented at the Conference on Economics of Training. Cardiff Business School.

Philippi, J. (1989). *U.S. Department of Labor technology transfer partnership project: JESP, application in the private sector, lessons learned report.* Washington, DC: National Alliance of Business.

Philippi, J., Mikulecky, L., & Kloosterman, P. (1991). *An evaluation of the UAW/Ford math enrichment program.* Dearborn, MI: UAW/Ford, National Developmental Education and Training Center.

Prais, S.J. (1991). Vocational qualifications in Britain and Europe: Theory and practice. *National Institute Economic Review, 136,* 86-92.

Prais, S., Jarvis, V., & Wagner, K. (1991). Productivity and vocational skills in Britain and Germany: Hotels. In P. Ryan (Ed.), *Information costs, training quality and trainee exploitation.* Presented to Project on Vocational Education and Training, Center for Economic Performance, London School of Economics.

Raizen, S. (1991, March). *Learning and work: The research base.* Unpublished paper presented at the International Seminar on Vocational-Technical Education and Training, Phoenix, AZ.

Rasmussen, J. (1986). *Information processing and human machine interaction: An approach to cognitive engineering.* New York: North-Holland.

Resnick, L B. (1987). Learning in school and out. *Educational Researcher, 16,* 13-20.

Resnick, L. B. (1989). Introduction. In L.B. Resnick (Ed.), *Knowing, learning and instruction.* Hillsdale, NJ: Erlbaum.

Rockhill, K. (1986, March). *Literacy as threat/desire.* Paper presented at the meeting of the Comparative and International Education Society, Toronto, Canada.

Ross, D.P. (1990, August). *Functional literacy and labour markets: Some findings and policy implications* (Report to Statistics Canada).

Ryan, P. (1980, November). The costs of job training for a transferable skill. *British Journal of Industrial Relations, 18,* 334-51.

Ryan, P. (1984). Job training, employment practices and the large enterprise: The case of costly transferable skills. In P. Osterman (Ed.), *Internal labor markets.* Cambridge, MA: MIT Press.

Ryan, P. (1990). Job training, individual opportunity and low pay. In A. Bowen & K. Mayhew (Eds.), *Improving incentives for the low paid*. London: Macmillan.

Ryan, P. (1991a). How much do employers spend on training? An assessment of the 'training in Britain' estimates. *Human Resource Management Journal, 1*(4), 55-76.

Ryan, P. (Ed.). (1991b). *International comparisons of vocational education and training for intermediate skills*. Lewes, England: Falmer.

Ryan, P. (1993). *Information costs, training quality and trainee exploitation*. Paper presented to Project on Vocational Education and Training, Center for Economic Performance, London School of Economics.

Sadowski, D. (1982). Corporate training investment decisions. In G. Mensch & R. Nichaus (Eds.), *Manpower planning and technological change*. New York: Plenum.

Secretary of Labor's Commission on Achieving Necessary Skills (SCANS). (1991). *What work requires of schools*. Washington, DC: U.S. Department of Labor.

Shaeffer, S. (1991). *A framework for collaborating for educational change* (IIEP Research Studies Program, Increasing and Improving the Quality of Basic Education). Paris: IIEP.

Shengena, J.J. (1982). Workers' education. In H. Hinzen & V.H. Hundsdorfer (Eds.), *Education for liberation and development: The Tanzanian experience*. Hamburg: Unesco Institute for Education.

Sincoff, J.B., & Sternberg, R.J. (1989). The development of cognitive skills: An examination of recent theories. In M.A. Colley & J.R. Beech (Eds.), *Acquisition and performance of cognitive skills*. New York: Wiley.

Singh, S. (1989, July 2). The hidden costs of illiteracy. *Business Review Weekly*, pp. 72-74.

Sköld, M. (1989). Everyday learning: The basis for adult education. In H. Leymann & H. Kornbluh (Eds.), *Socialization and learning at work*. Aldershot, England: Avebury.

Smith, A. (1976). *An inquiry into the nature and causes of the wealth of nations* (E. Cannan, ed.). Chicago: University of Chicago Press.

Socialist Movement. (1990). *Education: Towards a socialist perspective*. Chesterfield, Derbyshire, England: Author.

Sorge, A. (1981). *Micro-electronics and vocational education and training*. Berlin: International Management Institute.

Stafford, A. (1991). *Trying work: Gender, youth and work experience*. Edinburgh, UK: Edinburgh University Press.

Statistics Canada (1989). *Survey of literacy skills used in daily activities*.

Steedman, H., & Wagner, K. (1989, May). Productivity, machinery and skills: Clothing manufacture in Britain and Germany. *National Institute Economic Review, 109*, 40-57.

Stein, S.G. (1989). *The Massachusetts workplace education initiative: Program summary*. Boston, MA: Commonwealth Literacy Campaign. (ERIC Documentation Reproduction Report No. ED 313 917)

Sternberg, R. J. (1985). *Beyond I.Q: A triarchic theory of human intelligence*.

Cambridge: Cambridge University Press.

Sticht, T.G. (1975). *Reading for working: A functional literacy anthology.* Alexandria, VA: Human Resources Research Organization.

Sticht, T.G. (1982). *Basic skills in defense.* Alexandria, VA: Human Resources Research Organization.

Sticht, T.G. (1983). *Literacy and human resources development at work: Investing in the education of adults to improve the educability of children.* Alexandria, VA: Human Resources Research Organization.

Sticht, T.G. (1989). *Functional context education: Policy and training methods from the military experience.* (Background paper No. 41). Washington, DC: U.S. Department of Labor.

Sticht, T.G. (1991a). *Remmele's philosophy: Basic skills training is good business.* Scarsdale, NY: The Work in America Institute.

Sticht, T.G. (1991b). *Briggs & Stratton's employee educational learning center.* Scarsdale, NY: The Work in America Institute.

Sticht, T.G., Armstrong, W.B., Hickey, D.T., & Caylor, J.S. (1987). *Cast-off youth: Policy and training methods from the military experience.* New York: Praeger.

Sticht, T.G., & Hickey, D.T. (1991). Functional context theory, literacy and electronics training. In R. F. Dillon & J. W. Pellegrino (Eds.), *Instruction: Theoretical and applied perspectives.* New York: Praeger.

Streeck, W. (1988). *Skills and the limits of neo-liberalism: The enterprise of the future as a place of learning* (Discussion paper). Berlin: Science Centre, Research Unit on Labour Market and Employment.

Streeck, W., Hilbert, J., Van Kevelaer, K., Maier, F., & Weber, H. (1987). *The role of the social partners in vocational training and further training in the FRG.* Berlin: CEDEFOP.

Stromquist, N.P. (1989). Determinants of educational participation and achievement of women in the Third World: A review of the evidence and a theoretical critique. *Review of Educational Research, 59*(2), 143-183.

Stromquist, N.P. (1992a). *The intersection of gender and social marginality in adult literacy.* Unpublished manuscript, University of Southern California, Los Angeles.

Stromquist, N.P. (1992b). Women and literacy: Promises and constraints. In D.A. Wagner & L.D. Puchner (Eds.), *World literacy in the year 2000* (Vol. 520, The Annals of the American Academy of Political and Social Science). Newbury Park, CA: Sage.

Survey of Consumer Finances. (1984, September). *Federal Reserve Bulletin, 70,* p. 686. Washington, DC: Author.

Survey of Consumer Finances. (1984, December). *Federal Reserve Bulletin, 70,* p. 863. Washington, DC: Author.

Tan, H. (1989). *Private sector training in the United States: Who gets it and why* (Working paper). New York: Teachers College, Columbia University.

Taw, R. (1990). *Basic skills in the workplace.* London, England: Adult Literacy and Basic Skills Unit. (ERIC Documentation Reproduction Service No. ED 323 388)

Taylor, M., Lewe, G., & Draper, J. (1991). *Basic skills for the workplace.* Toronto, Canada: Culture Concepts, Inc.

Thurow, L. (1975). *Generating inequality*. New York: Basic Books.

Torres, C. (1990). *The politics of nonformal education in Latin America*. New York: Praeger.

Triton College. (1990). *POWER for progress: A model for partnerships in workplace literacy*. River Grove, IL: Office of Vocational and Adult Education. (ERIC Documentation Reproduction Service No. ED 324 458)

Unesco. (1976). *The experimental world literacy programme*. Paris: Unesco Press.

U.S. Department of Education. (1991). *Adult Literacy and Learning Bulletin*, 3(4), 5.

U.S. General Accounting Office (GAO). (1990). *The urban underclass: Disturbing problems demanding attention*. Washington, DC: Author.

Van Fossen, S., & Sticht, T. (1991, July). *Teach the mother and reach the child: Results of the intergenerational literacy action research project of wider opportunities for women*. Washington, DC: Wider Opportunities for Women.

Van Tilburg, E., & DuBois, J.E. (1989). *Literacy students' perceptions of successful participation in adult education: A cross-cultural approach through expectant values*. Paper presented at the Annual Adult Education Research Conference, Madison, WI. (ERIC Documentation Reproduction Service No. ED 321 030)

Volpert, W. (1989). Work and personality development from the viewpoint of the action regulation theory. In H. Leymann & H. Kornbluh (Eds.), *Socialization and learning at work*. Aldershot, England: Avebury.

Von Freyhold, M. (1982). Some observations on adult education in Tanzania. In H. Hinzen & V.H. Hundsdorfer (Eds.), *Education for liberation and development: The Tanzanian experience*. Hamburg: Unesco Institute for Education.

Wagner, D.A. (1990). Literacy assessment in the Third World: An overview and proposed schema for survey use. *Comparative Education Review*, 34(1), 112-138.

Wagner, R.K. (1992). Intelligence. In T. Sticht, M. Beeler, & B. McDonald (Eds.), *The intergenerational transfer of cognitive skills: Vol. II. Theory and research in cognitive science*. Norwood, NJ: Ablex.

Watanabe, S. (1991). The Japanese quality control circle. *International Labour Review*, 130(1), 57-80.

Westberry, S. (1990). *The BEST blueprint: Quality ABE in the workplace*. Columbia, TN: Maury County Board of Education. (ERIC Documentation Reproduction Service No. ED 324 427)

Winch, G. (1983). *Information technology in manufacturing processes*. London: Rossendale.

Wolf, A. (1990). Unwrapping knowledge and understanding from standards of competence. In H. Black & A. Wolf (Eds.), *Knowledge and competence: Current issues in training and education*. London: HMSO.

Workbase. (1990). *Setting up workplace basic skills training: Guidelines for practitioners*. London: ALBSU.

Zuboff, S. (1988). *In the age of the smart machine. The future of work and power*. New York: Basic Books.

Author Index

Subject Index